THE LONG AND
THE SHORT OF IT

ALSO BY JOHN KAY

The Truth about Markets, 2003
Culture and Prosperity (USA), 2004
Foundations of Corporate Success, 1993
Why Firms Succeed (USA), 1995

Collections
The Hare and the Tortoise, 2006
Everlasting Light Bulbs, 2004
The Business of Economics, 1996

THE LONG AND THE SHORT OF IT

A guide to finance and investment
for normally intelligent people
who aren't in the industry

John Kay

ep

THE ERASMUS PRESS

First published in Great Britain in 2009 by

The Erasmus Press Ltd
PO Box 4026
London W1A 6NZ

The moral right of the author has been asserted

A catalogue record for this book is available
from the British Library

ISBN 978-0-9548093-2-4

Text designed by Briony Hartley

Printed in Great Britain by
CPI William Clowes
Beccles NR34 7TL

CONTENTS

TABLES

ACKNOWLEDGEMENTS

Many people have helped in the preparation of this book. I would like to thank the people who have helped me understand the financial services industry over the past twenty-five years. This book is critical of that industry, and of what it offers to small customers. Yet while there are people in the City who are beyond contempt, there are also many who consistently display exceptional intelligence and unquestionable integrity. I have been privileged to work with, and learn from, some of them.

I am grateful to the people who commented on earlier drafts; in particular, Alistair Blair, Tony Boyce, Jonathan Davis, Roman Frydman, Tim Harford, Chris Hughes, Chris Llewellyn Smith, Callum McCarthy, Vaclav Potesil, Jorim Schraven, Robert Tann, Mark White, and Martin White. To Lipper and the WM Company for the proprietary data they have provided. The production team has not only done a wonderful job, but has shared my enthusiasm for the project. Thanks to Flo Bayley, Briony Hartley and Sheila Thompson. To Johanna Vorholz, for research assistance. And especially to Jo Charrington, who has not only organised the process from first draft to finished book but, by keeping my life in order, has made the whole venture possible.

And an especial thank you to Mika Oldham. She suggested the idea in the first place and has been a source of encouragement throughout.

FOREWORD

This book is a self-contained guide to finance and investment for the intelligent reader and the concerned citizen.

I'll describe investment options and financial institutions. Twice in the last decade – the New Economy bubble of 1998-2000 and the credit expansion of 2003-7 – financial follies have threatened the stability of the world economy. I'll explain the market developments and products that provided the background to these events.

The modern financial world is complex and sophisticated, but also greedy, cynical and self-interested. The only way to cope is to acquire your own knowledge and form your own judgment. You cannot, unfortunately, trust people who offer financial advice. If you can trust me, it is because the only product I am trying to sell you – this book – is one you have already bought.

I'll explain the principles of profitable investment. I'll distinguish profitable investment from gambling – which can be profitable, but mostly isn't. Profitable investment is ultimately based on returns from productive assets. The revenues of the financial services industry come from creaming off some of these returns through intermediation. Some of that intermediation is essential to the modern world economy; much of it merely creates opacity and generates fees. You will need to pay for the first and do not want to pay for the second. Ensuring that the largest possible slice of the underlying return goes to you is a fundamental principle of profitable investment.

Choosing investments that are indeed profitable is even more important. In a modern economy, productive assets are mostly owned by companies. I'll describe how businesses succeed (and fail) in creating value, thus generating the profits that create returns.

Amateur investors lost a lot of money in the New Economy bubble. Professional investors lost even more in the credit bubble. These outcomes appeared to come as a surprise to many involved. Profitable investment involves risks. Economic theories tell us that financial markets are a means of controlling and dispersing risks; practical experience suggests that financial markets aggravate and concentrate risks. The world is inevitably uncertain. But the events that cost participants so much money in the New Economy and the credit bubbles were not natural hazards. The risks and uncertainties were mainly created by financial markets themselves.

The victims of the credit bubble were large financial institutions employing sophisticated risk management tools. I'll explain why these control mechanisms failed. The critical issues are, as so often, to do with people and incentives. Most people in large organisations are not really interested in minimising risk. Their objective is to take as much as possible of the credit when things go right, and as little as possible of the blame when things go wrong. Everywhere you go in the world of business and finance, you confront the problem of agents whose interests differ from yours. You have to take responsibility for your own decisions. I'll develop a practical investment strategy for the intelligent investor, based on three fundamental principles: pay less, diversify more, and be contrarian.

Most investment books advise you to get to know the mind of the market; I suggest you think for yourself instead. Most investment books advise you how to trade; I suggest you trade as little as possible. Most investment books take for granted that your search for new investments is a search for stocks that are likely to go up. I'm certainly not going to dissuade you from that search. But I suggest you give equal weight to a different question: Is this investment different in character from those I already own?

I'll give you the specific information you need to implement such a strategy. The world of the small investor has been transformed in the last decade. The internet gives ready access both to financial products and financial information. Innovation in financial markets has provided many attractive new opportunities (as well as many unattractive ones). As a result, a small investor can now build a diversified portfolio of investments easily and cheaply with a modest sum. That is what the intelligent investor should do.

If the modern world is full of people anxious to muscle in on the credit and deflect the blame, we need to be blunt about the relationship between you, as reader, and me, as author. I am not making any specific investment recommendations to you – given the slowness of publication schedules and the speed of markets, that would be daft anyway. I take no responsibility for the consequences of your investment decisions. When events go well for you, you will no doubt take the credit; when they go badly, you will have to shoulder the blame.

The term 'intelligent investor' originates with Benjamin Graham. Graham's modern disciple is Warren Buffett, the most successful investor in history and, as a direct result, now the world's richest man. Buffett has claimed that

> 'Observing correctly that the market was frequently efficient, they (the
> academics – and many investment professionals and corporate managers)
> went on to conclude incorrectly that it was always efficient. The difference
> between these propositions is night and day.' (Buffett, p 78 in Cunningham
> (2002))

Buffett is talking about the efficient market hypothesis (EMH), the central tenet of modern financial analysis. I'll paraphrase Buffett's remark by saying that the efficient market hypothesis is illuminating, but not true. Such a statement may be puzzling for people who are used to the relative certainties of hard sciences like physics and chemistry. But the world of business and finance is comprehensible only with the aid of theories, like market efficiency, which are illuminating but not true.

This is intended to be a practical book. I'm not going to pursue the issues in the philosophy of science which that statement raises (though I'll tell you where you can). I shall simply make the pragmatic assertion that you cannot be an intelligent investor if you believe that markets are always efficient or deny that they are mostly efficient. It is a big mistake to believe that the efficient market hypothesis is true, and a bigger mistake to believe that it is false.

I will describe several other theories that are illuminating but not true – most of all, the theories that are used in risk analysis. You can make money in financial markets at the expense of people who don't under-stand these – illuminating – theories; such people often make elemen-tary mistakes. But you can also make money in financial markets at the expense of people who make the more sophisticated error of believing that these theories are true. The practical advice that I shall give exploits both opportunities.

This book is for normally intelligent people who are not in the financial services industry. Most such people will have been successful in some other activity. They read books of popular history or popular science, and expect to deal with issues of finance and investment at the same intellectual level. My aim has been to make things as simple as possible, but no simpler. Many issues of finance and investment are, necessarily, technical, and their explanation involves jargon. I've provided a glossary at the end of the book which offers quick definitions of possibly unfa-miliar terms. But I have kept references and footnotes to a minimum. I've provided a guide to some further reading and useful websites.

But I'm commercially minded – otherwise I wouldn't be qualified to write this book – and I hope to sell quite a few copies to people who do work in the financial services industry. They can skip the first three chapters, which review institutions and products, and perhaps Chapter 9, which describes modern developments in financial markets – derivatives, hedge funds, private equity and structured credit – and go directly to the heart of the book which describes what financial economics teaches about the determinants of risks and returns. Chapters 4 to 6 are concerned with the value of productive assets and the securities that are based on them. Chapters 7 and 8 describe approaches to risk and uncertainty.

Some readers may prefer to turn immediately to Chapters 10 through 12, which are intended to offer practical advice for intelligent investors. But if they do they will miss most of what is important, and potentially helpful, in the book. Intelligent investment is not a matter of rules and routines, but a style of thought. It requires an analytic, detached approach to everyday issues that comes naturally to very few people, including those in financial markets, where greed and fear often predominate.

As often, we experience the paradox of obliquity: the people who are, in the long run, the most successful at making money are not generally people who are exclusively interested in money. There are many people in financial markets who, although not necessarily stupid, are character-ised by extreme vulgarity of mind and expression. But people who have a sustained record of successful investment, some of whom we will meet in this book, are not like that. They are not only intellectually sophisticated, but also display a breadth of erudition unusual in any walk of life.

Successful investors are constantly receptive to new ideas, in search of insights that are illuminating, but they do not make the mistake of believing that they have stumbled across any unique insight into truth. It is in part because the world of investment is attractive to frauds, thieves, bullies and charlatans that the people who are very good at investment are often those who have the mental and moral capacity to see further.

The contents of this book raise issues for its readers not just in the management of their personal financial affairs but in their role as citi-zens in a democracy. So I have written two concluding chapters. Chapter 13 is addressed to the intelligent investor, Chapter 14 to the concerned citizen.

This book was written in 2007–8, a period of exceptional turbulence in the financial services industry. Its broad theme – that you should put little trust in the financial services industry whether you are an intel-ligent investor or concerned citizen – seemed more controversial when I began than when I finished. Factual statements have been checked up to 10 October 2008 – just after the collapse of several major financial insti-tutions on both sides of the Atlantic and the announcement of various rescue packages. But although the context will continue to change, the underlying arguments – the principles of intelligent investment – remain as valid in this crisis, and this century, as in the last.

CHAPTER 1

SENSE AND THE CITY

Can you be your own investment manager?

Many people think that successful investment is about hot tips. If someone rings you with a hot tip, ask yourself 'Why is he calling me?' and put down the phone. If you act on a hot tip from a friend, you may lose a friend and some money. If you act on a hot tip from a stranger, you will just lose some money.

Books tell you how to become rich from stocks. Software programs and training courses claim to help you trade successfully. The authors assert that, with their assistance, you can make a comfortable living playing the market. Before you succumb, ask the following question: If I had a system that held the secret of lazy riches, would I publicise it in a book from which I will earn – at most – a few thousand pounds? Writing a book is hard work, believe me.

You might already have asked a similar question: Why would anyone who could write a book like this one choose to do so? I am one of a minority, perhaps eccentric, who find the study of financial markets intellectually engaging. And I enjoy writing, and hope that you enjoy reading this book as much as I have enjoyed writing it.

My target reader wants to make good returns on investments without worry. He or she probably thinks that managing money is a chore, and that people obsessed by the stock market are sad. My target reader's financial objective is to have enough financial security not to have to worry about money. My target reader would be happy to go on holiday, even for months, and not look at his or her portfolio. My target reader is willing to take risks, but only with small amounts.

The purpose of this book is to help such a reader become an intelligent investor who can be his or her own investment manager. If you are hesitant about taking on that responsibility, you should, by the end of this book, be able to ask penetrating questions of anyone who offers you financial advice. This book is not for people who want to become professional traders, but for those who want to sleep securely, knowing that their portfolio is in the most trustworthy of hands – their own.

A book that told you how to be your own doctor or lawyer would be an irresponsible book. 'The man who is his own lawyer has a fool for a client.' Is it possible to be your own investment manager? The financial services industry attracts many of the smartest people in the country, and certainly comprises many of the best paid people in the country. The City of London contains office blocks accommodating thousands of professionals. Traders in the City spend long days dealing in securities, with access to unlimited computing power and extensive data resources. How can you compete with them? You can't, and you shouldn't. But you can fend successfully in their world. There are reasons why DIY investing is possible, even necessary, unlike DIY law or medicine.

An obvious and depressing reason for relying on your own judgment is that most people who offer financial advice to small and medium investors aren't much good. A doctor or lawyer may not always get it right, but you can be confident that their opinions are based on extensive knowledge derived from a rigorous training programme with demanding entry requirements. You can also expect that the doctor or lawyer will have real concern for your interests, not just his or her own.

Traditionally, financial advisers were neither expert nor disinterested. People who called themselves financial advisers were salesmen (overwhelmingly they were men) remunerated by commissions and selected for bonhomie and persuasiveness rather than financial acumen. They were financial advisers in the same sense that car dealers are transport consultants. Most of these financial advisers knew little that their customers did not know – except one piece of information they did not share: how much the adviser would be paid to make a sale.

Things are getting better. Comprehensive regulation of the sale of retail financial services began in Britain only in 1987. As the new regulators dug into the affairs of the businesses they supervised, they found that high-pressure selling by silver-tongued but ignorant and avaricious salespeople was not just bad practice at the fringes of the industry, but widespread in supposedly reputable companies.

In the late 1980s personal pensions and endowment mortgages were sold to customers who did not understand them by salespeople who did not understand them. Many buyers of personal pensions exchanged good and secure company pension schemes for uncertain, and often disappointing, returns from arrangements that paid commission to the advisers who recommended them. Many buyers of endowment mortgages did not really know what these products were, and were shocked when their investments failed to produce enough cash to repay their mortgages. They had good reason to be shocked. Market returns were high in the 1990s, and the shortfall was largely attributable to poor investment management and high charges.

In the end, well-known financial services businesses paid billions of pounds in compensation to their victims. The mighty Prudential, which for a time refused to cooperate with the regulatory system on the grounds that it was offensive for the affairs of such an estimable company to be scrutinised, was eventually forced to pay fines and reimburse customers.

Financial advisers must now disclose what they are paid, and how. They must also 'know their customer', a requirement that obliges advisers to obtain basic information about the client's situation and needs, and understand key features of the products they sell. New recruits must undergo training, although there are still many financial advisers whose expertise has been acquired in the school of life, over a drink, or several.

There is still a long way to go. Training courses are not demanding and are largely concerned with the mechanics of regulation rather than financial economics. After reading this book, you will understand the principles of investment better than most people who offer financial advice to retail investors. You do not have to worry about 'knowing your customer' if you are your own customer. You need not fear that the advice you give yourself will be biased by the prospect of a fat commission.

You can also benefit from the way the internet has given the individual investor a wider set of opportunities. Financial services can not only be bought and sold electronically, but can also be delivered electronically. From home or office, you can now obtain a wide range of information, buy and sell securities very cheaply, and access many investment products that did not exist a decade ago. Comparison sites enable you to scan a range of providers.

The internet will never replace the truly skilled intermediary, just as it will never replace the doctor or lawyer, though it may change the roles of these intermediaries. But the search engine and the comparison site can now do much of what intermediaries would once have done. Unfortunately, the search engine and the comparison site are also corruptible. Like the salespeople, they are paid by product providers. What these sites display may not be comprehensive; what they highlight is not necessarily what is best for you.

The divergence between your interests and the interests of those who would sell you financial products is pervasive. One of the oldest anecdotes in the financial world tells of a visitor to Newport, Rhode Island, weekend home of American plutocrats, who is shown the symbols of the wealth of financial titans. There is Mr Morgan's yacht, and there is Mr Mellon's yacht. But, he asks, where are the customers' yachts? The question is as pertinent today.

For a time, I served on the board of the statutory body that paid compensation to retail investors who had lost money through fraudulent or incompetent financial advisers. One such business was run by a flamboyant and persuasive individual who drove a Rolls-Royce and entertained his customers at lavish parties. In the small town in the north of England where he had lived all his life, his extravagant lifestyle was interpreted as evidence of his financial acumen. In a sense, it was: the money received from customers went directly into his pocket and paid for the chauffeur and champagne.

Crude theft is, fortunately, rare in the financial services industry, although some practices, especially during the New Economy bubble of 1998-2000, came close to what an ordinary person would describe as theft. But the lawful earnings of many people in the industry seem ludicrous to an ordinary person, and are. In the course of this book you will learn how activities of little social value are so profitable for the individuals engaged in them.

No complex analysis is required to see that every penny that people take home from the City is derived from fees, commissions and trading profits obtained from outside the City. This is a simple matter of accounting. You and I, and people like us around the world, pay the large salaries and bonuses of people who work in the financial sector. We do so in our various roles as investors, as prospective pensioners, as customers of financial institutions, and as consumers of the products of businesses that use financial services.

There may be consolation for British readers in the knowledge that the City of London is a very large exporter, so that much of what the City takes is paid by foreigners. In Britain, even people who do not work in the City benefit from the foreign exchange earned and the tax paid by City individuals and City institutions, although they also have to compete with City folk to buy houses and hail taxis.

This consolation may, however, turn to anger when it emerges that some of the best rewarded City people pay little or no UK tax – the result of unwisely generous concessions on capital gains tax and liberal interpretation of rules governing residence and domicile. New Labour politicians have preferred the company of rich people and clever financiers to attendance at constituency Labour party functions, and, while it is hard to blame them, the effect on policy has been excessive and inappropriate. Government has become a soft touch for what serves the interests not just of the City of London, as an industry, but of individuals within it.

The massive rewards available in financial services are sometimes defended as the result of competition to attract talented people. The observation is true. The City of London recruits many of the best minds in the country. In my experience, only a few top academics and lawyers rival the best minds in the City for raw intelligence.

The mechanism that achieves this result is indirect. Massive rewards attract greedy people. If the number of greedy people is large, then financial services businesses can select the most talented among them. Within the City you find many who are greedy and talented, many who are greedy and untalented, but few who are talented but not greedy. Interest in ideas is generally secondary to interest in money. That is why these people are in the City. So it is, unfortunately, necessary to be suspicious of the motives of everyone who offers you financial advice.

People in the financial world whose concerns are primarily intellectual do exist. You will find some in the finance departments of universities and business schools. Others are behind the scenes in banks and financial institutions, where they are described as 'quants' or 'rocket scientists'. Modern financial markets are sufficiently complex, and the relevant analytic tools sufficiently sophisticated, that some people find observation of these markets interesting for its own sake.

The good news is that the retail investor can take a free ride on all these skills and activities. You can be a beneficiary of the efficiency of financial markets. Efficiency has both a wide and a narrow interpretation. Financial markets, though costly and imperfect, proved to be a more effective mechanism for promoting economic growth than central direction of production and investment. But in investment circles market efficiency has a specific technical meaning. That meaning relates to the 'efficient market hypothesis' (EMH), the bedrock of financial economics. Much of this book will be concerned with the implications of that hypothesis and its limitations.

The professional expertise of everyone in financial markets is focused on the value of stocks and shares, bonds, currencies and properties, and advising on when to buy and sell. These market prices reflect a consensus of informed opinions. The information that Tesco is a good retailer or that the economy of Zimbabwe is in a mess is known to everyone who trades Tesco stock or Zimbabwean dollars.

The efficient market hypothesis posits that all such information is absorbed in the market-place – it is 'in the price'. The market is a voting machine in which the opinions of all participants about the prospects of companies, the value of currencies, and the future of interest rates, are registered, and the result is publicly announced. The corollary of the efficient market hypothesis is that the result of the painstaking research of everyone in the City is available to you for free.

If that conclusion seems startling, and it should, then imagine going to an auction – a fine wine auction, for example – dominated by professionals. At first, you might be intimidated by the assembled expertise. But if you behave prudently, the dominance of professionals ensures you can't go too far wrong, because their bids will be the main influence on the price you pay.

You may not be convinced by this analogy. You may fear that there will be collusion amongst the dealers at the auction, that the market is rigged against the little guy. You may well be right. Fifty years ago, you would have been justified in having similar suspicions about securities markets. But, over recent decades, extensive public resources have been devoted to securing the integrity and transparency of financial transactions. This is partly because of popular revulsion at corrupt and fraudulent practice, and also because a reputation for honest dealing is a real competitive advantage in international markets, in which the City trades so successfully.

These regulatory provisions don't work perfectly, and never will. When you trade, your broker must normally secure 'best execution', which means you get the best price available in the market. The reality is that a bank dealing on its own account will often do better. But not so much better. The edge that the skilled and experienced buyer may have can be more than offset by the advantages you have in trading for yourself. You have greater knowledge of your own needs, you know that you can trust yourself. Best of all, you don't have to pay yourself. Your bonus is already in your pocket.

From gentlemen to players

The efficient market hypothesis describes how the market handles information. Information has always been the life-blood of markets, but the manner in which information is handled has changed. The old City of London was founded on relationships. Who you knew, who you had been to school with, determined how you did business and especially whom you did business with. The City of London was one of the last areas of English public life in which social class played a major role in career advancement and commercial activity.

For the gentleman stockbroker of yesteryear, information meant gossip. The broker would arrive in the office at nine-thirty or ten in the morning to enjoy leisurely conversations with clients, business contacts and colleagues before the alcoholic lunch that was an essential part of the working day. He – invariably he – was an agency broker. He would receive orders from an individual investor or a fund manager, and transmit those orders to 'the market'. A jobber on the floor of the stock exchange would seek to match potential buyers and sellers. All brokers charged the same high commissions.

The atmosphere of today's financial markets is very different. The London Stock Exchange no longer has a trading floor where buyers and sellers meet. Now, the large investment banks have their own raucous trading floors, which may contain hundreds of desks, each linked to the market via a screen. The visual display has several parts, designed to convey the impression of an unmanageable flow of new information.

Gentlemanly capitalism has given way to the professional City of London. The modern institution encompasses a mixture of people and approaches: the urbane sophistication of the investment bankers who plan new issues and plot mergers and acquisitions; the rocket scientists and the quants – frequently intellectually sophisticated but often lacking in common sense; the traders – some of them graduates of the finest universities and business schools, some with no higher education at all – demonstrating the aggression and ethics of the market stall. The organisations that combine these functions are an explosive mix which frequently explodes. The overall change is from benign amateurism, based on what would now be called insider trading, to specialised professionalism, based on the most sophisticated of analytic tools.

Technology, globalisation and the erosion of English class distinctions drove this transition. The process of change was, in London, mostly handled well, although with results that no one predicted. Today, the City of London is a successful international institution, a major exporter, and the country's highest paying employer. It is dominated by American-owned firms that have a global outlook but retain an American culture.

The players who ousted the gentlemen were a diverse group. Sigmund Warburg, who arrived in Britain in 1935 as a refugee from Nazi persecution, founded an investment bank whose determinedly meritocratic and unconventional approach resulted in London's newest financial institution becoming its most respected. Warburg's fund management arm, Mercury, was at the same time the leading asset management business.

Gordon Borrie, an academic lawyer from Birmingham University, was the first head of a new competition agency, the Office of Fair Trading. Given the power in 1976 to investigate services, he aimed his fire at the rule book of the London Stock Exchange. The Exchange faced the probably hopeless task of defending in the courts the proposition that its extensive restrictive practices benefited not only its members but the public at large. Borrie paved the way for competition.

Borrie came close to resignation after a deal in 1983 between two gentlemen – the Chairman of the Stock Exchange, Nicholas Goodison, and the Secretary of State for Trade and Industry, Cecil Parkinson. The outcome of the agreement between Goodison – a traditional City grandee whose exterior masked a sophisticated intellect, and Parkinson – an irresistible charmer whose career was ended by the squalid details of an extra-marital affair, was known as 'Big Bang'. The immediate consequence of Big Bang, which ended the rules and conventions that defined the separate territory of different types of City institution, was that specialist firms, including stockbrokers, were integrated into retail and investment banks. Goodison and Parkinson allowed the development of financial conglomerates.

But the retail banks mismanaged their acquisitions, and the British investment banks were outsmarted by their US competitors. Today, some of the dominant firms in the City of London are owned by retail banks domiciled elsewhere, such as Union Bank of Switzerland (which absorbed Warburg), Deutsche Bank, HSBC, and Citigroup (the largest US retail bank). But the leaders are mainly US investment banks – Goldman Sachs, Morgan Stanley, Merrill Lynch.

American influence led to a more analytic investment style. The development of quantitative techniques in investment analysis goes back more than a century. The first index of stock prices – an average of the prices of twelve leading stocks – was created in the US in 1896 by Charles Dow. A few years later, the Frenchman Louis Bachelier presented a thesis on the mathematics of securities prices that is generally celebrated as the foundation of mathematical finance. Bachelier encountered resistance, both from practitioners, who ignored his work, and from his examiners, who gave it the modest accolade of honourable – insufficient to enable the author to pursue an academic career.

Other seminal contributors to quantitative finance – such as Harry Markowitz, Fischer Black and Myron Scholes – would also initially encounter negative reactions. I'll describe their theories and these responses in later chapters. Their work, like that of Bachelier, is now fundamental not just to the analysis but to the operation of modern financial markets. The University of Chicago was where much of this work originated, and Chicago was also where new derivative markets were created. Both the graduates and the techniques were taken up by Wall Street, and subsequently by the City of London.

The change in the structure of the financial services industry was paralleled by a change in the structure of regulation. At the beginning of the 1980s, the reputation of the City of London was dented by fraud on retail investors. One notorious scandal involved a Gibraltar-based entrepreneur who spent the money that suckers poured into his 'guaranteed' bonds on yachts and other forms of high living. Following that episode, a law professor, Jim Gower, was asked to recommend reforms. Gower proposed a comprehensive regulatory regime. The publication of his recommendations coincided with the Goodison-Parkinson agreement, which plainly had far-reaching implications for the regulation of financial services. New legislation was enacted and what was then described as 'self-regulation with a statutory basis' came into force in 1987. This regime would evolve into the single supervisory body that is the Financial Services Authority (FSA).

The target reader of this book is a retail investor who will never knowingly or directly deal with Goldman Sachs. The term 'retail investor' has a technical meaning under FSA rules. Retail investors receive certain regulatory protections and rights to compensation.

You may be able to certify that you are a sophisticated or high net worth investor, which means that you lose some of these entitlements but you will be able to access some more complex investment options. The retail investor most frequently buys financial services from a retail bank. These retail banks have become financial conglomerates, with a wide range of investment products as well as their traditional roles of providing payment services for large and small customers and lending, mostly to corporate clients.

All kinds of financial institution – retail banks, investment banks, insurance companies – have similarly broadened the range of their activities. The rationale of such conglomeration lies in cross-subsidy and cross-selling. Cross-subsidy involves selling some products below cost to enhance the sales of other more profitable lines; cross-selling involves use of the customer list for one group of products to promote others. Both practices generally operate to the long-term, and frequently immediate, disadvantage of customers. I'll discuss the conflicts of interest between investment banking and retail banking, and advise you to resist cross-selling.

Many commentators have anticipated the consolidation of retail banks into a smaller number of global firms, and the demise of the bank branch. Both of these developments will probably happen, but far more slowly than has been generally supposed.

The cry of 'the foreigners are coming' – which proved true in investment banking – has been heard frequently in retail banking. But the foreigners have not come. For almost two decades there have been rumours that Crédit Lyonnais, or Deutsche Bank, then Citibank, or Bank of America, plan to become a major force in British banking. None of these plans has materialised.

The two weakest British banks – Midland and NatWest – were taken over. Midland was bought by HSBC which, whatever its name (Hong Kong and Shanghai Banking Corporation) suggests, has always been essentially a British, even a Scottish, bank. NatWest was acquired by Royal Bank of Scotland, emphatically a Scottish bank. An enterprising Spanish financial institution, Santander, bought the former Abbey National Building Society. But the structure of retail banking, in contrast to wholesale banking, remains largely unchanged. Still, the manner in which it is conducted has altered radically.

The traditional bank manager was an independent financial adviser. He was an active participant in the local community, to which he would usually be attached for many years. He might meet his customer at the golf or Rotary club and the modern obligation to 'know your customer' would be met implicitly and automatically. The caricature of Captain Mainwaring in *Dad's Army* – self-important, unimaginative, but scrupulously honest and reliable – identifies the qualities that banks sought, and found, in their managers.

Personalised banking is today prohibitively costly for a mass market. While the cost of processing transactions has fallen with the development of information technology, the cost of employing people to handle them has risen. The costs of employing knowledge-able people to handle them has risen rapidly since the scope of the financial services industry became such that people of mediocre abilities began to command large salaries. A vestige of relationship-based advice survives in private banking for high net worth individuals. But the modern bank branch is a shop and, like other shops, is staffed by pleasant sales assistants with limited knowledge and training. The physical environment has been remodelled accordingly.

Despite the efforts of designers, the bank branch is less inviting than most shops – security precludes too inviting a display of the goods. Few products are more suited to online retailing than financial services, and that is how I suggest you buy them. Still, the branches remain busy, as you discover if you try to visit one at lunch-time. Many people dislike dealing with money and managing financial services and need personal reassurance when they do. Many readers will continue to feel this need for reassurance at the end of this book. Take advice, then, but do not pay much for it. Adopt the same sceptical attitude towards your advisers as you would towards a sales assistant in a shop.

The triumph of players over gentlemen was not confined to banking. The London insurance market would similarly lose much of its competitive position in the face of more professional competitors from continental Europe (southern Germany and Switzerland) and the United States. London would remain a primary location for financial services business even as ownership of the businesses passed out of British hands and the personnel became increasingly cosmopolitan. When Nicolas Sarkozy successfully contested the French presidency in 2007 his campaign speech in the City of London attracted an audience of his voters larger than he could have anticipated in the financial centre of Paris.

While the passing of the old City of London was inevitable, there were losses as well as gains. Much of the old City was characterised by a certain rigid integrity. It wasn't exactly that people wouldn't steal from or cheat each other, rather that they would do so only in certain well-defined and tolerated ways. This carefully modulated self-regulation – its ultimate sanction, as the saying went, was the devastating rebuke of the raised eyebrows of the Governor of the Bank of England that could end a City career – could not survive the globalisation of financial markets.

In 1985 Norman Tebbit, Parkinson's successor, was responsible for deciding whether there should be an investigation into a proposed takeover of Harrods, the iconic London department store. He rang the chairman of Kleinwort Benson (as it then was) to seek advice on the *bona fides* of the purchasers. Tebbit was told that the reputation of the bank was associated with that of its clients. What Tebbit was told was true, but did not have the meaning he attributed to it. Reputation had become another commodity, to be bought and sold.

In buying investment products or trading in financial markets today, you are dealing with players, not gentlemen. Events of the last twenty years – the misselling of personal pensions and endowment mortgages in the 1980s, the New Economy bubble in the 1990s, the promotion of complex packaged securities in the years after 2000 – have shown the need for scepticism and wariness in dealing with even the most apparently reputable institutions. The intelligent investor needs to develop his or her own strategy.

CHAPTER 2

BASICS OF INVESTMENT

Before you begin

I'll start with the preliminaries you should go through before you even think about investment principles or investment options. Compile a list of your financial assets and liabilities. Do it with your spouse or partner. (In Britain the legal status of the relationship matters for some financial issues, though not many.) Whether you manage your financial affairs separately or collectively, plan together.

If you subtract your liabilities from your assets, the balance is your net worth. High net worth is the new euphemism for rich, but what people mean by high net worth varies. You are well off, it is often said, if you earn more than your brother-in-law. The FSA allows you to certify yourself as a high net worth investor if you have net assets of £250,000, but few people in the City will be impressed.

Most people will find that their house, with the associated mortgage, dominates the calculation. The FSA definition of high net worth excludes your main residence and associated mortgage. I suggest that for most purposes you do the same.

But don't put house and mortgage out of your mind altogether. Borrowing on mortgage is the only form of borrowing appropriate for anyone planning an investment portfolio. I am going to suggest later in this chapter that you aim for a 10% rate of return on your portfolio. Even if you fall short of this, mortgage borrowing is so cheap that it is realistic to expect to earn more on your investment portfolio than the cost of the mortgage. Many conservative people want to reduce their mortgage as quickly as they can, but such a strategy isn't necessarily wise.

If you have any debts other than a mortgage, repay them before you undertake any investment. In particular, repay outstanding credit card balances. The interest rate on almost all credit cards is well above 10% and certainly above the return you can realistically expect on your investments.

You will pay income tax. Most people with an investment portfolio pay income tax at the higher rate of 40%, which applies to incomes above around £45,000 a year. Income tax in Britain is assessed on an individual basis. If one partner pays higher rate tax, the couple will gain if the lower income partner receives more of the investment income.

In most of what follows, I generally assume that you expect to pay tax at 40%. Only around 10% of the population does but readers of this book are not average. The 40% tax rate also applies to interest income but, in recognition of the corporation tax the company has already paid, dividends are taxed at a lower rate of around 25%.

Two other taxes may be relevant to an investment portfolio: inheritance tax and capital gains tax. In 2008 the threshold for inheritance tax (charged at 40%) for a married couple was increased to £624,000. The previously complex capital gains tax rules were replaced by a single tax rate of 18%, payable when you sell. You can deduct losses from gains, and the first £9600 of gains in any tax year are tax free. Taking income tax and capital gains together, you might expect the average tax rate on your investments to be around 20%. That means that a 10% return before tax would be 8% after tax.

You need a current bank account, a savings account, a credit card, and a mortgage. Most people have been with the same provider for years. This is usually a mistake. Financial institutions rely on inertia and give introductory incentives to buy what later become uncompetitive products. The problem originates with consumers rather than with institutions. Banks or insurers who provide everyday good-value pricing find their customers drift away to the introductory bargains offered by other companies.

If you are willing to be a 'rate tart', sitting regularly at your computer pursuing the best deals, you can benefit permanently from introductory incentives. Most readers have better things to do. I would prefer to find a provider who offers competitive terms and good service, and so I suspect would you.

The best buys are often from 'monoliners' – firms that specialise in a single product group – because their future depends on their reputation in these products. Examples of monoliners are Fidelity (funds), Capital One (credit cards), Mortgage Express (what the name suggests). Monoliners are often owned by big institutions but that usually doesn't matter to the consumer because the business model remains the same.

Unless you have an offset mortgage (which I describe below), you need a current account and a savings account. Internet providers are usually the most competitive. Stand-alone savings accounts frequently advertise excellent rates, but beware the introductory offer – providers reduce rates once sufficient funds have been attracted to the accounts. Financial services conglomerates, especially the major banks, will try to cross-sell you products. They are not very successful at this, but they emphasise this business strategy to themselves and the City. The products they cross-sell are rarely competitive and the sales pitch will waste your time.

Since the modern bank branch is a shop selling products you probably don't want to buy, you do not need to pay fees – in the form of charges for a branch-based current or savings account – to go there. An internet account or an offset mortgage will operate on the platforms of the major banks so that processing of everyday transactions should proceed in exactly the same way. Banks seeking new current accounts now offer services designed to make switching accounts easy.

An offset account takes the balances on your current and savings accounts and offsets them against your mortgage. If you have a mortgage of £200,000 and a current account balance of £10,000, you pay interest not on £200,000 but on £190,000. The offset means that if the mortgage interest rate is 5% you, in effect, earn 5% on your savings and current account balances. This rate compares favourably with the

0.1% that some major banks pay on current account balances. It even compares well with a savings account which pays 5%, because you have to pay tax on savings interest.

The disadvantage of an offset mortgage is that the interest rate is not usually as good as the best rate you can obtain on a conventional mortgage. The offset is profitable to you only if you anticipate that the savings balance will usually be a significant proportion of the outstanding debt.

You should be able to borrow on a conventional mortgage at about the same rate at which banks buy and lend to each other.[1] You may wonder how such a bargain is possible. Banks make money on arrangement fees, but they make more from customer inertia. Introductory offers usually revert to what the bank describes as its standard variable rate, which will be much higher.

Do not allow this reversion to happen. One phone call should be enough. Lenders have mortgage retention teams which offer competitive rates to competitive customers. The phone call may save you literally thousands of pounds. You may be able to do better still by shopping around but, once more, you probably have better things to do. If your existing lender makes a reasonable offer, save yourself hassle.[2]

On a conventional mortgage you will usually be offered a choice of a rate fixed for two, three, or even five years, or a variable rate that will change with (and may even be linked to) the Bank of England's base rate.

---

1 There is a subtle reason why quoted mortgage rates seem so low. You may notice that mortgage lenders frequently charge interest on the amount outstanding at the beginning of the year, while a savings account will pay you interest only after six months or even a year. A simple calculation shows that if you charge a year in advance and pay a year in arrears, and the interest rate on both accounts is 5%, you will make 0.25% a year in margin which, on a large mortgage book, is a lot of money. Whenever an annual rate is quoted, consider the frequency with which the return is added to the principal. The Annual Percentage Rate (APR), a legal attempt to standardise this calculation, assumes that the return is added each year, in arrears.

2 As this book was completed, in the summer of 2008, the mortgage market had ceased to be competitive as banks in a state of near panic reined in mortgage lending. While mortgage rates will probably never be as finely priced as in 2007, the text, rather than the exceptional 2008 situation, is the normal position.

A lot of fuss is made about the choice and you may be asked whether you think interest rates will go up or down over the next two, three, or five years. You don't know, and nor does anyone else. These fixed and variable rates reflect underlying market 'swap' rates. (I'll explain swaps in Chapter 9.) If you are persuaded by the metaphor of market as voting machine (although I'll suggest several reasons why you might not be), then you will recognise that the market has voted on the future of interest rates and you probably have nothing to add. Probably more important – and certainly more under your control – is the up-front fee you are charged. The lender may offer complex combinations of interest rates, fixed fees, percentage fees and valuation and legal costs, so a calculator is needed to work out which combination is best.

If these calculations sound tedious, they are not complex, and, per minute, may be the best paid work you ever do. A mortgage broker may be able to help you get some deals that are not available in other ways. It is unlikely that he will offer any other useful advice, unless you are a bad credit risk – but bad credit risks are probably not readers of this book.

The benefits of getting these preliminaries of banking arrangements and mortgages right are so large that anyone who fails to do so isn't serious about managing money. Obtaining a better deal may involve moving away from an established high street provider (although frequently moving to a subsidiary of an established high street provider). You don't need to be a rate tart; a comprehensive review of your arrangements every few years will be enough.

Review financial risks outside your investment portfolio. Households generally cover some risks by insurance – risks such as domestic fire or theft, car accidents, travel disruption. I'll come back to insurance in Chapter 10, after discussing the ways people think about risk. Most people take out insurances they shouldn't and most people fail to take out insurances they should. Here are a few preliminary pointers.

If you have dependent children, you should consider insurance on the life of both parents. The low take-up of such policies is a legacy of the sale of costly savings products under the label 'life insurance' by salespeople on commission. The policyholders could rarely afford the premiums so most policies lapsed, leaving children without protection and creating a well-founded perception that life insurance was expensive.

A more appropriate form of insurance – life insurance that has no savings component but lasts for the period of the child's dependence – is cheap, since young parents rarely die, although the financial consequences can be extremely serious if they do. Policies that cover costs and loss of earnings from long-term illness or disability are also worth considering, although far from cheap.

Do not buy insurance from someone who offers it when you are buying something else. Examples are payment protection insurance when you take out a loan; extended warranties on domestic appliances; and travel insurance when you buy a holiday. Because the purchaser has little opportunity to compare prices, or even to consider the purchase carefully, these policies are almost always bad value. You are, unfortunately, depriving the salesperson of income, since he or she receives large commissions for selling these policies. That is why the policies are expensive and the seller persistent. If you want such insurance – mostly you don't – buy it elsewhere.

Insurance can cover some of the financial risks of everyday life – accidents at home and on the road, theft, sudden death. But the most serious financial risks most households face come from redundancy and unemployment, old age and chronic illness, marriage and relationship breakdown. Such risks cannot be insured and can only be mitigated through effective money management and successful investment. That's the main subject of this book.

Investment choices

When people discuss investment at clubs and dinner parties, in pubs and lunch rooms, they generally mean investment in securities – stocks and shares, bonds and deposits. But investment finds another meaning in the creation of the physical infrastructure of the economy. Companies invest in plant and machinery. They must finance inventories and pay for work in progress. They operate from offices and shops. The government invests in schools and hospitals, bridges and roads. People used to make a sharper distinction between savings – putting money aside for later, and investment – putting that money to use. But these words have lost this differentiated meaning. I'll talk instead about financial investment and productive investment.

The return on financial investment must, ultimately, be generated by the return on productive investment. The quest for financial perpetual motion machines is unending, but the basic principle of bookkeeping – money that goes out equals money that comes in – is as immutable as the natural laws of thermodynamics. Financial investments fund physical investments, and the two principal means by which they do so are shares and loans.

A share (an equity) gives you a portion, for better or worse, of earnings and realisations from the productive activities of a company. Secured loans give the lender the right to seize some or all of the company's assets if it fails to pay agreed interest and the original money lent.[1] Unsecured loans give the lender a legal claim against the borrower for payment, which will be met only after secured creditors have realised the value of the assets pledged to them.[2]

Physical objects, such as offices and machinery, are not the only productive assets. Many of the assets of modern companies are intangible. Companies own brands, and build reputations. They acquire licences and intellectual property, and they build internal systems and structures. These assets earn a return, just as plant and buildings earn a return; many such assets can be bought and sold, and can even provide security for loans.

Some financial assets are not directly associated with productive assets. Governments discovered – hundreds, even thousands, of years ago – that they could borrow to finance wars and profligate consumption because lenders knew that states could raise taxes to repay the

1 A mortgage – the loan most familiar to readers – allows the unpaid lender to repossess the mortgaged house. If the sale of the house does not realise enough money to pay the debt, the bank remains an unsecured creditor for the balance.

2 The distinctions between shares, equities and secured and unsecured loans, have become much less clear-cut than formerly as a result of financial innovation. A non-recourse loan gives the lender rights over the asset on which the borrowing is secured, but not over the other assets of the borrower. Junior, mezzanine or subordinated debt will be paid only after other lenders have been repaid. Such debt may, in recompense, enjoy some share of the profits.

loans. (This did not always mean they would, as lenders continue to rediscover.) Individuals can, more modestly, borrow to spend now on the strength of their ability to earn income in future. So some investments are backed by what economists coyly call 'time preference' – the premium that impatient or hard-pressed people will pay to spend now rather than later.

Lending to government, or a credit card borrower, must compete with lending to a company, so the returns you can earn on these financial investments are ultimately governed by what productive investments can earn. None of the complexity of modern financial markets, which package and repackage securities in ever more elaborate ways, can alter that essential truth.

While investors mostly own indirect claims on productive assets, through shares and loans, investors can also own a direct claim on the productive investments of businesses, governments and households. They sometimes do so by owning the buildings – shops, offices, warehouses, factories and houses – from which businesses, governments and households operate. Shares, loans and property are the main investment choices.

What choices should you make? The strategy I will propose in Chapters 10 to 12 is that you should begin as a conventional investor – relying on the illumination of efficient markets to provide you with the assembled wisdom of the financial services industry. Recognising that this theory is only illuminating, not true, you will want, over time, to become an intelligent investor, employing your own judgment – to pay less, diversify more, and take contrarian stances.

The conventional investor follows the average of what professional investors do. The power of conventional thinking in the City is so pervasive that this is, in reality, what the vast majority of professional investors do themselves. You can follow that consensus with the aid of publicly available information and the properties of efficient markets. Instead of paying heavily for conventional thinking, you can use conventional thinking for free.

What do conventional investors do? The largest investors in Britain are pension funds. UK pension funds hold total assets of around £1000bn, and dominate the British investment scene. These funds are required to keep detailed accounts of their activities. Most of them provide reports in standardised form to their regulators, the Occupational Pensions Board; to their trade association, the National Association of Pension Funds; and to a private company, the WM Company, which provides performance monitoring services to its subscribers.

I shall use local authority pension funds as the benchmark for the conventional investor. This sounds unadventurous; it is meant to be. Local authority pension funds are meticulous in obtaining the best possible and widest range of advice, and in acting on it. They pay close attention to their own performance, and that of other similar funds. Moreover, they are interested in total return, and are long-term investors; local authorities know that they will still be around in ten, twenty, even fifty years' time, and will be responsible then for the consequences of their actions today.

I have chosen local authority pension funds, rather than pension funds as a whole, because many private sector pension funds have closed their schemes to new entrants and are beginning to run down their activities. In many cases, the sponsoring company is now mainly concerned with minimising its involvement and its liabilities. In fact, there are not very large differences between the historic performance of local authority and all pension funds. Both seem to have done better than the average charitable endowment, which is the other main category of investment institutions whose activities are well reported.

Table 1: Total returns earned by local authority pension funds, 1987–2006

	last 10 years %	previous 10 years %	complete 20 years %
Shares*	7.6	12.2	9.9
Bonds*	7.2	10.6	8.9
Property	13.7	9.3	11.5
Overall	7.7	10.9	9.3
Inflation (RPI)	2.8	4.4	3.6

Source: WM Company
* UK shares and bonds. Returns on non-UK shares and bonds were lower in all periods

Table 1 shows the returns local authority funds have earned in different asset classes over the last twenty years (1987-2006).

Outperformance seems to be followed by underperformance and vice versa. Shares did better in the first period than the second, property better in the second period than the first. No asset category stands out for its high return or low volatility. A portfolio spread across the three asset categories, as these pension fund portfolios were, would have experienced good and stable returns.

You would have done better if you had invested heavily in equities in the first period and property in the second. Of course, you would have had to know, without hindsight, that this was the right thing to do. Most people thought the opposite; shares were in fashion in the 1990s, and property unappreciated. In the new virtual world, economic power would lie with the young titans who had been the first to 'get it', and bricks and mortar would play a minor role in commerce. But you would have been better off – over the long run – with a sceptical stance.

Shares, bonds and property are the main asset categories available to investors. In addition, most investors will need some cash for immediate needs, and to exploit investment opportunities, as they become available. In gloomy economic circumstances, cash may be an investment class in its own right.

There are other options. Some large educational endowments in the United States – particularly Harvard and Yale Universities – pioneered the use of a wider range of investment categories to diversify their investments. Yale's investment manager, David Swenson, attracted a following, first in the United States and then internationally, for his innovative approach. After the New Economy bubble burst in 2000, many investors, having learned that shares did not always go up, turned their attention to other investment possibilities.

What was the next new thing? If you couldn't rely on equities any more, what was the new source of easy wealth? This search would be the dominant investment theme of the first years of the twenty-first century. Like a caravan of prospectors, huddled together for mutual support and security, investment institutions moved from one asset class to another, bidding up each – property, minerals, emerging market bonds, energy and foodstuffs – to new highs. An older meaning of the term 'alternative investment' also described investments in objects, like fine art, vintage cars, or wine, and in commodities, such as gold, copper, or coffee. The most widely favoured alternative assets today are private equity and hedge funds. I'll discuss these further in Chapter 9.

Realistic expectations

The returns described in Table 1 are total returns. An earlier generation of investors was taught (in some cases compelled) to limit their spending to their income – the interest and dividends they received each year from their portfolio. When interest rates rose to 15% or more in the 1970s, and inflation was running at 27%, anyone spending their income was wildly imprudent. Conversely, if your investments have a low yield but continue to generate capital gains – as with many investments in the last two decades – then it may be sensible to anticipate the value of some of that growth.

A modern maxim is 'Think total return'. Both income and capital gain are part of the yield on your investment. The average total return earned by local authority pension funds was 7.7% per annum over the last ten years. With inflation at 2.8%, this meant that the average fund increased the purchasing power of its assets by an average of 4.8% per year. The nominal return is 7.7%; 4.8% is the real return. Over the twenty years, the nominal return earned by the funds was 9.3% but, with inflation over the period somewhat higher at 3.6%, the real return, at 5.6%, was about 1% greater than in the more recent decade.

These returns were obtained by conventional – and tax-exempt – investors in what has generally been perceived as a good period for savers. Some readers will think such figures are disappointing. They have heard many stories about people who have made a killing on the stock market through hot tips and inspired timing. If you click on internet bulletin boards, you will read about the search for 'ten and twenty baggers' – stocks that will rise, or have risen, to ten and twenty times their initial value.

If you open an online stockbroking account – and you should – you will soon be seduced by bulletin boards and offered hot tips. The stocks promoted there may be 'concept stocks', based on unproven technologies or bright ideas. Penny shares are priced so low that any movement seems to have a large effect on the wealth of the holders. When you begin investing, you may be inclined to back some of these tips, and I wouldn't discourage new investors from doing so with a very small proportion of their available funds. It is a cheap means of beginning to learn about the mechanics and the psychology of the market. A few people, possessed of ill-founded self-confidence or books or courses on how to trade, set out to make a fortune in this way. The New Economy bubble saw the emergence of 'day traders', who bought and sold stocks several times a day. Stockbrokers established offices to service them.

As with many forms of professional gambling, there do seem to be small numbers of people who are good at it. To good luck they add exceptional psychological insight and rigorous self-control. But surveys of day traders show that after a few months most give up, or are obliged to do so by their families. Not all. Besides the few who develop successful careers, a larger group of people become addicts, whose financial stability and family lives may be destroyed by their obsession.

Financial innovations, especially in derivative markets, have greatly increased the opportunities and risks of market-related gambling for both amateurs and professionals. In securities markets, many people are in a position to gamble, legally, with their employers' money. Some become hooked; a few corporate and municipal treasurers have lost large sums; and a personal tragedy has become an expensive disaster for shareholders or taxpayers. The most sophisticated punters are managers of hedge funds and operators in the proprietary trading operations – 'prop desks' – of investment banks. Even here, there is a heady mix of real skill, addiction, obsession and self-delusion on the part of both individuals and organisations.

If you are tempted to make a living from stock market speculation, this is not the book for you. There are many other books aimed at the seekers after twenty baggers. The target reader of this book is concerned, as local authority pension funds are, with the careful and responsible stewardship of assets – your own.

Retail investors – people like you and me – don't have the same opportunity to measure and compare performance as do these pension funds. The sketchy evidence we have is that we have done worse. The return on the average balanced fund managed for retail investors is below the average return on local authority pension funds. (Table 2) This is not surprising, since the funds are managed by the same people and the charges are higher, sometimes much higher.

Table 2: Average returns to retail investors, 1987-2007

Total return to 31 May 2007 (% p.a.)	10 years	20 years
Balanced managed fund	6.6	7.6
Life insurance policy	2.7	7.0
Instant access account	3.4	5.0

Source: *Money Management*

The return on with profits life insurance policies, the most common balanced investment held by retail investors, has over the last ten years been a shocking 2.7%. Although the twenty-year return is better, it is difficult to understand why anyone would want to pay substantial charges, or anything at all, to the people who achieved this result. Perhaps retail investors, who make their own choices, do better. Perhaps. Hindsight and selective memory play a large role in anecdotal accounts of investment successes.

Both equity and property markets have fallen since 2007, and the most recent data on the performance of UK retail investment funds is shown in Table 3.

Table 3: Performance of UK retail investment funds, 1998-2008

Total return to 31 July 2008 (%p.a.)	5 years	10 years
Median UK equity fund	9.0	2.5
Median Sterling bond fund	3.0	5.0
Median UK real estate fund	5.5	9.5

Source: Lipper

Realism can be depressing. You may want to close the book at this point, and either continue, alone, the search for the twenty bagger, or decide you might as well leave your money in the bank. Both decisions would be mistakes. Intelligent investment is rewarding over the long run.

Albert Einstein is reported as saying that compound interest is the most powerful force in the universe. There is no evidence that Einstein said this, and it is unlikely that he did, but the sentiment has some truth. The reinvestment of returns over a long period has dramatic consequences. Over ten years, £100 invested at the average instant access rate of that decade, 3.4%, would become £140. At the local authority pension fund return of 7.7%, £100 becomes £210. While many amateur investors tend to be attracted by capital gains and attach little weight to dividends, reinvested dividends play a large role in long-term capital accumulation. You might do better than the 7.7% performance of the average local authority pension fund, with its bevy of well-paid advisors. I shall describe why you can and how you might. If you do, you will be doing better than most investors and investment professionals.

Let's be optimistic. An average return of 10% pa before tax and before inflation is a demanding, but not impossible, target for the intelligent investor. The typical reader should expect tax to reduce that return by perhaps 2% (20% of a 10% return). The Bank of England's inflation target (which has generally been achieved in the last decade) is 2%[5] so that the corresponding real after-tax return is between 5% and 6%. A 10% return will turn £100 into £260 in ten years. 10% may seem a disappointing rate of return to locker-room braggarts but viewed as a return on productive investment, rather than on financial investment, 10% appears high. While businesses often target higher returns on investment than this, they rarely achieve them.[6]

---

5 There are several different measures of inflation. Two that are relevant to intelligent investors are the Retail Prices Index (RPI) – used to determine the returns on index-linked bonds; and harmonised index of consumer prices – the basis of the Bank of England's inflation target. The RPI, which has more extensive coverage of housing costs and differs in technical details of construction, has generally risen faster.

6 The return on equity they say they earn is often much higher. After reading Chapter 6, you should understand why.

Look at it in another way. The return on secure assets such as cash and government bonds is around 5%. If you succeed in earning a 10% rate of return, that means you are receiving an additional 5% per annum for taking on risk – the risk premium. This is a handsome reward. Nevertheless, it is not unrealistic.

This generous level of return for risk has proved achievable over very long periods – a century or more. The question of why the risk premium is so high has puzzled financial economists, who call it the 'equity premium paradox'. I'll come back to the equity premium paradox in Chapters 7 and 8. The size of the premium is a reason why most investment institutions allocate very little to cash. You should do the same. (There are stronger reasons for making allocations to indexed bonds.)

If you set yourself a target rate of return of 10%, you are already differentiating yourself from many conventional and most professional investors. They are judged relative to the performance of their peers, and therefore focus, not on absolute return, but on relative return. It is not enough to have earned 20% if the benchmark index has returned 25% (as it often will, over a short period, and as it did over longer periods in the 1990s). It is defensible (even if uncomfortable) to have lost 15% if the benchmark has lost 20%. The manager can blame 'the market' for his poor performance.

When you become your own investment manager, the incentives and consequences are different. The money you manage is your own, and there is no one else to blame. Relative performance may pay the salary and bonus of a fund manager, but relative performance doesn't pay the bills of the investor. What pays bills, in the long run, is total return, in absolute terms, after tax and expenses. In the next chapter, I'll review the ways in which shares, bonds and property can contribute to that objective.

CHAPTER 3

INVESTMENT OPTIONS

Sense about shares

You might buy a share in an initial public offering (IPO), when a company raises capital by selling its shares to the public. It is much more likely that you will buy a share on a market, like the London Stock Exchange, which trades shares in established businesses, like BP, Britain's biggest company, which produces and distributes oil around the world. BP shares are quoted in London and, like many large British companies, BP makes its shares more accessible to American investors by having a New York listing for American Depository Receipts (ADRs). BP's share price varies every minute of the trading day.

You can get this price from a wide variety of internet sources (possibly the price as it was fifteen or twenty minutes ago). The real-time price is considered valuable information and typically available only to people who pay for the information or are clients of stockbrokers. As I write, the price to buy BP shares is 570.5p and the price to sell is 569.5p. The average of the two, 570p, is the mid-market price. In the course of the day, the mid-market price has varied between a low of 568p and a high of 575p. BP is a large company and its shares are actively traded. The spread between buying and selling prices is much wider for small companies.

What do you get for 570.5p? People often say that shareholders 'own' the company. They don't, at least in Britain, as you will find out if you turn up at BP's head office to assert your 'ownership'. In 2003, the House of Lords reaffirmed its 1948 ruling that 'shareholders are not, in the eyes of the law, part owners of the company'. As the court explained, what shareholders own is their shares, and ownership of shares confers a variety of rights. The value of a share is the value of these rights.

In 2006, BP made a profit after tax of about 60p per share, from which it paid quarterly dividends amounting in total to just over 20p.

The directors of the company decide how much will be paid to shareholders in dividends and how much will be retained for investment. The company doesn't have to pay the shareholders anything. What the directors decide to pay can be, and generally is, varied in line with the performance of the business. But if the company does declare a dividend, all shareholders have an equal right to receive it.

If the company is wound up, the shareholders are entitled to whatever is left – normally very little – when all the liabilities of the company have been met. Most companies are worth more as a going concern than the realisable value of their assets, and the usual reason a company is wound up is that the business is failing. But the possibility that the value of the business could be distributed to the shareholders influences the value of the stock, even if such a distribution rarely happens in practice.

Another right conferred by a share is the right to vote. At annual general meetings of companies, shareholders elect directors and can pass resolutions to determine the policy of the company. In practice, these meetings are agreeable but insignificant occasions attended by professional advisers and a few, mostly retired, small shareholders. All nominations and resolutions are put forward by incumbent management and approved by overwhelming majorities. The process resembles elections in totalitarian states.

These shareholder powers to elect and remove directors are important, even if rarely exercised. Someone – typically another company – who acquires a controlling block of shares in a company can appoint the senior managers of that company and take control of the direction of the business and of its assets and earnings. The threat of such a takeover means that the value of the stock is influenced not only by what the directors decide to pay out – the dividend policy – but also by the value of these underlying assets and earnings.

Let's look at the earnings and assets of BP. In 2006, the company made a profit of around £12bn after interest and tax. Since there are nearly 20bn shares in issue, earnings per share were 60p. With a share price of 570p, the PE ratio – the ratio of price to earnings – is 9.5. In 2007, BP paid dividends of about 20p, giving a dividend yield of 3.8% on an investment of 570p. These ratios – the price earnings ratio and the dividend yield – are key numbers for all investors.

BP's annual accounts record assets at the end of 2006 of around £45bn. The market value of BP's shares is much higher. With 20bn shares worth 570p each, the market capitalisation of the company – the total value of its outstanding shares – is more than £110bn. The gap between the value of the assets in the accounts and the total value of the company is large, but a difference of this magnitude is common.

The real value of BP's assets – which include cash in the bank, oil installations in remote and unstable parts of the world, and oil in the ground that will not be recovered for many years – is hard to assess or interpret. In 2006, BP invested almost £10bn and the company maintains approximately this level of spending year after year. BP also has substantial intangible assets in its brand, its systems, its experience and its relationships with governments around the world.

The return on a stock like BP will depend partly on the dividend yield but rather more on the capital gain, or loss, that shareholders make as a result of growth of the business and investment in it. In 2006, BP earned about 60p per share, and paid dividends of 20p per share. What did it do with the 40p difference? Retained profits are available to grow the business, but that isn't what BP did in 2006. The profit of £12bn is calculated after an allowance for depreciation and amortisation – the decline in the value of assets through exploitation and use – of almost £10bn. In the same year, new investment was about £10bn, the amount needed to maintain the value of the company's capital. The allowance for depreciation funded the new investment. The company spent the 40p per share difference between earnings and dividends – a total of almost £8bn – on buying back its own shares in the stock market.

The company gives no detailed explanation of why it made these share purchases. Since BP could have paid out 40p on dividends instead, the buy-back makes sense for shareholders only if it increased the value of the shares by at least 40p. Perhaps it did although, given the disappointing performance of the share price during the year, there is no evidence of such an effect.

In any event, BP generated 60p per share of cash in 2006 and distributed that 60p, directly and indirectly, to its shareholders. If that 60p were the total return to shareholders, as it would have been if the buy-backs had had an impact on the share price which matched the money spent, that total return would have exceeded 10%. The company's ability to generate cash makes it reasonable to hope that you might earn the 10% target return from an investment in BP. Most shareholders would be more readily convinced if distributions took the form of dividends rather than buy-backs, and so would I.

Given BP's policy, you will earn less than half of total return from the dividend. The potentially larger, but more volatile, component of total return comes from changes in the capital value of your investment. Even for a stable, well-established company like BP, the share price may rise, or fall, by more in a single month – even sometimes a single day – than the 20p annual dividend.

People in markets offer post hoc explanations for these constant fluctuations – the release of new economic data, say, or a Delphic utterance from the chairman of the Federal Reserve Board. The idea that these events can add or subtract £5bn to or from the value of BP's assets and earnings makes no sense. These share price fluctuations are what natural scientists call 'noise', random interference in physical processes. Developing this analogy, financial economists describe people who trade on hunch and gossip, with little skill or knowledge of what they are doing, as 'noise traders'. Most tip sheets, and many of the books on how to trade the market, are written for noise traders.

As the relevant time horizon extends beyond a few days, the rise and fall of the BP share price will reflect perceptions of the prospects of the company. These assessments will, in turn, depend on the prospects for the oil industry and BP's performance relative to other oil companies, and on market sentiment towards it. Do analysts rate the management team highly? Is a large institution attempting to buy, or sell, a large block of shares?

Behind statistics, there is always a story. BP seems cheap, on many indicators, and from 2003 to 2007 was one of the poorest performing shares among large UK companies. Price earnings ratios below ten are usually indicators of a company that is struggling. A dividend yield of almost 4% is, because of the reduced rate of income tax on dividends, equivalent to a return of 5% on a savings account. Part of the explanation for the low rating is that BP's earnings are boosted by current high oil prices and few investors think that the oil price will remain at current levels. But the company is out of favour with investors.

BP and Shell are Europe's leading oil companies. The world oil industry was for decades dominated by 'the seven sisters' – these two European businesses, and five of the American companies created by the break-up of John D Rockefeller's Standard Oil. In the 1990s, the industry went through a period of consolidation. John Browne, BP's then chief executive, masterminded bids for two large American companies, launched a 'Beyond Petroleum' initiative to position his business as environmentally friendly and socially aware, and produced rapid earnings growth by a vigorous cost-cutting programme. With these moves, Browne was seen as having outflanked both Shell and the company's largest American competitor, Exxon. For the best part of a decade, Browne was Britain's most admired businessman.

Then it all went wrong. Maintenance failures forced the closure of the pipeline to BP's huge Alaskan reserves at Prudhoe Bay, and an explosion at the company's Texas City refinery killed fifteen people. Cost cutting seemed to have had insufficient regard for long-term consequences. Browne lost out in an internal power struggle, and announced his retirement date. Then he resigned after revelations of false statements in court documents about a gay relationship.

This discussion of 'poor performance' and 'out of favour' is based on a comparison between BP and the overall market index. Ever since Charles Dow published the first share price index over a century ago, investors and market professionals have given constant attention to the indices. When they ask 'What is happening in the market?', they will begin by looking at what has happened to 'the index'.

The earliest indices were simply averages of share prices, but the calculation has become more refined. In Britain today, the two main indices are the FTSE (Financial Times Stock Exchange, pronounced *footsie*) 100 share and all-share indices. The first is an index of the prices of the 100 largest companies. It is revised quarterly, so that every three months some of the smaller constituents that have performed poorly are ejected and newcomers admitted. The all-share index includes all companies quoted on the London Stock Exchange. However, the constituents are weighted by their size, so that the 100 largest companies typically account for about 80% of the value of the index.

The value of shares in BP, as for other companies, depends partly on the fundamentals of the company – its assets, earnings, cash flow and dividends, its brand, competitive position, and management strengths – and partly on market sentiment towards it. Returns from shares are the result of the interacting influences of the company's fundamentals and the mind of the market. These issues will be the subject of the next three chapters.

Basics of bonds

Treasury 4.25% 2055 is possibly the most boring investment you could own. If you buy £100 of these bonds, the British government will pay you £4.25, in two half-yearly instalments, every year till 2055 and will then give you back your £100 (the principal).

If you are happy to sit in your armchair for almost fifty years, you can do so with absolute security. Well, nearly absolute security. There is a risk that the British government will not be able or willing to meet these obligations. This is not a very big risk, but it exists, and if the government were the government of Argentina or Zimbabwe, it would be a serious risk. The risk that the issuer will not pay is the credit risk of the bond.

Another risk is that you might stir from your chair and want your £100 back before the redemption date of 7 December 2055. The government not only need not but *may* not repay you a day earlier or a day later. If you want to realise your investment before 2055, you will have to sell your bond to someone else. This is easy to do, but the price you will get for it may be more or less than £100.

Treasury 8% 2021, which was issued at around £100 between 1995 and 1997 and will be repaid in 2021 at £100, currently sells for £131. Price fluctuations such as this are the result of interest rate risk associated with the bond. Interest rate risk may work in the investor's favour – as it has done for initial holders of this bond – or against.

The longer the life of the bond, the greater the interest rate risk. There are some outstanding bonds of the British government – such as 2.5% Consols, first issued in 1888 – that need never be redeemed. These carry the greatest interest rate risk of all. In 1897, and again in 1947, the price of Consols was above £100. By December 1974, it had fallen to £15. In February 2006, the price was back at £63, the highest figure of recent times.

Treasury 4.25% 2055 leaves you exposed to inflation until 2055 which will reduce the value of both the interest and capital repayment. Inflation almost wiped out the savings of people who invested in Consols. In 1888, you could have bought a house with £100; in 1974, you would have paid more than £15 to replace the front door.

Since 1981, you have been able to protect yourself against inflation risk through index-linked government bonds, an even more boring investment. Both the amount of interest and repayment of capital on Treasury 1.25% 2055 are linked to the Retail Prices Index (RPI). The guarantee comes at a price – the much lower interest rate of 1.25%. If inflation is more than 3%, the total return from the indexed bond will be greater; if inflation is less than 3%, you will get a better return from the conventional security.

Indexed bonds remove inflation risk, but all bonds are subject to interest rate and credit risks. Most British government bonds currently sell above their issue price, because interest rates have fallen over the last twenty-five years. Treasury 8% 2021 pays £8 per year, an 8% yield to someone who bought it at its £100 issue price. But for someone who pays £131 today, this return (called the 'running yield') is only 6% on their investment. And then you must factor in the inevitable capital loss between today and 2021. The price of the bond will decline, until it reaches £100 at maturity. The total return on such a bond, including both running yield and capital loss, is known as the gross redemption yield (GRY), and for Treasury 8% 2021 the GRY is less than 5%.

The market moves so that the gross redemption yields are much the same on all bonds with the same maturity, old and new. That outcome is the result of 'arbitrage', a process in which investors look at similar securities and buy those that are relatively cheap and sell those that are relatively expensive. Such arbitrage has pushed up the price of Treasury 8% 2021 to £131.

I have written as though there were a single interest rate, but there isn't. When I began writing this book, the gross redemption yield on a bond maturing in one year – which carries almost no interest rate risk – was 5.4%. This yield fell to 4.7% on bonds maturing in five years and 4.2% for bonds maturing in twenty-five years. This relationship between return and maturity is known as the yield curve.

Conventional wisdom once held that the 'normal' shape of the yield curve is upwards, because longer bonds carry more interest rate risk. But the modern world of bonds rarely seems to be 'normal'. The yield curve didn't slope upwards in 2007, and hasn't often done so since. The main influence on bonds with short maturities (the short end) is the Bank of England's interest rate policy, and the main influence on bonds with long maturities (the long end) is expectations about future inflation. Sometimes, when the Bank's Monetary Policy Committee reacts to worries about inflation by raising interest rates, yields rise at the short end and fall at the long end. By the time I was completing this book, the yield curve had returned to a more 'normal' shape. The yield on one-year and five-year bonds had fallen below that on 25-year bonds, which had changed little.

Even Treasury index-linked 1.25 % 2055 carries interest rate risk. The government will guarantee the purchasing power of your £100 only if you hold the bond through to 2055. As with a conventional bond, you can realise the value of your bond earlier only by selling it to another holder. The price of an indexed bond will vary with real interest rates, rather than nominal interest rate.

You might expect that real interest rates would not vary much, but they do. In 1998, during the New Economy bubble, conventional investors, expecting to become rich from their dot.com stocks, were not interested in securities that did little more than guarantee their holders against inflation. The price of index-linked stocks fell, and the real gross redemption yield on them rose above 4%.

After the bubble burst, more realistic expectations set in. The price of index-linked stocks rose and yields fell. Long-term investors were attracted to these assets. In 2006, Treasury index-linked 1.25% 2055 proved a racy investment. Pension funds looking for long-term security pushed the price of these bonds up by 30% in just a few months. The real yield on this bond fell below 0.5%.

British government securities have just about as low a credit risk as can be found. (Although people who bought Chinese and Russian bonds in the nineteenth century thought these involved little credit risk at the moment of issue.) The British government can borrow for fifty years at 4.25%, but only the governments of other large, rich and stable countries, and some international agencies like the World Bank, can match this rate.

The biggest and best industrial companies, like General Electric and Shell, rank a little way behind these governments and agencies, followed by the leading banks. Banks were once regarded as the best risks of all – houses like Rothschild prospered because their banks were more creditworthy than kings – but there have been too many instances in modern history of banks letting down their customers, bondholders and shareholders. The security you are right to feel when dealing with major banks should come, in large part, from the knowledge that governments will not allow such institutions to fail.

The downside of this implicit guarantee – more disturbing, therefore, to taxpayers than to investors – is that large retail banks use their deposit base to support complex speculative transactions that their senior management may not understand, or are too ready to accept. The successive collapses of financial institutions in 2008, and the costs of guarantees and bailouts to avert losses on further collapses, illustrated just how expensive the consequences might be.

Credit rating agencies, such as Moody's and Standard and Poors, make influential judgments of the quality of borrowers and their bonds. The very best corporate borrowers, along with the governments of rich countries in Europe and North America, enjoy credit ratings of 'triple A'. And, to the surprise of some and the ultimate disillusionment of others, many of the structured products, which I'll describe in Chapter 9, also qualified for the approval of these agencies. The top four credit ratings are described as 'investment grade' and many institutions will only buy investment grade bonds. Ratings below investment grade are known as 'junk'.

The initial yield on a bond reflects the credit risk when the bond is issued, but a bond which is prime investment grade when issued may deteriorate over its life. Ford and General Motors were once among the most respected companies in the world but, by 2006, fears over these companies' obligations and their weak current trading, meant their bonds were rated as junk.

Bonds were once the most staid and boring backwater of the financial system. The Government Broker, recognisable by his top hat, would assess the market on behalf of the Bank of England. He (a female Government Broker was even more improbable than a female Prime Minister) was a partner in Mullens & Co, and frequently bore the surname Mullens.

Mullens & Co disappeared in Big Bang and, within a very few years, the former backwater of bond markets had become the roughest of seas. Michael Lewis, whose account of life and work at Salomon described the City at its most raw, was a bond trader. So was Sherman McCoy, the fictional Master of the Universe in Tom Wolfe's *The Bonfire of the Vanities*. Volumes of bond trading grew explosively, and so did the profits of (some of) the firms that handled it.

The causes of the change in the nature of bond markets were not Big Bang itself, but financial innovations in the United States which were imitated in London. An early idea was the strip, which separated the income from the principal of a bond, so that one person might receive the £4.25 interest per year for fifty years and another the £100 at the end of fifty years. Some people might have needed income, while others wanted to secure a future liability. A rapid proliferation of more complex derivative products, whose commercial rationale seemed less compelling, followed.

In the 1970s, a graduate student wrote a thesis investigating the default rate on corporate bonds. He demonstrated that the premium on risky bonds seemed too high – the interest rate differential was more than sufficient to compensate for the default rate. That graduate student was Michael Milken and, in the following decade, his name would strike fear into the hearts (if they had them) of senior corporate executives across America.

Milken pioneered the issue of junk bonds, and for a few years the investment bank he worked for, Drexel Burnham Lambert, almost monopolised that market. The idea was to issue very large quantities of low-quality bonds to enable people without much money to take over very large companies. Using the results of his graduate school research, Milken argued that junk bonds would produce returns in excess of those available from conventional investments. Few students find, as Milken did, a thesis subject that will make them unimaginably rich.

Junk bonds allowed the takeover of RJR Nabisco, the food and tobacco conglomerate, by KKR, a private equity business, that would, for a decade, be the largest acquisition in history. The movement reached its apotheosis when an unstable Canadian of large ambition and smaller talent, Robert Campeau, used this financing mechanism to acquire many of America's largest department stores, including the iconic Bloomingdale's (and damaged those businesses, in some cases irreversibly, as he failed to stave off the bankruptcy of his fragile empire). The 1980s boom ultimately turned to bust. KKR made no profit from RJR Nabisco though many fees were paid on their transformative deal; Milken was sent to prison; Drexel Burnham Lambert collapsed. Salomon ran into trouble after deceiving the US Treasury in bond auctions, was rescued by Warren Buffett, and eventually absorbed into Citigroup. Few participants – not even Buffett – found the outcome a happy one.

There is no such thing as an absolutely safe long-term investment. If you know that you want to buy something in 2055, Treasury index-linked 1.25% 2055 is about as good as you can get. But not many of us are as certain about our future plans. In Chapter 7, I'll discuss more systematically what is meant by security and by risk. The key issue for the intelligent investor is that achieving security does not lie in avoiding all risk – which is impossible – but in diversification. Do not be too exposed to any particular contingency, however improbable. Hold as many options as possible against a necessarily unpredictable future.

The relevance of bonds to an investment portfolio is not that they are completely safe, but that they may do well in circumstances in which other investments will not. British government bonds served their holders well in the Great Depression of the early 1930s, and were the only major asset category to do so. Indexed bonds would perform strongly in circumstances – such as the oil crisis of 1973-4 – when shares and property tumbled in value. The conditions that would strongly favour indexed bonds have not occurred since they were created, but they have occurred in the past and they might occur in the future. They began to emerge in 2008.

Bonds ought to be boring. The market in shares is associated with, and contributes to, the growth of companies and their investment and expansion. Over time, businesses grow and investors and traders share these profits. But Treasury 4.25% 2055 is, well, just Treasury 4.25% 2055. However often you trade, however many derivative securities you construct on the back of it, the government will not pay a penny more, or a penny less.

But the excitement continues. In the new millennium, junk bonds re-emerged, on unprecedented scale, and in 2007 were the main component of a new series of financial crises. I'll come back to that resurgence, and its consequences, in Chapters 5 and 9.

Pillars of property

If you own a property, you own both the building and the land on which it stands. The insurance value of your house is its rebuilding cost. In Britain today, that rebuilding cost is generally less, and sometimes much less, than the market value of the house. My London house, for example, is worth more than three times its insurance value. The site is a great deal more valuable than the building itself.

Sometimes, however, the replacement cost is greater than the market value. This implies that if the building did not exist, no one would plan to construct it. Most stately homes are impractical for modern living and the rebuilding cost exceeds the market value. At the other end of the spectrum, a small terraced house in northern England may also be worth less than its rebuilding cost. The population has moved away and demand for property is weak. There is not much new construction and what there is is to much higher standards.

Housing has been a very good investment for most people in Britain. Over the last ten years, residential property has done better than any other major asset class, although the previous ten years were relatively disappointing.

If you draw up a personal balance sheet in the way a company would, you are very likely to find that your most valuable asset by far is your house. Yet your house is not quite like your other investments. You bought your house in order to live in it, and for the rest of your life you have to live somewhere. That doesn't mean you are indifferent to its value, as you will learn from the interminable dinner party bores who celebrated the rising value of their house with too much Sauvignon Blanc.

If you mentally separate yourself as investor from yourself as consumer, then you would have to charge yourself rent. The only rationale for higher house prices would be that, in the long run, you would be able to charge yourself more rent. If you are under forty-five, then you are probably worse off when house prices rise – you expect to live a long time, and pay a lot of rent. If you are older, then you have probably bought the most expensive house you are likely to buy. The value of the asset you own exceeds the value of the rent you must pay yourself. Much of the value of the house will accrue to your heirs. Only you can decide how you view that legacy. For all these reasons, your house, and the associated mortgage, cannot be treated in the same way as the assets you own for purely investment motives.

The mortgage on their house is the way in which most people first encounter the magic of gearing, or leverage. (The latter, American, term, is becoming increasingly common on both sides of the Atlantic.) Leverage allows you to have assets that exceed your net worth.

Suppose you own a house today worth £300,000 with a mortgage of £100,000. You might have begun by putting down a deposit of

£50,000 to buy that house for £150,000. The value of the house has doubled – from £150,000 to £300,000. But the equity in the house – the difference between the value of the property and the debt – has increased fourfold, from £50,000 to £200,000.

If leverage sounds too good to be true, it is, because it works in both directions. In the late 1980s, many young professionals in London were desperate to find a place on the housing ladder. They might have bought a £100,000 flat with a loan of £95,000. Their finances went spinning out of control when interest rates rose and house prices fell. If their flat would realise only £85,000, their savings of £5000 had become a debit of £10,000. If these individuals had been companies, they would have been required to declare themselves insolvent. As matters were, they were unable to move from their property because they could not repay the outstanding mortgage.

Folk wisdom in Britain has it that property prices always go up, an observation derived from an economic environment of steady inflation. German house prices have not risen in the last decade; those in Berlin have fallen by around half since reunification of the city. Finnish house prices fell by around 40% in the early 1990s, and those in Hong Kong fell by more after the 1997 handover. In the US in 2007, those who had hoped to spin a profit on newly built houses discovered their mistake.

'Safe as houses' may be true if you plan to live in one, but you should expect volatility in the value of property you plan to sell or let. The history of the property market is full of the stories of well-known names – from Donald Trump to the Reichmann brothers (who created the financial services centre at Canary Wharf) – who have discovered to their considerable cost that leverage can work both ways.

The positive experience of owner-occupiers has encouraged many individuals to buy houses and flats to let. Although an investment property of reasonable quality is likely to cost £100,000 or more, gearing means that such a property can be bought with a deposit of £20,000 to £25,000. While residential property is less volatile than most other asset classes, leverage multiplies the risk. Buy-to-let is a low-risk strategy only for someone rich enough to make it a modest part of a larger portfolio.

While individuals have recently been active in the purchase of buy-to-let investment properties, there has been little new institutional investment in residential property. Insurance companies and pension funds prefer commercial property – shops, offices and industrial premises – which only rich individuals can hold directly. Small investors can access these properties through funds, and they generally should.

The ownership of property was once bound up with power and status – landed estates were associated with aristocratic titles. The capitalist owned the premises – the mill, the shop, the factory – where the workers laboured. Today, great estates are liabilities, not assets, and businesses rarely own the premises they occupy. Financial markets have become more sophisticated, and premises have become less specialised. Once, a textile business or a steel company would build a mill or a plant to its own particular requirement. Today's companies will often rent space on an industrial estate, in a shed adaptable to many alternative uses.

On the main streets of provincial towns, shops and offices are little changed. You will pass the offices of solicitors and other small businesses, and shops occupied by chain retailers. The professional firms (or the pension funds of their partners) may own their premises; the retailers generally will not. If you pass to the side streets or even visit some of the less desirable high street sites – secondary locations – you will see charity shops, a familiar indicator of a location in decline. Trade has moved to out-of-town locations, and retailers have moved to retail warehouses on the outskirts.

In the City of London, office blocks built only twenty to thirty years ago are pulled down to make way for modern replacements with cabling and air conditioning, and in the style of internal layout that today's office workers require. Yesterday's office, like yesterday's shop, is outdated, and the implication for the investor is that even if the property does not physically decay its economic value does. In the most valuable locations – such as prime sites in the City – the value of the property lies mostly in the land, rather than the building, and that is why constant renewal of the building makes sense. For the shed on the outskirts of a northern town, however, the proportions are reversed – the property value lies mostly in the cost of the building.

Commercial property is leased from its owner to a tenant. A typical English lease has a fixed initial term – perhaps twenty-five years – with five-yearly rent reviews. At each five-year period, the rent is reset in line with the rent of comparable local properties, with arbitration if the parties cannot agree. Rent reviews are often 'upward only' – if the current market rent is below the actual rent, the actual rent remains at its previous level. A property for which the actual rent is below the market rent is called 'reversionary', while if the actual rent is above the market level the building is described as 'over-rented'.

A tenant who signs a twenty-five-year lease does not have to occupy the property for twenty-five years. The lease may be assigned to a different tenant, but the rent remains payable to the landlord (and by the original tenant if the new tenant fails to do so). A tenant may be able to assign a reversionary property at a premium, but would have to pay someone to take a lease on an over-rented property. These specifics of the terms of leases, the conventions of the property market, and the legal framework, are vital to property investors, and vary substantially from country to country.

For these reasons – tax complications are another – it is much more difficult to buy overseas property than overseas shares. Until recently, only the largest institutional investor could easily invest in property in other countries. This has now changed. Not only are the Saturday papers full of invitations to buy apartments in Bulgaria – invitations that should generally be resisted – but many funds invest in foreign property.

Facts about funds

The conventional retail investor usually holds securities indirectly, through investment funds. Funds may be open ended or closed end. Open-ended investment companies (OEICs)) are what used to be known as unit trusts in the UK (and often still are) and are called mutual funds in the US. Hedge funds and insurance bonds are also open-ended funds. Investment trusts, investment companies and real estate investment trusts are closed-end funds.

The manager of an open-ended fund computes the value of the

portfolio regularly and will buy or sell shares at a price that reflects that underlying value. These funds are called open ended because the size of the fund grows or shrinks as the fund attracts new investors, or as existing investors redeem their units. The size of the closed-end fund is determined by the amount the original shareholders subscribed. Some funds, especially hedge funds, may be closed to new investors. They will redeem shares from their existing holders, but will not expand the fund to accommodate new ones.

You can dispose of your share of the portfolio in a closed-end fund only by selling it to someone else. Traditionally, this meant a closed-end fund could be more adventurous – you could borrow, or invest in assets that were not easily realisable. But open-ended hedge funds, have recently been far more adventurous than any closed-end fund. Hedge funds deal with the potential problem of realising illiquid assets by imposing conditions that allow them to delay pay-outs to their investors. Sometimes they exercise such conditions. When the property market fell at the end of 2007, many open-ended property funds suspended redemptions.

The value of your share in a closed-end fund can be more or less than the value of your share of the underlying assets in the portfolio. The possibility of variability in this discount or premium to asset value compounds the investment risk. If property is currently a fashionable investment, then real estate investment trust shares may sell at a premium to their asset value – the value of the shares is greater than the value of the properties the company owns. If emerging market stocks are unfashionable, it may be possible to buy shares at a large discount in investment companies specialising in emerging market stocks. You can sometimes buy out-of-favour funds at discounts of 20% or more. Closed-end funds involve extra risks but also extra opportunities.

In practice, most closed-end funds sell at discounts to their asset value. If the fund is at a premium, the manager can issue more shares to satisfy demand, and often does since fees can be earned from the new issue and from managing the additional assets. If the shares are at a discount, then there might be a potential gain to the holders in winding up the fund and giving them back their money. Managers are usually not keen to do this. Some people – arbitrageurs – try to make a profit by taking control of companies with large discounts to asset value. But the costs of taking control may be large, and there may be taxes and other costs to pay in realising the portfolio. The prospect of liquidation limits the size of the discount, but not by much. Buying shares in closed-end funds at a discount may sometimes be an attractive way of investing in out-of-favour assets. There is rarely a case for buying a closed-end fund at a premium.

Most funds, open or closed ended, are actively managed. Passive funds simply replicate the performance of an index. A computer buys and sells shares to minimise the tracking error – the difference between the index and the value of the assets the fund holds. A more recent innovation is the exchange traded fund (ETF). The mechanics of ETFs are slightly more complex but the outcome is that the investor can buy or sell a share that will reproduce almost exactly the performance of an index – the FT all-share index, an index of Brazilian stocks, or a basket of commodities. Both index funds and exchange traded funds have low expenses and dealing costs and should play a major role in the investment strategies of intelligent investors.

In this chapter, I've described the three main asset categories available and the choice of direct or indirect investment. In the next three, I will review the relationship between prices and values – the fundamental issues of intelligent investment. In Chapters 10 to 13 I'll explain how to build these different assets into an investment portfolio.

CHAPTER 4

EFFICIENT MARKETS

Efficient markets and asset values

Few of the many jokes about economists are funny. One tells of the finance professor walking down the street with his wife. 'There's a ten pound note on the pavement,' she says. 'Don't be silly,' he replies, 'if there was, someone would already have picked it up.'

The joke refers to the efficient market hypothesis (EMH), but the joke is on the teller. There are few £10 notes on the street, for the reason the professor elucidates. People rarely drop £10 notes, and when they do, the notes are quickly picked up. Most pieces of litter that look like £10 notes are, indeed, litter. The professor's theory of why there are no £10 notes on the pavement is illuminating. It will save considerable time for anyone who plans to make a living searching for £10 notes on the streets of London. The theory is not, however, true. There *are* occasional discarded £10 notes. There are also people who make profits by picking them up. Otherwise, £10 notes in the street would be easier to find.

In a securities market, the £10 note is the difference between the price and the value of an asset. Since the efficient market hypothesis is illuminating but not true, such differences occur, but rarely, and they are hard to identify with confidence. So what determines the relationship between price and value?

An economist, another joke goes, knows the price of everything and the value of nothing. The relationship between price and value is a subject with a long history – particularly amongst accountants.

There are two basic approaches:
- the value of an asset is what someone is willing to pay for it;
- the value of an asset is the cash it will generate over its life.

I'll call these the 'mark to market' principle and the 'fundamental value' principle. Almost all valuation methods are based on one or both of these principles.

If you are appraising a property, you might call in a valuer to mark it to market. The valuer will have experience of transactions in similar properties in the area and should have a good idea of what the building will fetch. The mark to market principle is easy to apply in this case.

The fundamental value principle looks instead at the cash generated over the life of the asset. Begin with the flow of quarterly rents from a property, taking account of possible increases at future rent reviews, then deduct any expenses you might need to incur to preserve the value of the property.

Perhaps the building has a finite life, like an industrial warehouse or modern office block; you will need to consider what the property will be worth when the structure needs to be replaced. Other buildings can, with some attention, maintain a satisfactory flow of rental income for ever.

The fundamental value of a company is calculated in a similar way. Look at either the path of dividends or the stream of earnings. If you focus on dividends, observe the current dividend level and conjecture how rapidly the company will increase that dividend in future years. If you focus on earnings, you need to estimate their probable growth, bearing in mind the growth rate of the economy, the industry, and the specific prospects of the business.

The mark to market principle and fundamental value principle are certainly different, and seem incompatible. They involve different styles of thinking and lead to different approaches to investment. The mark to market principle is easier, and less speculative. But it is a common mistake to emphasise what you can measure at the expense of more important things you can't. It is generally better to be approximately right than precisely wrong.

Which of these principles should be applied? Market prices can't be completely independent of fundamental value because opinions about fundamental value influence market prices. This is the metaphor of markets as 'voting machine'. Everyone who trades registers an opinion. The results of this survey of opinion are reported in the financial papers every day. The metaphor contains a possible reconciliation of the mark to market and fundamental value principles: the market price is the result of a plebiscite on fundamental value.

The market is democratic in the sense that everyone is allowed to vote, but it is not a fair election. The weight given to your opinion depends on the amount of money you can put behind your vote. The votes of Citigroup and Goldman Sachs count more than the votes of you and me. Perhaps this is as it should be. If you are really confident of your opinion, you can make that opinion count by putting a lot of money behind it. I shall describe how George Soros brought off a spectacular coup by doing exactly that.

The concept of the market as voting machine provides a justification for my claim that every investor can access, without charge, all the expertise that the financial services industry can bring to bear. That idea leads to the efficient market hypothesis. If the market price were an average of informed estimates of fundamental value, markets would be efficient, not only in the narrow technical sense that all available information is in the price, but also in a broader sense – market prices provide signals that guide the efficient allocation of investment funds.

In this chapter I'll focus on the narrower interpretation, the one relevant to investors. Or rather three interpretations, because there are three variants of the efficient market hypothesis (EMH) involving progressively more demanding assumptions:

- the weak form – past movements of prices convey no information about future price movements;
- the semi-strong form – all public information about securities is already reflected in their price; and
- the strong form – everything that could be known about securities is already reflected in their price.

Louis Bachelier, the pioneer of mathematical analysis of security prices, discovered his data resembled the observations of natural processes, such as the movement of small particles suspended in a fluid. Physicists call this behaviour Brownian motion. Financial economists, more engagingly, employ the term random walk. A random walk is directionless. Every step is independent of every previous step and equally likely to be in one direction as another. All three versions of the efficient market hypothesis claim that securities prices will follow a random walk. The random walk is a mathematical concept inseparable from the EMH.

Most of the evidence observed by early researchers was favourable to the random walk theory. The earliest evaluations were undertaken by statisticians – until the 1950s, Wall Street and the City of London were innumerate and there was no serious finance theory in business schools. At Stanford, Holbrook Working showed that long series of commodity prices followed a random walk. The British statistician, Maurice Kendall, analysed long series of stock prices, and more than 100 years of cotton price data. He concluded that 'The Stock Exchange, it would appear, has a memory lasting less than a week.'

While none of the three versions of the efficient market hypothesis is true, each offers its own shafts of illumination. Markets may have no memory, but commentators on markets do, and the random walk theory suggests that most of their observations and analysis are of little use. 'Shares are 20% lower than a year ago – this is a buying opportunity.' 'The market needs to pause for breath after its recent rise.' 'The dollar is experiencing a technical correction, which will continue.' You regularly hear statements like these in popular discussion.

The weak form of the efficient market hypothesis claims that no such statement can ever be justified because prices move without knowledge of their history. The probability that they will rise next year, or next month, or today, is unaffected by whether prices rose yesterday afternoon, or last week, or in the first quarter of 2008.

The weak EMH is a blow for people who rely on projections of historic trends, or identification of recurrent patterns, to make their investment decisions – most of all for chartists, whom I'll describe in the next chapter. But the weak version does nothing to discourage people from looking at fundamental values. Rather the opposite – the weak EMH encourages you to believe that you might make money at the expense of noise traders by close attention to fundamentals.

There is a considerable practical difference between weak and strong EMH. Strong EMH – that everything that could be known about securities is already in their price – essentially rules out any possibility of investment skill. Legendary investors like Buffett have simply been lucky. No research or analysis can be useful, because its results will be reflected in the market. Put like this, the theory seems absurd.

Indeed, the strong version of EMH contains an inherent contradiction. If it were the case that research and analysis could never be profitable, because the result of that research and analysis would always be 'in the price', why would anyone undertake such research and analysis? If prices were always efficient, what could be the process by which they become efficient?

The semi-strong version of the efficient market hypothesis is less extreme, claiming only that information is 'in the price' if publicly available. Thus the semi-strong version does not exclude the possibility that insightful new analysis, unpublished or not yet widely circulated, might be valuable to those who possess it. It certainly permits possibilities of profit from trading on private information. The investment banker who knows of a planned takeover, the corporate executive who knows that the coming results will be worse than is generally expected, can both deal advantageously on the basis of this inside information.

Such insider trading was once the daily practice of brokers and fund managers, and put small investors at a substantial disadvantage. But most countries, including Britain, have made it illegal for people who have inside knowledge to deal. These laws do not cover all forms of trading on private information, nor can they ever be perfectly effective, but they have probably reduced the incidence of these practices.

Few people are convicted of insider trading. This is because evidence is hard to obtain not because the activity is rare. The cases that have come to court show that criminal insiders often made little profit from their unlawful activities because their actions moved market prices against them. Information held by insiders does not have to be announced to percolate into the market-place.

That observation has important implications for intelligent investors. Be very wary of sustained individual price movements that seem to have no explanation. A falling share price may be the result of inside knowledge; a rise that cannot be accounted for may herald a possible takeover. Perhaps information the investor does not know, and may never know, is already reflected in the market. Be suspicious of advisers whose predictions are based on extrapolations from past price movements, or who claim to see patterns in data.

Information asymmetry

Market prices measure prevailing market sentiment, incorporating all the analysis, prejudice, skills and irrationality of market players. What is general knowledge will normally be 'in the price' and of little value to investors. Information such as 'Tesco is a well-managed business', 'Philip Green is an outstanding retailer', or 'Utilities are a sound business', though true, does not provide a reason to buy related stocks. This information is in the market.

'General knowledge' includes such knowledge as we have of the future as well as knowledge of the present and past. The term 'consensus forecast' is used to describe the common expectations of City people about economic prospects. There usually isn't a very wide spread of opinions. The canard that economists always disagree is much exaggerated. (Although there are many other, well-founded, criticisms of economists, especially of zealots who embrace the EMH with fundamentalist fervour.) You don't have to pay for the consensus forecast, or spend time reading about it – it's already 'in the market'.

The glossy descriptions of economic prospects that financial advisers, investment managers and banks circulate to clients may be illuminating (I rarely find them so) but not as a guide to investment decisions. You don't have any valuable insight into the future – and nor do they. I've sometimes asked people in business and finance, who crave accurate economic forecasts, 'If I gave you the exact figure for national income three years from now, what would you do with the information?' Useful economic knowledge is usually specific rather than general.

This central role of information, and the dependence of trade on differential information, distinguishes securities markets from other markets. Trade in modern economies is mostly the result of specialisation. I grow apples, you grow pears, and each of us gains by swapping one for the other. We call on the plumber for his specialist skills. We buy from General Motors because the company is organised to produce cars, and we are not. America sells computers in return for Saudi oil. All these exchanges normally benefit both parties to the trade.

Sometimes trade in financial markets has a similar character. An importer buys foreign currency because he and his customers are based in the UK, and his supplier is based in China. The commercial transaction requires a foreign exchange transaction.

But most trade in securities markets – even in foreign currency markets – is not like that. Both parties to the transaction have the same need – to make as much money as possible; they just have different ideas about how to do it. I think the dollar will rise in value, you think it will fall. I think Tesco shares are underpriced, you think they are overvalued. In each of these trades, one of us will be proved right, the other wrong.

In any market in which there is wide and irresolvable uncertainty, in any market where participants have different information and beliefs, many trades will be the result of mistakes. And in financial markets, uncertainty and differential information are endemic.

A brilliant exposition of the problems this would create for market efficiency – in both a narrow and a wide sense – was provided in 1970 by George Akerlof, who would receive the Nobel Prize for his analysis. Akerlof used the metaphor of the market for lemons. Some cars are 'lemons', prone to faults. The seller knows whether the car is a lemon, the buyer does not. If the price of the used car reflects the average probability that the car is a lemon, that is a good price for owners of lemons and a bad price for everyone else. Sellers will be inclined to sell lemons, but not good cars. The proportion of cars on used car lots that are lemons will be much greater than the proportion of lemons in the population as a whole.

As buyers realise this, the price they will pay for any second-hand car, lemon or not, will fall. The result of this will be to reduce still further the proportion of good cars on sale. The outcome is a market characterised by mutual mistrust, low prices, low-quality products, and buyer dissatisfaction. As I was writing this book, that realisation and that outcome are exactly what happened in the market for structured credit products.

If you fail to understand the problem of imperfect information, you may fall victim to the 'winner's curse': you think you have won, only to discover subsequently that you wish you hadn't. This problem was first identified when the US government auctioned offshore oil blocks. The bidders in all cases were the same large oil companies. Both the government and the companies quickly realised that the successful bids were higher than had been expected, or were justified. All the companies wanted the oil and had similar access to funds. Their preferences and resources were the same, but their assessments differed. All judgments were to some degree in error, but the successful bidder was – by the nature of the auction – the one who bid highest. The most common reason one estimate was higher than the rest was that the winning company's geologists had made a mistake.

The notorious auction of British mobile phone licences in 2000 was carefully designed to avoid this version of the winner's curse. Yet the same problem emerged, in somewhat different form. Assets will always tend to be held by people who are too optimistic about their value rather than people who are too pessimistic.

Strategic trading, moral hazard and market manipulation

An experiment by Joe Stiglitz focused on the consequence of that observation. The professor would invite a class to bid for the money contained in his wallet. Respondents were invited to estimate the likely value of the contents, and bid accordingly. To participate would be a mistake. If a bidder offers less than the amount in the wallet, the professor can refuse to trade. If the bid is more than that sum, it will be accepted. If the seller is willing to sell, the buyer is foolish to buy. Why do I want to buy what they want to sell? In such a market, you never do. Anyone tempted to buy securities in an IPO, or to purchase a complex derivative from an investment bank, should ponder the lesson of the wallet auction.

These structures give rise to a problem known as 'moral hazard'. Wherever there are imperfections of information, people with superior information can use that knowledge to sell products for more than they are worth, or rid themselves of risks which others underestimate. As the lemon example illustrates, the result is a decline in the average quality of products and risks. Moral hazard has always been evident in insurance and credit markets (there is no divorce insurance because only unhappy couples would pay the premium) and is widespread in financial services.

Sellers of securities usually have the advantage over buyers. The people who run a company know more about it than the people who plan to invest in it. The people who issue a bond know more about the issuer than the buyer. The people who construct a complex derivative understand its characteristics better than the people who buy these securities. Some of the derivatives and structured products of modern finance can only be valued – if at all – by the banks that devised them. This not only leaves the purchasers vulnerable, but leaves the banks themselves at the mercy of the few employees who understand the models.

Once oil companies understood the winner's curse, they adjusted their bids downwards. Markets characterised by differential information are reflexive, because prices reveal information about the behaviour and the expectations of other parties, and these may in turn affect their assessments of fundamental values. Ultimately, this may give rise to strategic behaviour. The motive for trade is to influence the expectations of others, and hence their business or trading decisions.

When Guinness successfully bid for Distillers in 1986, the management of the company secretly organised a group of rich individuals to buy shares in the brewery. The objective was to give a flattering impression of the value of the shares that would be provided in exchange for Distillers' stock. The implicit calculation was that it was cheaper to pay the losses on these transactions than to make a higher offer to all the shareholders. The scheme was exposed and several of the participants, including the former chief executive, Ernest Saunders, went to prison.

In 2004, Citigroup bond traders hatched a scheme called 'Dr Evil', which placed 188 sell orders simultaneously. Their – correct – judgment was that they could buy back a larger volume of bonds cheaply in the ensuing panic. The bank paid a £13m fine after its actions were disclosed.

The most entertaining form of market manipulation is 'the corner', in which a bidder attempts to dominate the whole of the available supply and force buyers (especially short sellers, who have sold shares they do not own and may be obliged to buy) to pay whatever price the bidder chooses. The most famous instance was an attempt by the Hunt family, Texas oil billionaires, to corner the world silver market in 1980. Individuals rooted through their attics to buy silver to add to the Hunts' hoard, but in the end the oil fortune was inadequate to achieve the corner, and the price (and the fortune) collapsed.

An outrageous case of market manipulation at the expense of retail investors was the practice in which some mutual fund managers allowed friends and associates to trade in the funds on a favoured basis, making profits at the expense of fund investors. As with insider dealing, extensive regulation seeks to protect you – and market professionals – from abuses that involve the fraudulent exploitation – or creation – of differential information. This regulation is less than perfectly effective. Necessarily so – the financial services industry exists because of differential information.

Illuminating but not true

The prevalence and persistence of information asymmetry is the reason no one should accept that securities markets are efficient in either a broad or a narrow sense. Yet the efficient market hypothesis has a sufficiently strong hold on the investment world – particularly among finance academics – that deviations are still described as 'anomalies'. Over the last two decades, evidence of anomalies has accumulated steadily. One collection of essays is provocatively titled *A Non-Random Walk down Wall Street*, (Lo and MacKinlay, 1999), in deliberate contrast to Burton Malkiel's popular introduction to the efficient market theory in *A Random Walk down Wall Street* (Malkiel, 2007). Robert Shiller, who achieved wide attention by publishing

Irrational Exuberance (Shiller, 2000) at the peak of the New Economy boom, has become intellectual leader of the sceptics.

Some investment rules and systems seem to be systematically profitable, at least for a time. 'Sell in May and go away.' Benefit from 'the small company effect' – consistently higher returns on smaller companies that may be the subject of less intensive research. Buy 'the dogs of the Dow' – the worst performing large companies of the previous year.

These ideas rarely work. There are several problems. It is always possible to find some such pattern by studying the past; that doesn't mean that the same pattern will persist in future. Even if the scheme appears profitable, profits may be inadequate to offset the costs of turning over a portfolio. And the very fact of publishing these seemingly attractive investment ideas may lead others to follow them, and reduce the potential gains the investor sought. The efficient market hypothesis strikes back.

So, is the empirical claim that prices follow a random walk correct? You may still be puzzled by the equivalence of the weak EMH and the random walk theory. Why does the assumption that all information is 'in the price' imply that prices follow a random walk? Bachelier's empirical observation of the random walk, and Kendall's supporting analysis, preceded a comprehensive explanation of the relationship by several decades.

The definitive account of that relationship came in 1953 from the Nobel Prize winning economist Paul Samuelson, whose introductory textbook is familiar to everyone who has taken a basic economics course. Return to that metaphor of markets as voting machine. The result of every election depends on the question you put to the voters. The question that is put to the voters here is not 'What do you think the Federal Reserve should do?' It is not even 'What do you think the Federal Reserve will do?' The question is 'How do you think the bond market and the currency market will react to what the Federal Reserve will do?'

Suppose people think that the Federal Reserve Board will raise American interest rates or Marks and Spencer will announce good results. These expectations lead them to sell American bonds, and buy dollars, or to buy Marks and Spencer shares. Views about the future are therefore built into the level of prices we see in the market today. If the Federal Reserve Board is expected to act, bond yields and currencies will already reflect this, and will move only if these expectations change. If Marks and Spencer's business is improving, the market price will already acknowledge the improvement. The price will move only if people think that outcomes will be better still, or that these outcomes will not, after all, be as good as previously expected. Traders are not voting on what Marks and Spencer's results will be, or whether Marks and Spencer is a good business; they are voting on what they think will happen to Marks and Spencer's share price. They vote 'up' when they buy, and 'down' when they sell.

Keynes described this process through the analogy of a newspaper beauty contest. Competitors were asked to choose the most beautiful faces, and the most beautiful were those selected by the majority choices of all competitors. As Keynes explained, what thoughtful entrants are trying to do is not to choose the most beautiful, but what they think others will find most beautiful, or even what they think people will think other people will find most beautiful – and so on.

Samuelson elaborated this idea. If unanticipated events were more likely to increase prices than to lower them, then that expectation would itself be anticipated, and prices would rise immediately. If unanticipated events were likely to lower prices, then prices would fall until that ceased to be true. That is why, Samuelson claimed, properly anticipated prices fluctuate randomly.

Market reactions to events and to changes in the trading environment are not easy to predict and may seem disproportionate to the events that trigger them. Certainly they may be larger than can possibly be explained by reference to assessments of fundamental value. The worst day in the history of modern stock markets was 19 October 1987, when the Dow Jones Industrial Average, the most widely followed US stock index, dropped 22%. The Brady Commission, established by the government to investigate, concluded that the fall was triggered by a higher than expected trade deficit and a rumour of higher taxes, magnified by the use of portfolio insurance – computerised trading systems that sold large quantities of stocks when markets fell.

Perhaps. In any event, none of these factors was directly relevant to the British stock market, which fell by almost as much. Within a few days, and for no obvious reasons, market sentiment switched from sanguine optimism to unreasonable pessimism. On days such as 19 October 1987, market movements can only be explained by reference to market psychology; attempts to explain them by reference to changes in fundamental value are simply rationalisations. Prices rise or fall in the short run on ephemeral changes in sentiment, with little if any basis in fundamental value.

In some markets, such as that for Old Master paintings, concepts of fundamental value are themselves elusive. These market prices are the result of the whims of a small number of very rich men. The principle that an asset is worth what someone will pay remains dominant in this market. But it is implausible that the prices of bonds, shares or properties can for ever remain unrelated to fundamental value.

Prices move around fundamental value – sometimes violently so, as on 19 October 1987 or in the New Economy bubble. Constantly changing, prices are influenced, but not determined, by a fundamental value that is itself unknown and constantly changing. From time to time, the path of market prices strays far from the path of fundamental value, but these divergences are ultimately corrected. Prices display 'short-term positive serial correlation' – if you examine prices over a day, a week, or a month, then upward price movements are slightly more likely to be followed by further upward price movements. Downward price movements are also more likely to lead to further downward price movements. This feature of short-term price change is called 'momentum'.

There is also evidence of 'long-term negative serial correlation'. If you look at prices over much longer periods – three or five years – upward movements are more than averagely likely to be followed by downward movements, while periods of underperformance of this length are more than averagely likely to be followed by periods of outperformance. This feature of long-term price movements is called mean reversion.

Investment strategies for imperfectly efficient markets

The efficient market hypothesis, although illuminating, is not true. Momentum rules in the short run mean reversion in the long run. A day is short run, five years is long, run. If there were a means of telling just when the short run becomes the long run, there would be a sure-fire route to making money: ride the wave, jump off before it breaks. This isn't possible. The two phenomena of momentum – short-run positive serial correlation – and mean reversion – long-run negative serial correlation – map into two basic investment techniques. One is understanding the vagaries of market sentiment; the other, analysing the sources of fundamental value.

The first strategy seeks to understand the mind of the market and the psychology of its participants – exploit momentum, buy into market rises, sell ahead of market falls. The alternative approach ignores these fluctuations, focuses attention on fundamental value, and anticipates that, in the long run, truth will out through mean reversion. The first of these strategies can be associated with George Soros, the second with Warren Buffett. These two men are the best known and most successful investors of recent decades. Both are now over seventy, having begun their public investment careers in the 1960s.

Soros left East Europe as a child refugee. A devotee of Karl Popper, he would prefer to be remembered for his philosophy rather than his fortune. But Soros will go down in history as the man who broke the Bank of England in 1992. His massive bet against sterling on world currency markets proved decisive in forcing Britain out of the European Monetary System. Soros' Open Society network has made large philanthropic contributions to the promotion of education and democracy in post-Communist Eastern Europe. His Quantum Fund – an early example of what is now known as a hedge fund – returned an average of 30% pa to its investors over the period from 1970 to 2000. The Quantum Fund traded actively, buying and selling currencies or commodities and any other assets that appealed, or failed to appeal, to Soros and his colleagues.

Buffett's investment vehicle is Berkshire Hathaway, an American corporation. Anyone can buy shares in it, although a single share will set you back over $100,000. Berkshire Hathaway was a textile company when Buffett took control, but insurance is now its largest business. Insurance premiums are received well before claims are paid, so insurance generates a large float of investable cash. This facilitates investment and Berkshire owns large stakes in businesses such as Procter and Gamble and the *Washington Post*. Buffett's investment success has taken him from modest beginnings to over-taking Bill Gates (to whose foundation he plans to donate most of his fortune) as the world's richest man. Despite that, Buffett still lives in the bungalow in Omaha that he bought fifty years ago, and regu-larly enjoys a meal at a local steak house washed down with a glass of cherry Coke (he switched brands after buying a 10% stake in the Coca-Cola Corporation).

There will always be individuals who have outperformed the market – just as there will always be winners of the lottery. I'll observe in Chapter 8 how exceptional investment performance rarely persists. Most people who do well are lucky rather than clever. But Buffett and Soros not only established outstanding records, but continued to demonstrate remarkable performance even after they had been widely recognised as the most talented managers of their generation. To win the lottery once may be evidence of either luck or skill; to win it repeatedly is evidence of skill.

You might think that the strategies of the folksy Buffett and the philosophical Soros would be the subject of intense study by students of finance and investment professionals. You would be wrong. These individuals receive a lot of journalistic attention but no academic attention. Since Buffett and Soros cannot exist, according to the strong efficient market hypothesis, they are treated as if they don't. A lot of ink has been spilt on the proposition that what plainly exists in practice can't exist in theory.

In turn, Buffett and Soros are open in their contempt for most academic work in finance. They can afford that contempt. But their contempt is not simply the practical man's disdain for the intellec-tual – they are both smart and well-read people. They simply believe that much of this academic work is misdirected, engaged in obsessive pursuit of narrow ideas of limited application. The distinction between the market as a mechanism for voting on events and the market as a mechanism for voting on market reactions to events was understood and expressed generations ago by Keynes and Samuelson – and by Benjamin Graham, the first intelligent investor. But the distinction is not understood by many commentators who regard market judgments as a repository of wisdom, not just about the market judgments of other market participants, but about the real economy.

The distinction between the anticipation of events and the anticipation of beliefs about events is elided by most finance academics. They understand that there might be such a distinction, but have developed a group of arguments – known, in extreme form, as 'rational expectations' – to suggest that the difference does not matter. The rational expectations school is associated with the strong form of the efficient market hypothesis – all information that is capable of being known is already incorporated in prices.

But the distinction between market judgments and underlying realities, the distinction between prices and values, and the distinction between the mind of the market and economic and business fundamentals, manifestly *do* matter. By exploiting divergences between them, Buffett and Soros have made billions of dollars. Both individuals recognise that such divergences are the basis of their success. Buffett shouts from the rooftops that markets are only imperfectly efficient. Soros, quoting Keynes's metaphor of the beauty contest, writes that 'The fact that a theory is flawed does not mean that we should not invest in it as long as other people believe in it and there is a large group of people left to be convinced …. we are ahead of the game because we can limit our losses when the market also discovers what we already know.' (Soros, 2003, p 25)

The essence of Soros's investment strategy is to read, and anticipate, the changing mind of the market more successfully than other traders. The essence of Buffett's investment strategy is to emphasise fundamental values and use the volatile mind of the market as an opportunity to buy assets that are underpriced relative to their fundamental value. I'll discuss these two broad approaches in the two chapters that follow.

CHAPTER 5

THE MIND OF THE MARKET

Market psychology

People in the City use phrases such as 'The market thinks', 'The view of the market is', or even, if the person is very senior, 'We could ask the market'. Of course, the market does not think; only people can think. But the anthropomorphic view, which treats 'the market' as if it were a person, is so pervasive that the metaphor is part of everyday language. Benjamin Graham formulated the anthropomorphic analogy when he wrote of the moody, volatile Mr Market. Mr Market has grown in influence in subsequent decades. Mr Market features regularly in Warren Buffett's homilies.

This metaphor contrasts with the metaphor of market as voting machine, which aggregates and weighs the different views of different players. Although there is some similarity between the two, there is also a fundamental difference. The market as voting machine is democratic – the analogy supposes a diversity of views, in which all judgments are relevant (if not necessarily equal). The personal analogy is hierarchical – the market view can be ascertained and interpreted, but not questioned. City players talk of 'confidence', by which they mean the standing of an individual, organisation or opinion in the eyes of the market – in much the same way as commentators identify the confidantes at the court of an autocratic politician or chief executive. Such confidence needs to be earned, and can easily be forfeited.

And yet the person who inspires such deference, whom it is perilous to defy, has no tangible existence. There is no Mr Market. 'The mind of the market' is what people believe the mind of the market to be, and the evolution of what 'the market thinks' is a process of convergence of these common beliefs. Understanding 'the mind of the market' – a deep appreciation of the psychology of Mr Market – is a potentially rewarding investment strategy, and some people are good at it. Not, however, as many as those who *think* they are good at it.

Trading once took place in physical markets, where buyers and sellers would meet to exchange securities and to exchange information. Some of the information might have been true, other parts of it false; some information would be contained in what they said, some of it contained in the way they behaved. In the crudest versions of face-to-face market making, such as the 'pit' of the Chicago Mercantile Exchange, the physical capacity of the traders to elbow aside their colleagues would contribute to their success. This short-term trading environment was a testosterone-laden world.

Technology transferred trading from meeting places to screens. The rise of financial conglomerates means that dealing rooms are now the places where the traders of Goldman Sachs or Morgan Stanley sit beside each other and make electronic contact with their competitors at other firms. The atmosphere is still frenzied – and still very masculine, even though there are now some women traders. You will still hear frequent obscenities on trading floors; many City firms have faced claims of sex discrimination and harassment; and lap-dancing clubs can be found around the fringes of the City.

Most traders are now employees of major investment banks. These conglomerate institutions manage assets for investment clients, execute deals for fund managers, and provide advice to major corporations, as well as trading on their own account through what is called their 'prop desks'. Bankers are required to maintain 'Chinese walls' in order to prevent people in these different departments communicating with each other. There are differing views on the effectiveness of the Chinese walls. Within these institutions are assembled expertise and information, unparalleled elsewhere, about all aspects of securities markets and, indeed, about wider economic and geopolitical events.

It is difficult, even for the banks themselves, to judge the long-run profitability of their proprietary trading activities. Traders use the capital, credit and reputation of their employers. They take a significant share of the profits from their activities, but not the losses. The penalty for making large losses is being fired. This asymmetric structure of incentives encourages trading strategies and styles that return regular profits while countenancing occasional exceptional losses that may, over time, swamp the profits. These structures play a central role in modern finance and I'll come back to them in Chapter 8.

If markets are characterised by weak positive short-term serial correlation – momentum – and weak negative long-term serial correlation – mean reversion – then it ought to be possible to analyse the processes that give rise to these 'anomalies'. George Soros describes the boom and bust process associated with momentum and mean reversion. He illustrates how in a variety of markets, from conglomerate acquisition to real estate investment trusts, a momentum-driven boom creates the seeds of its own destruction and leads to an inevitable downturn.

But describing the cycle is not at all the same as picking accurately the turning point of the cycle. Soros did, indeed, identify correctly the broad shape of some large swings in behaviour during the 1970s and 1980s to profit both on the upswing – following the momentum-driven herd – and on the downswing – benefiting by anticipating a period of mean reversion. These judgments proved very profitable. But such success became harder to achieve.

Can mathematical techniques help with understanding past and future cycles? Many amateur speculators rely on charts or other forms of what is known as technical analysis. This approach to investment analysis involves the identification of recurrent patterns in price series. The technical analyst looks at a chart of recent prices and identifies trends, believing that it is possible to identify buy and sell signals from inspection of the chart.

Purists among chartists do not care what the chart records – whether it is the stock price of BP, the exchange value of the dollar, or the price of an index-linked bond. Chartists look for pictures in the data – the 'head and shoulders' is an especially popular image. They draw trend lines through market rises and declines and horizontal resistance levels across more stationary ones. They see recurrent cycles. The Kondratieff fifty-year cycle has been discussed since the 1920s and there is just enough evidence of long-term fluctuation to make continued attention to it plausible. The Elliott 'long wave', the discovery of an accountant and amateur investor, is a favourite of many chartists.

Among the community of finance academics in universities, technical analysis has a terrible reputation. Most textbooks simply refuse even to acknowledge that the technique exists. But chartism continues to have a cult-like following, and market prognostications based on technical analysis are regularly found in the financial press and business journals.

There are good reasons for professional disdain. Many of the statements made by chartists resemble those of astrologers. The analytic component is ascientific and the predictions sufficiently ambiguous not to be falsified by any likely events. Chartists make use of the natural human inclination to see patterns in data – the same tendency that leads us to see images in ink-blots and interpret rocks as sculptures.

Technical analysts are often associated with investment gurus, more common in the United States, where there are many published investment newsletters, or tip sheets. The guru makes an outlandish prediction. Sometimes the prediction comes true, so the newsletter attracts subscriptions, the seminars are oversubscribed. The guru continues to make predictions – often the same prediction – but when these are falsified, the audience and reputation gradually drift away. The relatively few gurus who have a long-term track record of success – or indeed of employment – are generally based in large institutions with substantial resources devoted to fundamental research, such as Barton Biggs, formerly of Morgan Stanley.

Chartists, gurus and people with proprietary and secret systems are, overwhelmingly, charlatans. But the story is not quite so simple. The slogan of this book is that the efficient market hypothesis, although illuminating, is not true. And so the assertion that since the EMH is true, no claim made by chartists, gurus, or for mechanical rules or trading systems, can ever be valid is not good enough. At most, what can be said is that there is little evidence that any individuals or systems use these methods with sustained success.

Perhaps the difficulty of identifying patterns in historic price series is the result, not of the absence of such patterns, but of the absence of techniques sufficiently powerful to identify them. At some level, this must be correct. No one really believes that price movements are truly random – the most that might be claimed is that explanations of price movements are so complex and so varied that we can never do better than to describe them as a random process.

Much of this book describes the theory of finance that originated in Chicago around fifty years ago and has been developed by economists since. Today, that body of analysis is subject to a pincer movement, pressured from one side by behavioural economics – the applied psychology that emphasises the ways in which the beliefs of traders influence the determination of prices – and from the other side by higher-powered mathematics.

Techniques brought to bear on financial markets more recently push towards, even beyond, the frontiers of applied mathematics. Some analysis makes use of very large computers to analyse patterns in data. Statistical arbitrage identifies divergences in the prices of closely related securities on a minute-by-minute basis. Both approaches use models to reproduce what the most skilled traders may be able to do instinctively. In what is superficially a paradox, soft revisions from psychology and hard revisions from mathematics turn out to be two sides of the same coin. The mathematics of complex systems may help to provide the formation of expectations and the dissemination of beliefs in markets. If it does, then these processes will change. Watch this space. My guess is that there will be more on this heady mix of psychology and mathematics in subsequent editions of this book. Maybe the chartists will have the last laugh.

In the first chapter, I suggested that the intelligent investor could fend for him or herself in a world populated by financial professionals. But in the world I have described in this chapter, the intelligent but amateur investor cannot fend for him or herself. A minority of successful traders in hedge funds and investment banks have an intuitive feel for market psychology. These few individuals have honed their skills over years of experience and are exposed to a wide range of market information every minute of the trading day.

The mathematicians who build trading systems have access to the best brains and most powerful computing resources available. Successfully riding market momentum involves frequent trading, and investment banks have much lower trading costs than retail investors. Even with all these advantages it is not at all clear that over the long run the activity is profitable for investment banks. You need to set the losses from supposedly unforeseeable events and allegedly unauthorised trading against the profits. We simply don't know whether over a period of years banks make money out of these market judgments (as distinct from making money out of their customers' transactions), and nor do they. Most people who are described as successful traders blow up after a long lucky run.

The David and Goliath notion that with a home computer, a proprietary software package and a book of trading rules, you are likely to succeed where the best resourced institutions in the world have largely failed is laughable. Most people who claim to trade successfully in this way are themselves on a lucky run in a rising market, or engaged in self-delusion, or both.

The intelligent investor cannot match the professionals in understanding market psychology. But he or she does have advantages when it comes to fundamental value. In the remainder of this chapter, and the next one, I'll explain why and how.

When the market lost its mind

The World Economic Forum, held annually in the pretty Swiss ski resort of Davos, is the foremost networking event for business, political and economic leaders. In February 2000, the hot air it produced threatened to melt the snow on the meadows above. The New Economy boom was reaching its climax.

I dined with a shooting star of the New Economy, who explained how Webvan (an internet-based grocery delivery service, which closed a few months later) would shortly overtake Tesco and even Wal-Mart. I recognised the fixed grin, the shaking of the head, the incredulity with which he would intersperse his remarks with 'You just don't get it!'

There was, in the end, nothing to get – or not quite nothing. The internet is not only an important social innovation but an important commercial one. It is transforming industries such as entertainment, financial services, and classified advertising. The internet is changing, in a more modest way, the structure of all business. A great deal of money was made in the course of the New Economy bubble. But mostly by stock promoters, not investors in businesses such as Webvan. Where are the customers' yachts?

The two enduring general principles of asset valuation described in the preceding chapter are:

- an asset is worth what someone is willing to pay for it; and
- the value of an asset is the cash it will generate over its life.

Rarely have these two bases of valuation become as divorced as in the last decade. In the New Economy bubble, billions were spent buying shares in companies that had never generated any cash and were never likely to. These shares were mostly bought by people who believed that they could subsequently sell them to someone else at a higher price. They were often right. In the credit bubble, trillions were spent buying complex securities, whose underlying value could not be ascertained. The bonds were mostly bought by people who believed that they would, at least for the moment, yield a higher return than the securities that had been issued to pay for them. They were often right. Assets were worth what someone was willing to pay even if they had no fundamental value, or it was impossible to determine what that fundamental value was. These transactions always raise in acute form the question Why do I want to buy what they want to sell? The answer was obvious: Because so many other people want to buy them. Eventually, the supply of people willing to buy was exhausted and the bubble burst.

The New Economy bubble began with the initial public offering of Netscape in 1995. Such IPOs were once the means by which growing private companies raised capital for new investment. Today it is not usual to raise much new capital through IPOs. The primary purpose of the modern IPO is to enable the existing owners to cash in.

Netscape offered the first browser, which enabled users without technical skills to access the worldwide web. But the $2.2bn valuation attached to Netscape – a company with negligible sales and no profits – would soon pale into insignificance. Priceline, which offered discounted air tickets, was valued at more than the entire US airline industry. Analysts became heroic figures. Mary Meeker of Morgan Stanley, whose 1995 report had helped start the boom, was described as 'the internet goddess', her sponsorship 'a laying on of hands'. Henry Blodget, who had presciently anticipated the soaring share price of Amazon.com, became Merrill Lynch's internet spokesman.

Meeker worked for, and Blodget was recruited by, a financial conglomerate. As a result of the structural changes in the financial services industry, these companies sought banking and issuing business from the corporations on which their analysts did research. Once brokers were owned by banks, their new bosses feared that research critical of customers might jeopardise other, more lucrative relationships between banks and large corporations. The language of the City distinguishes the 'buy side' – investment managers – from the 'sell side' – financial advisers to companies that issue securities. Integrated banks combined the buy side and the sell side. These banks generally concluded that the sell side mattered more to their revenues. Certainly the representatives of the sell side – the investment bankers – were usually decisive in the politics of these institutions. So the analyst became part of the sales force of investment banking business. The expectation of enthusiastic promotion of a company's virtues through 'research' provided to prospective investors would attract lucrative corporate deals to the banks.

The conflict between buy side and sell side has a long history. America's Glass-Steagall Act, passed in 1933, required the separation of investment and commercial banking operations, following the excesses of the 1920s and the crash of 1929. Senators Glass and Steagall argued, with considerable justification, that banks had pleased their corporate clients by plying their retail customers with worthless stock.

The Glass-Steagall Act was successively relaxed in the face of industry lobbying. In 1998, the legislation was the last remaining obstacle to the achievement of the well-connected and ambitious

Sandy Weill's aspiration to become chief executive of Citibank. His telecoms analyst, Jack Grubman, maintained that what had once been a conflict of interest was now a synergy – investors were able to benefit from the exceptional insights derived from Grubman's close contact with corporate clients. This privileged knowledge enabled Grubman to maintain his enthusiastic recommendation of World.com and admiration for its then chairman, former basketball coach and future convict, Bernie Ebbers, until the day the company went bust.

The disgraced former Governor of New York, Eliot Spitzer, made his once stellar reputation by exposing these New Economy deceptions. Spitzer uncovered details of how the analyst's insights had pleased Michael Armstrong, a Citigroup board member who was CEO of AT & T, and whose support was needed to secure Weill's elevation over rival John Reed. Grubman had been unenthusiastic about America's oldest and dullest telecommunications company, but he suddenly formed a more favourable opinion. Contemporaneously, the bank's generous donation to the 92nd Street Y school helped secure the admission of Grubman's child to a Manhattan nursery rumoured to be more selective than Harvard.

Britain had no Spitzer; its internet boom came later; and criminal prosecutions not at all. Few European internet companies made it through to their IPO before fundamental values reasserted themselves. The aptly named lastminute.com came to market as the boom was subsiding. Boo.com, a fashion site and perhaps the most absurd of all internet businesses (whose founders blew over £100m on air travel, hotels and parties before the business collapsed) sold few clothes to the public and no shares.

None of this had much to do with fundamental value and no serious investor could become successfully involved in the madness of 1999-2000. Soros's Quantum Fund attempted to read the cycle of boom and bust but, after a late plunge into internet shares, incurred heavy losses when the bubble burst. Buffett simply stood on the sidelines, professing unwillingness to be involved with investments he did not understand.

The New Economy episode was not the first great asset bubble, nor will it be the last, but its scale is unprecedented. The tulip mania which afflicted the Netherlands in 1636 is so much part of popular history that the cry of 'It's not like tulips' needed to be reiterated often in 1999. But it *was* like tulips. Isaac Newton – who overcame his initial scepticism about the South Sea Bubble and invested – declared that 'I can predict the motion of heavenly bodies, but not the madness of crowds'. The railway boom, 100 years later, not only created and destroyed fortunes but give rise to what remains even today a definitive study of the psychology of bubbles (Mackay, 1843).

The best account of bubble psychology and behaviour remains J K Galbraith's *The Great Crash* (1997), which describes the speculative mania of the 1920s that parallels, not just in broad outline but in considerable detail, the events that would unfold seventy years later. When I read that book as a student many years ago, I wondered how people could have been so foolish. Eventually, among the business and political élite of Davos 2000, I would know.

Two months later, the New Economy bubble burst. Within eighteen months, the NASDAQ index had lost three-quarters of its price, if not its value. But it would take less than five years for the next market folly to begin.

The mind of the market, jaundiced by stocks, turned to bonds. While the puffery of the New Economy bubble had been aimed largely at retail investors, the puffery of the credit expansion was aimed at more sophisticated professional investors. In the New Economy bubble financial institutions plied junk to third parties. In the credit bubble they plied junk to each other. For a time, the boost to profits was just as satisfactory. Their employees earned bonuses by plying junk, and it did not matter to whom they sold it. But the consequences of the credit bubble would be more profound. Its bursting would bring down many of these financial institutions themselves.

The traditional activity of a bank was to borrow short and lend long – to collect deposits from wealthy individuals and businesses and lend it on for house purchase and productive investment. Such banks were vulnerable to runs – depositors could demand their money back sooner than the loans could be recovered from borrowers. But while occasional runs occurred, the combination of the scale of banks' operations and the ultimate support of central banks such as the Bank of England protected the depositors and shareholders of essentially sound institutions.

Enter intermediation, a process in which banks borrowed and lent, not just to and from their customers, but to and from each other. Banks began to securitise. They would take packages of loans and parcel them into bonds of shorter or longer maturity. There were fees to be earned by issuing and trading in these packages. As bonds became exciting, from the 1980s, the pace of securitisation accelerated. In the years that followed the New Economy bubble, such securitisation became one of the most fashionable areas of the financial services industry. Bankers talked of the 'originate and distribute' model, in which the role of the bank was to originate loans which would immediately be distributed in wholesale markets.

As the tempo gathered pace, financial institutions learned to securitise their securities, parcelling their packages of bonds into yet more complex packages, and collecting a commission on each round of repackaging. The fundamental value of these debt obligations depended on the quality of the loans that underpinned them. But it became difficult, and ultimately impossible, to penetrate the layers of complication and determine the fundamental value that lay beneath. Originators therefore became less and less concerned to monitor the quality of the loans they originated. The most notorious result was the development of 'sub-prime mortgages' for indigent borrowers. But the funding of property purchases and private equity deals with unaffordable levels of debt was larger in scale.

If the fundamental value of these securities could not be established, the mind of the market determined their price. The bond rating agencies played the cheerleading role that analysts had fulfilled in the New Economy bubble. On 9 August 2007, the credit bubble burst. Doubts over the fundamental value of asset-backed securities had been rumbling ever since defaults had started to grow on sub-prime mortgages. Traders had assumed, as in the New Economy bubble, that the value of an asset was set by the price that someone else was willing to pay for it. But if there were no buyers, you would have to rely on its fundamental value – and no one knew what that was.

So the market simply dried up. In the first instance, banks were left with loans they had originated but could not distribute – that caused the rapid collapse of Northern Rock. But over time, the consequences spread more widely. Since banks held large portfolios of asset-backed securities, inability to determine the value of asset-backed securities meant that it was impossible to determine the value of banks themselves. Bank shares fell, and fell again, as the scale of the problems became apparent. The credit ratings of their own debts deteriorated sharply. Investment banks, with little capital relative to the overall scale of their assets and liabilities, ceased to be creditworthy. Of the five large US investment banks, two – Bear Stearns and Lehman – folded, and one – Merrill Lynch – was rescued by Bank of America. At the moment of writing, the two strongest – Morgan Stanley and Goldman Sachs – have survived by raising external funds and tapping government funding.

Even the retail banks, with large deposit bases provided by small savers, fell under suspicion. These events demonstrated another problem that resulted from the repeal of Glass-Steagall. Retail banks around the world had, in effect, used their deposit base – on which there was an implicit government guarantee – as collateral for their speculative trading. Politicians were fearful – with some justification – of a replay of the events of 1932–3, when the entire US banking system stood on the verge of collapse. The threat was enough to induce massive support operations from the US government to remove doubtful assets from bank balance sheets.

In 1999–2000 I had learnt how people could indeed be so foolish; in 2007-8, I learned that such foolishness was ineradicable in modern financial services markets. Its origins lie not so much in innate stupidity, but in the capacity of clever people to fall victim to the power of conventional thinking.

The power of conventional thinking

In the New Economy and credit bubbles, conventional, yet magical, thinking created its own reality. It is hard to overstate the power of group thinking in business and finance. People repeat to each other the same transitorily fashionable views in mutual reinforcement. What matters is not to have a well-informed opinion of one's own, but to have a good knowledge of currently prevailing opinion, of 'what the market thinks'. For most investment professionals, that is the only thing that matters. That is the force of Keynes' metaphor of the beauty contest.

The market judgment that emerges from this process need have no foundation in objective reality. Both truths and falsehoods spread contagiously, forming what Galbraith called 'the conventional wisdom'. Such processes can lead people to believe absurd things – that Salem was besieged by witches, that the US was endangered by Communist subversion, that boo.com and Webvan would dominate their industries, and that securitisation could conjure wealth from thin air. It is not only common, but reasonable, to believe what is widely believed, especially among business and political leaders, who have little time for reflection. I believe the world is round, not because I have myself verified it, but because the general belief is that the world is round. If I had lived 1000 years ago, I would have believed the earth was flat, and for the same reasons.

In the complex and uncertain world of modern finance, such behaviour takes us far away from market efficiency and fundamental value. In all market bubbles – tulips or the South Sea, the New Economy or the credit bubble – distortions are supported by commercial interests that benefit from their promotion. There was always a kernel of truth in the exaggerated propositions. Speculators in the South Sea Bubble were on the verge of an industrial revolution and an explosion of world trade. Railways, electricity and modern information technology were transforming discoveries. Financial innovation did create opportunities for better risk management. The people who lost money in these bubbles were not mistaken in their basic thesis but they greatly overestimated both the pace of change and the extent to which individual companies would benefit from it.

Beliefs – true or false – affect prices and may even affect fundamental values themselves. George Soros describes this phenomenon as 'reflexivity'. Although the development of the internet was not an event of great significance for Tesco and Wal-Mart, the belief that it was a significant event had a large influence on their businesses. There was an even larger effect on the investment climate within which these companies operated. The New Economy bubble led to large overinvestment in telecommunications capacity, which itself made nemesis more likely. The massive overpayments by European telecoms companies for mobile phone licences were the result of misperceptions of reality generated by the New Economy bubble.

The senior executives of these businesses were captured by these misconceptions and could not have escaped them even if they had been more thoughtful people. The senior executives of banks, five years later, were in the same position. In the distorting mirror provided by ostensibly sophisticated risk management models, they saw irresistible profit opportunities. The 'originate and distribute' model was a new paradigm for banks, as the New Economy had been a new paradigm for retailers and phone companies, and the winners would be the ones to pursue their fantastic vision most vigorously. The price of contradicting the mind of the market was to lose one's job.

The price of going along with the market would also be to lose one's job, but at a later date. Many bank and telecoms executives were left with more time to spend with their families (though they were also left with a great deal more money to spend with their families). After the New Economy bubble a few individuals, like Skilling and Ebbers, were thrown to the wolves. Men such as Blodget and Grubman, leaders among the analysts who puffed hopeless shares, and Frank Quattrone – the leading investment banker of the technology sector – were barred from the financial services industry. But they were nailed by regulators for specific misconduct, not fired by their employers for professional incompetence. The merely naïve – people like Mary Meeker, with more enthusiasm than judgment – continued in similar well-paid employment. I expect that the outcome of the credit crunch for individuals will be much the same, though the effects on institutions have already proved more severe.

The mind of the market is its own reality. Investors sought insight into 'the mind of the market' and that was what they received – and continued to receive. What was true was what was believed, and what was believed was true. And, when the bubbles burst, what had once been believed and was therefore true was no longer believed and therefore no longer true. The dot.com shares that were once stars were now dogs; there was nothing more to be said.

Practical men of the financial world, who would be appalled at the suggestion that they might be influenced by French philosophy, are the most determined of postmodernists. In financial centres across the world, truth is in the eye of the observer. Jean Baudrillard notoriously remarked that 'the (first) Gulf War took place only on television'; in much the same sense, the New Economy was observed only on Wall Street.

Not everyone was deceived. But risk for a fund manager is not volatility, but underperformance relative to an index. It is, as Keynes observed, better for a career to be conventionally wrong than unconventionally right, and disastrous to be unconventionally wrong. The control of the manager's perceived risk leads to the practice of 'closet indexation'. Although the fund manager is paid for stock selection, the composition of his fund mirrors closely the composition of the index. Most fund managers receive daily reports of their overweight and underweight positions, relative to the benchmark index. As a result, many allegedly 'actively managed' funds virtually replicate an index.

The successful fund manager is one who can stay close to his benchmark index but be consistently slightly ahead of it. You might think that this could be achieved by close attention to fundamental value. If performance were measured every five years, when mean reversion would have asserted itself, this would probably be true. But performance isn't measured every five years, but much more often – commonly every three months, often more frequently. Over such short periods, momentum dominates mean reversion – this quarter's outperforming stocks are more than averagely likely to have been last quarter's outperforming stocks. Knowing the mind of the market trumps fundamental value.

If you were a professional investment manager, and you had made the – good – call that shares in 1996 were overvalued relative to property, you would almost certainly have been fired. From 1996 to 2000, shares rose steadily while property stagnated. The reversal came afterwards. If you are managing other people's money, three years is a long time – too long to be, or appear to be, wrong.

Managers who are doing markedly worse than their peers for as long as three years will find their jobs in jeopardy. Tony Dye, who once had a large, admiring following, was a notorious sceptic during the New Economy bubble, and lost his job only days before the bubble burst. All the great investors were out of favour in 1999. Where have all the geniuses gone? *Fortune* asked. Warren Buffett 'didn't get it', and shares in Berkshire Hathaway fell by almost 50% in that year. George Soros failed to read the timing of boom and bust correctly, and retired from active involvement in managing other people's money, content to devote himself to the philanthropic management of his own.

Keynes said that the market can be wrong for longer than you can stay solvent, warning of the risks associated with ignoring the mind of the market in favour of fundamental value. Writing today, he would say that the market can be wrong for longer than a contrarian fund manager can hold his or her job. And so it proved.

While three years is a long time-scale for an investment manager, it isn't a long time-scale for the intelligent investor. This difference in the time-scale on which you are judged gives a big advantage to the DIY portfolio manager. Patience pays.

The emphasis by institutional investors on quarterly figures has led analysts and fund managers into a symbiotic relationship with corporate executives known as 'earnings guidance'. In pre-war days, the great figures who headed large companies, like Harry McGowan of ICI, or Alfred Sloan of General Motors, had virtually no contact with shareholders. The emergence of the hostile takeover was probably the most important single factor in changing this behaviour. Senior managers of large companies began to pay closer attention to the share price – their jobs depended on it. The growth of stock options as a means of payment reinforced the trend. It provided an additional reason for executives to pay close attention to the share price – their wealth depended on it.

Now, most large companies will have an investor relations department, or employ a specialist firm to handle these issues. The chairman, chief executive and chief financial officer will expect to devote a substantial proportion of their time to investor relations. That means pitching the company to analysts, and talking to the investment managers who are the principal shareholders. Sometimes, analysts will benefit from lavish hospitality in the course of learning about the company's affairs.

The market responds, not to good and bad news from companies, but to news that is better or worse than market expectations. Therefore many businesses want to manage both outcome and expectation themselves. They seek steady earnings growth just a little faster than the market is anticipating, and manage their quarterly reporting in order to achieve this. I will describe in the next chapter how much scope finance directors have for keeping their reported earnings on a steady path. Often the main criterion by which analysts judge the quality of management is whether executives do the things they say they will do. This mutually rewarding process of earnings guidance has only the loosest of connections with how the business is actually performing.

Occasionally, fund managers have developed such a strong reputation with investors that they can ignore these pressures. While Buffett was criticised for refusing to participate in the New Economy bubble, he could laugh all the way to the bank, and the steak house. Eventually, of course, fundamental value breaks through. There is a stock exchange regulated process – the profit warning – by which companies abandon informal earnings guidance, and confirm that things are not as everyone would like them to be. Profit warnings are often followed by second, and even third, profit warnings. The favoured analysts of companies like WorldCom and Enron – such as Grubman and Curt Hamner of CSFB – continued to puff these stocks until the companies collapsed.

A major part – in many cases much the largest part – of the remuneration of senior executives is now related to movements in the company's share price. That makes it inevitable that the mind of the market takes precedence over fundamental value. In tribute to the power of Mr Market, many companies display the constantly fluctuating share price in their reception area. Some chief executives have it on their desks, and it is not unknown for them to check it several times a day. Their business plans are heavily influenced by the conventional wisdom of their peers, analysts and bankers, rather than their own judgment. Success, as measured by the market, is being able to anticipate the new fashion slightly more quickly than other people. Advance insight into the conventional wisdom is the commodity that many consultants, business gurus, journalists and investment analysts now sell.

Boards appoint non-executive directors with 'appropriate experience', which in practice means the directors seek out people with backgrounds and opinions indistinguishable from their own. Closer links between politics and business mean that the statements of politicians and leaders of business and finance increasingly echo each other. In the New Economy bubble, politicians and business leaders, journalists and investment professionals vied with each other in talking nonsense. The power of conventional thinking asserts itself in the reiteration of banal opinions on fashionable issues. Today these include the excitement and paranoia over China's economic development, the obsession with climate change, and the scramble for alternative assets in hedge funds and private equity.

The unproductive contact between finance directors and analysts provides an opportunity for the individual investor – the rewarding opportunity to ignore it. You aren't party to earnings guidance, but it doesn't matter, because the information such guidance provides has little to do with the substance of the business. You don't have to remain popular with company management to do your job. You don't have to worry that you will be fired if you underperform the market in one quarter, or several. Being close to the market is not necessarily an advantage. Remember that Warren Buffett lives in Omaha.

Best of all, you can emphasise absolute, rather than relative, returns. That emphasis enables the intelligent investor to focus on the analysis of fundamental value, rather than the mind of the market. For the intelligent – and therefore patient – investor, there is a simple reconciliation between the mark to market and fundamental value principles: an asset is worth the higher of its fundamental value and its market price.

If the market price is above fundamental value, an intelligent investor can sell for the market price and look for something else. If the market price is below fundamental value, an intelligent investor can continue to hold and enjoy the benefit of the projected stream of cash returns.

This freedom gives the intelligent investor an immediate advantage over the majority of professional fund managers, bound by the routine of quarterly performance measurement. For the professional fund manager, the mark to market principle rules – an asset is worth what someone is willing to pay for it.

Being able to take a detached view of fundamental value is a big advantage. But it is not easy. Estimating fundamental value requires a view on the long-term future prospects of the company. The information you need is extensive, difficult to obtain, and changes constantly. The analysis of fundamental value is speculative, and different people are likely to come up with different answers. In the next chapter, I'll look at what is required.

CHAPTER 6

IN SEARCH OF FUNDAMENTAL VALUE

Accounting for earnings

Fundamental analysis of a company begins with its profits. With earnings of around 60p per share, and a share price of 570p, BP's price-earnings ratio in 2007 was 9.5. This is a low figure for a sound business. In the long run a normal PE ratio is between 10 and 15. Sometimes, when investors are optimistic and economic conditions are thought to remain favourable, the average PE ratio for the market is above 15. Sometimes, in gloom and recession, the market average is below 10. Such fluctuations are usually followed by long-term mean reversion – either earnings catch up, or prices adjust. At the height of the bubble in 2000, the FTSE all-share price-earnings ratio was 27. Eight years later, the PE ratio had returned to 11. Although earnings were more than 50% higher, prices were more than 25% lower.

When the price-earnings ratio rises outside its conventional range, analysts opine that historic experience is no longer relevant. When Japanese share prices soared in the 1980s, they advised that Japanese companies should not be looked at in the same way as companies elsewhere. A decade later, the New Economy and the economic and political environment that followed the end of the Cold War had, many financial commentators argued, changed the basic principles of stock valuation. Securitisation wrote new rules for credit risk assessment.

Once again, the world had not changed, only opinion. Long-term mean reversion struck and PE ratios returned to more normal levels. There is a saying that the most expensive words in investment are 'It's different this time'. Sceptics who were reluctant to believe the rules had changed avoided the bubbles in Japan, the New Economy and credit to their ultimate benefit.

Broad market averages conceal large variation in the PE ratios of individual stocks. Generally, high PE ratios indicate industries or individual companies thought to have better than average growth prospects; low PE ratios attach to sectors or businesses thought to have worse than average growth prospects. Table 4 illustrates.

Some people look at the ratio between the price-earnings ratio and the growth rate or earnings ratio (the PEG ratio). Their reasoning is that a low PEG ratio suggests that future growth can be bought at a relatively modest price. It's not that easy: measures such as PEG are simply ways of beginning to frame questions about the fundamentals of a company. The PEG ratio is a simple screen for identifying companies whose fundamentals deserve further examination.

If a stock has earnings of 60p, and a price of 570p, then the PE ratio is 9.5. The earnings attributable to each share, 60p, are equal to 10.5% of the share price. This ratio, the inverse of the PE ratio, is known as the earnings yield. If a normal PE ratio is between 10 and 15, a normal earnings yield lies between 6.7% and 10%.

Table 4: Market sector PE ratios, 2 January 2008

Technology	26.7
Leisure goods	25.6
Consumer goods	16.9
General retailers	12.6
Auto and auto parts	11.1
Banks	8.1

Source: FTSE

Since shareholders do not receive the company's earnings, the earnings yield is not directly relevant to the shareholder. However, it is indirectly relevant, since earnings determine the dividends the company can pay. The earnings yield is a guide to the long-run rate of return that it is reasonable to expect from owning shares.

Creative accounting

But the value of such a guide depends on the value of the information on which it is based. The collapse of Enron brought to the attention of a wider public what market professionals and companies have always known. Companies have a lot of scope to make their reported earnings and assets what they want them to be. What is the profit of a company? It all depends on the meaning of 'is', as Bill Clinton explained to the Grand Jury. Creative accounting is the quantitative equivalent of the modern politician's lie – a statement that is in some narrow technical sense true, but is substantively false.

The jury decided that the practices at Enron constituted fraud, and former chief executive, Jeff Skilling, and former chief financial officer, Andy Fastow, went to jail for their part in one of America's most spectacular corporate collapses. The methods Skilling and Fastow employed were aggressive versions of financial techniques used by the most respectable companies.

Wall Street wanted companies to report a steady stream of increased earnings (part of the process of managing investor expectations that I described in the previous chapter). So that is what companies reported. How were companies able to manage, not their businesses, but their declared earnings, in this way?

Most large businesses are, from a legal perspective, a group of companies under common ownership. Consolidated accounts add the individual accounts of all these companies and report the overall result as if the business were a single entity. Since shareholders are, indirectly, shareholders in all the companies within the group, this is the only sensible way to present the figures in a manageable, comprehensible form.

But companies often give stakes in associated businesses to outsiders. In a joint venture between two or more companies, each cooperating company will usually have a share of the legal entity that conducts the business. A firm establishing a new business venture may want to give shares to key individuals. Or a company may simply own shares in another business as a strategic investment.

The general principle – and it is a sensible one – is that if a company manages and controls a subsidiary or associate company, the consolidated accounts of the parent should include the relevant share of assets and earnings of the subsidiary or associate. If the parent doesn't manage and control the other company, then its interest should be treated as if it were an investment. The asset is the value of the shares and the income is the dividend.

So far so good, if not so simple. But what exactly is meant by management and control? US accounting standards – known as Generally Accepted Accounting Principles (GAAP) – try to pin this down. But whenever standards try to pin down a concept, the creature flies away. Creating subsidiaries that you do, in fact, manage and control, but that you do not manage and control for the purposes of generally accepted accounting principles, has many advantages for the creative accountant. You can use transactions between the parent and subsidiary to create profits, or to make them disappear. This doesn't work for ever; sooner or later these manoeuvres will have to be reversed. But you can make it later rather than sooner. And, remember, in the long run we are all dead. Or, in some cases, in the penitentiary.

Enron created hundreds of these subsidiaries. If you went through the detail of the company's accounting filings, you would find all this out. But to do so would involve burying yourself in thousands of pages of figures. Some analysts did figure it out. I'll come back to them in Chapter 9.

But most analysts were employed by investment banks that earned, or hoped to earn, large fees from Enron's hyperactive transactions. A decade before Enron's fall, Terry Smith was forced out of his job at investment bank UBS after publishing a book (Smith (1992)) that offended the bank's large corporate clients by explaining some of the most common abuses. 'The Chinese wall fell on me,' he said. The outcome benefited both parties: Smith went on to establish his own broking firm, and made far more money than he could have expected as salary from his former employer; UBS continued to derive large revenues from the businesses it had placated; and the practice of earnings management became still more common The fate of Terry Smith indicates that diligent inquiry is not just time consuming, but can be damaging to careers. It is easier and more rewarding to be impressed by a company's slick presentation and generous hospitality.

Another contemporary fraudster, Bernie Ebbers of WorldCom, reduced the slick presentation to bare essentials. He would arrive at meetings and simply point to a graph of the company's rising share price before inviting questions. Any more extensive account of what the company was doing might have taxed his business knowledge and financial expertise. The accountants of both Enron and WorldCom, encouraged to support that rising share price, made extensive use of two other common devices – 'revenue recognition' and 'acquisition accounting'.

A long-term contract or project will incur costs and accrue revenues over several years. A conservative approach recognises the profit when the books have closed and the money is banked, acknowledging only the bird in the hand. An optimistic frame of mind takes credit for the anticipated profit on the deal the moment it is signed, chalking up many birds in the bush as soon as the hunter's gun is primed.

A true and fair view would strike a position somewhere in between. The right balance requires careful, and subjective, judgment. But the exercise of careful judgment was not the activity in which self-aggrandising executives were engaged. Some companies of the New Economy era would simply exchange long-term contracts to supply each other with the same thing, enabling both to credit turnover and profits even though no real transaction took place – or ever would.

Vanco was a pioneer in the supply of 'virtual network' services headed by an aggressive and publicity-conscious CEO called Allen Timpany. The company did not own its own network, but would buy capacity from the major carriers (companies like BT and France Telecom) and use it to offer services to large corporations. The contracts last for several years, so that the principles used to allocate revenue and costs are crucial to the determination of profits.

The terms of the contracts are, for good reasons, confidential. However, the company's method of allocating revenues was not directly related either to the payments made by its customers or by its suppliers. We do know that the company reported regular profits but negative cash flow. In its annual report for 2007, Vanco explained 'In the six months 2006 total debtors (amounts owing to the company) rose to £111m from £99m at 31 January 2006. This is an increase of 12.1% while revenue fell by 9% in the same period. In the six months ended 31 January 2007, this trend was reversed with revenue increasing by 33% and debtors increasing to £141m which represents a 27% increase over the position at 31 July 2006. The Directors expect this relative improvement in debtors (*sic*) to continue.'

Early in 2008, the auditors resigned. In May 2008, the company failed to produce its annual report and accounts; the shares were suspended by the London Stock Exchange; and the entire business was purchased for £1 by another company.

The issue of revenue recognition is an aspect of a much larger problem. Managers given a target of finding 5% or 10% cost savings, a frequent corporate practice, can usually deliver. Sometimes this can be done with little effect on the efficiency of the business or the quality of its product. We have all encountered people who reduce, rather than increase, the effectiveness of the organisation that employs them. You can always spend less on maintenance, or on customer service, or press employees to work harder. These actions will have consequences for future profits, but the consequences will be some time ahead, and may prove to be more or less expensive than the initial cost savings.

Most large companies have engaged in successive rounds of these cost savings in the last decade, either to enhance measured efficiency or to produce the 'synergies' that justify their merger activity. This is the main reason why corporate earnings have grown faster than revenues or the economy as a whole. Some of the cost savings represent real efficiency gains, others enhance current profits at the expense of future profits. Often, only time will tell.

BP had taken cost cutting too far at Texas City and in Alaska, with damaging long-term consequences both for profits and corporate reputation. Through the 1990s, Marks and Spencer steadily increased margins at the expense of the company's famous value for money until, in 1998, the business earned record profits. Then sales dropped sharply. Within a period of only a few months, the iconic reputation had evaporated.

The privatised Railtrack penny-pinched on maintenance until, following serious accidents, the inept company threw money at its problems in a desperate, and unsuccessful, attempt to restore the confidence of passengers and government.

Pharmaceutical companies stressed marketing and cost reduction and spent their ample profits on buying each other rather than on new research, leaving empty their pipelines of new drugs and endangering the fragile implicit contract between the industry and the public.

Despite these regrettable examples, there are many British businesses that are far better and more tightly run today than two decades ago. Almost every company can reduce cost at the expense of future revenues and, if analysts project this growth of earnings into the future, the stock price gets a double bonus. The key issue in every case – BP, Marks and Spencer, Railtrack and others – is to look at the sustainability of the business strategy and, above all, the sustainability of the firm's competitive advantage: the reputation of BP and of the pharmaceutical industry; Marks and Spencer's relationship with its customers; Railtrack's franchise. Competitive advantage can only be understood by going behind the earnings statement.

A prudent business that acquires another will take a careful look at the assets it has acquired. So will an imprudent one. The imprudent one writes down the value of these assets to low levels and then attributes the gains made when these undervalued assets are sold or used in the business to its own superior management skills. The 'restoration' of value can be used to enhance profits for many years. This practice is called 'acquisition accounting'.

In the 1980s, several companies – such as BTR, which bought businesses as diverse as Dunlop's sports goods and Tilling's transport activities – presented a consistent picture of growing earnings to pave the way for the next large acquisition. Every takeover had to be larger still to maintain the momentum. Eventually, the music stopped.

Advisers and accountants connived in these schemes. It is impossible to believe that sophisticated, intelligent investment bankers did not realise that Kenneth Lay, Enron's chairman, was an affable, skilful political operator with little grasp of business detail; that Jeff Skilling, the chief executive, was as corrupt as he was brilliant; or that Bernie Ebbers of World.com had none of the attributes needed to run a global telecoms company. But Enron's complex financial transactions and World.com's constant acquisitions generated large fees.

Accountants were once the butt of jokes – stuffy people with a rigid professional ethic. In the 1980s, the large global firms that audit virtually all major corporations in Britain and the United States consolidated into what is now the big four of KPMG, PwC, Ernst & Young, and Deloitte. Their partners became hungry for consulting revenue as fee levels from their traditional audit business came under pressure. Pleasing corporate clients received greater emphasis.

'Eat what you kill' – partners taking home the revenues they have personally earned rather than a share of the collective profits – was an increasingly common slogan in law and accountancy firms. The characterisation of clients as prey is revealing. Arthur Andersen, always the most commercial of the major firms, would pursue new clients most aggressively – and would be destroyed by its acquiescence in Enron's frauds.

The main counteracting force to the effect of competitive pressures in reducing standards is public regulation of accounting standards and the sale of securities. The most important accounting standards bodies are America's Federal Accounting Standards Board and the global International Accounting Standards Board. All countries have financial regulators. America's Securities and Exchange Commission is the most formidable and Britain's Financial Services Authority has influence which extends beyond national borders.

These organisations have done much to rein in abuses and, as a result, formal accounting statements now contain much less rubbish than they did even a decade ago. Still, the presentation of company accounts remains confusing. Many companies highlight partial or misleading information, and commercial pressures on analysts to join in corporate self-congratulation and facilitate the process of earnings guidance remain strong.

Beware of EBITDA (Earnings Before Interest, Tax, Depreciation, Amortisation), pro-forma earnings or any numbers that include or exclude supposedly non-recurring items. The figures that company executives present are sometimes described as 'earnings before bad stuff'.

One clear pointer to the problems of Enron and Vanco was that the company, while supposedly very profitable, was not generating the cash that matched its reported earnings. Cash is a good reality check. If the people at Barings ostensibly supervising rogue trader Nick Leeson had stopped to ask themselves why his trading successes needed to be financed by repeated injections of money from the rest of the group, Barings might still be in business today. A common feature of all the accounting wheezes described above – dubious transactions between the company and its subsidiaries, premature revenue recognition, inappropriate writing down of acquired assets – is that increased reported earnings have no cash counterpart.

Tax is also a clue to what is really going on. Revenue authorities have many faults but they do not often levy tax on profits that do not exist. High profits and a low tax charge may be explained by clever tax planning, or by large investment programmes that produce large deductions. Another possible explanation is that profits are not what they seem.

There are ways of piercing the fog created by earnings reports. One is to focus on the ability of a business to generate cash. Another is to look in a more qualitative way at the inherent capabilities of a company's business. I'll look at each of these approaches in turn.

Cash is king
Most thoughtful analysts look at cash flow and assets rather than reported earnings when they try to assess the fundamental value of a business. The general principles of asset valuation apply just as much to a company, and to the assets of a company, as to a security:
- an asset is worth what someone is willing to pay for it; and
- the value of an asset is the cash it will generate for its owner over its life.

Applying the second of these principles requires a process for trans-lating a stream of cash that accrues continuously over time into a value at a particular point in time. The cash flow will come from the dividends on a share or on the earnings of a company. The standard method is called 'discounted cash flow' (DCF), the first and indispensable tool for any quantitative investment analyst.

Compound interest at 10% per year means that £100 now will be worth £110 a year from now, £121 in two years' time, and so on. If £100 is worth £110 a year from now, then £100 a year from now is today worth £91 (£100 x $\frac{100}{110}$). A similar calculation would make £100 two years from now worth £83 today (£100 x $\frac{100}{121}$). The method of discounted cash flow derives in this way a set of conversion factors, like exchange rates, which can be used to convert cash at any future date into an equivalent value of cash today (£100 of 2010 correspond to £83 of 2008.) A promise to pay £300 in three equal annual instalments, starting now, is worth not £300, but £100 + £91 + £83, or £274. All you need do is choose an appropriate discount rate. The choice of an appropriate discount rate is not a minor problem, as we shall see.

The method of DCF valuation can be applied either to the cash flow accruing to the shareholder – the dividends to be paid – or to the cash accruing to the business itself. I'll look in turn at each of these approaches.

Suppose a company, like BP, is paying a dividend of 20p per share. We need to estimate the likely growth of that dividend. If dividends grow at 7%, next year's dividend might be 21.4p, rising to 22.9p the year after, and so on. All we need to do is write down that stream of cash flows, discount it at, say, 10% and we can calculate the fundamental value.

If 7% growth is the long-term average, there is a simplifying trick. Subtract 7%, the growth rate, from 10%, the discount rate. The difference, 3%, should be the dividend yield on the share. It is easy to work through the mathematics but you may prefer just to believe the result. A dividend yield of 3% would give BP shares a fundamental value of 667p, about 20% above the current share price.

The DCF approach requires knowledge of the appropriate discount rate and of the appropriate cash flows. The usual approach is to say that future cash flows should be discounted at the rate the company has to pay to raise money – the cost of capital. In the calculation above I used an arbitrary 10% as discount rate (a common procedure) but if the technique is to have scientific value the number requires a more scientific basis.

The yield on long-dated Treasury 2055 stocks – 4.25% nominal, 1.25% real – might be a good starting point. Payments of interest and principal by the British government are secure. But since the future dividends of BP are speculative it is common practice to use a much higher discount rate to reflect the greater risk associated with investment in shares. This allowance for business risk is the 'equity risk premium'. The simplest and commonest way of measuring the equity risk premium is the average historic difference between returns on shares and the return on safe assets. The data in Chapter 2 might justify a figure of about 5%, which is broadly consistent with a 10% figure for the cost of capital. A 10% figure for the cost of capital is also consistent with the intelligent investor's target rate of return. I'll come back to the calculation of this risk element of the cost of capital in the next chapter.

The alternative approach to DCF appraisal for a company like BP is to look at cash flows generated within the business itself. The free cash flow approach subtracts necessary investment in productive assets from the cash generated by a company's operations. The balance – the free cash flow – is the relevant amount for the DCF calculation. If we had a sufficiently long series of future free cash flows, the DCF technique would enable us to calculate the fundamental value of the business. But that is a big if.

A rapidly growing business may have negative free cash flow, because the company is spending more building the business than it is currently earning. Most new companies are in this position. Only after several years will projected cash flows become positive. Many years of data are therefore required before any clear assessment of fundamental value can be made.

A further difficulty then emerges. As illustration, go back to the DCF valuation of BP, and use the dividend growth approach. Over the next five years, the DCF value generated from dividends will be less than 100p, only around 15% of the hypothetical value of the share. Most of the projected cash flow lies in a far distant future.

Worse still, the result of the calculation is extremely sensitive to the assumptions. Suppose the dividend growth projection is 5%, rather than 7% and the discount rate is 11% rather than 10%. These aren't large adjustments – just a move from a good growth assumption to a fairly good one, from a benign economic scenario to a slightly less favourable one. But such adjustments halve the projected share price from 667p to 333p. Optimism can have an even more spectacular effect. Raise your dividend growth expectation to 8%, lower the discount rate from 10% to 9%: the fundamental value of the share soars from 667p to 2000p.

At this point, you may be inclined to give up on the use of DCF measures of fundamental value. Yet the DCF technique doesn't create the problem – it reveals it. Most of the value of today's major businesses really does lie in a future beyond the five or ten years that seem reasonably foreseeable. Small changes in assumptions, compounded far into the future, have large effects on current values. DCF calculations are illuminating, but don't make the mistake of believing that any particular DCF calculation is true.

There is a partial solution to these problems, which is to cut off the cash flow analysis after a period – five years is a common choice – and make an assumption about the value of the business at that date. This is not a very satisfactory answer. It resolves the difficult question posed initially – What is the fundamental value of the business now? – by requiring an answer to a more difficult question – What will be the fundamental value of the business five years from now? At this point, the first principle of asset valuation – the value of an asset is the cash it generates for its owner – becomes confounded with the second – an asset is worth what someone is willing to pay for it.

That emphasis on asset value suggests another approach to valuing a business. Look, not at the earnings, but at the assets the business owns. Every company you might invest in produces a balance sheet, an accounting statement of the value of the assets it owns. Normal accounting practice is that the balance sheet should report the *lower* of the amount the company paid for an asset and the value of the cash the asset will generate over its life. While this formulation closely mirrors the general principles of asset valuation, it does so in a deliberately cautious way. This caution comes firstly from insisting that the lower of the possible answers is used, and secondly by substituting the amount the company paid for the asset for the amount someone else would be willing to pay for it.

The accounting valuation principle is more cautious still. If the market value of the asset – the maximum amount anyone else is willing to pay for it – is lower than the amount the company was willing to pay for it, and that loss of value is likely to be permanent, the company should substitute the market value for the historic cost.

These exceptions to the historic cost principle have always been controversial. The company must substitute market values for the price paid when asset values decline, but may not substitute market values for the price paid when asset values increase. The asymmetry leads to systematic understatement and many exceptions exist to prevent distortion. Companies are allowed to revalue assets – such as property – that have a realisable value when it is reasonable to think the increase in value is permanent. Another important exception is for financial companies, and other companies that have an investment business, which are generally required to report these investments at their market value.[1]

Still, accountants have always tended to revert to the historic cost principle, and for good reasons. The principle is conservative – it tends to value assets at less than they are worth rather than more than they are worth. It is relatively objective – free of the flights of fancy of imaginative financial officers. And it doesn't require constant reassessment of asset values.

The pioneers of securities analysis, such as Graham and Dodd, operated successfully by simply having the skills and energy to penetrate accounting statements. Since the assets reported in the balance sheet were generally estimated conservatively, shares whose prices were below the reported asset value were generally good buys. Some investors became rich by identifying companies where the value of the assets the company owned – shops or land – was greater than the value of the company as a trading entity.

1 This issue gained significance in the 2007–8 with the collapse of the credit bubble, when many assets became virtually unmarketable.

Charles Clore became Britain's largest shoe retailer, not because he was interested in shoes, but because he was interested in the shops in which shoes were sold. Jim Slater enjoyed a meteoric career as the whiz-kid of the late 1960s before his sprawling business empire collapsed in the economic crisis that followed the 1973 oil shock. Slater looked at the business not as a trading concern, but as a collection of assets. The term 'asset stripper', coined for him, remains a term of abuse today.

Those days of easy returns have gone. Today, most companies have stripped their own assets. When assets have a value separable from the company that uses them, companies have generally realised that value. I have already explained that modern businesses rarely own the premises from which they operate and usually don't own the computers and the vehicles that their employees use.

The important assets of modern businesses are no longer their buildings, their plant and machinery, but their intangible property – their reputation with customers, their relationships with suppliers. When pompous executives proclaim that 'Our people are our greatest asset' what they say is often true. Most other assets are owned by, or pledged to, the financial sector.

Financial companies directly or indirectly own much of the plant or the property occupied by other industrial and commercial businesses. For banks and insurance companies and for property and investment companies, it remains important to understand the structure of their assets. There are a few sectors, such as oil and house building, where the market position of the company will depend on its control of future reserves of petroleum or of land. But while company accounts report a figure for the net assets of the company, the asset value is usually now a poor guide to the value of its shares. Investment analysts used to distinguish value and growth investing. Broadly speaking, value focused on companies with strong tangible assets, growth on companies with strong intangible assets. Nowadays these categories have become too blurred to be useful.

Some people think that more systematic attempts should be made to include the value of intangible assets in company accounts. Accounting theorists want to revive the balance sheet for a modern era; creative finance directors want to present the most favourable impression of the company's affairs. But the goodwill you find on corporate balance sheets is usually an accounting fiction that arises when a company pays, or overpays, in the acquisition of another business. These numbers should be disregarded. Corporate accounts reveal imperfectly, or not at all, the most important determinant of a company's fundamental value – its competitive advantage.

Competitive advantage

In the nineteenth-century businesses that Karl Marx described, the capitalist owned the factory and the plant in which workers produced the goods, and that state of affairs defined both the economic and political relationship between them. The analytic framework of that era lingers although the modern business environment is quite different. The bosses of large corporations have authority because of their job titles, not their wealth (though they are increasingly inclined to use the former to secure the latter). They don't own the place where they work and nor, as a rule, does the company that employs them.

The modern company is best viewed as a collection of capabilities. It is defined by its brands and its products; through its internal systems and its relationships with customers and suppliers; by the resources to which it has access and the operating licences it holds; and by its reputation with the public, governments and prospective employees. We have capitalism without capital.

When the company's most valuable assets descend in the lift at the end of the month, they take their pay cheques with them. The ability of the company to generate returns for shareholders depends on its ability to add value to its employees through its own capabilities. In a competitive market-place, a business can add such value only if there is something distinctive about these capabilities that yields a competitive advantage.

A distinctive capability becomes valuable when it yields a sustainable competitive advantage. That is what Warren Buffett understood when he bought stakes in Coca-Cola, Gillette and the *Washington Post*. He didn't think he was buying a head office in Atlanta, a razor blade manufacturing line, or a printing press. He was buying powerful brands and irreproducible market positions.

The largest of Britain's companies by market capitalisation (the blue chips) are BP, Shell, HSBC, Glaxo and Vodafone. The two oil companies, BP and Shell, are similar in many respects. They are integrated businesses with activities that include exploration and production; trading, transportation and refining; and selling petrol, heating oil, aviation fuel and other petroleum products to final consumers. Historically, BP's strengths have been more upstream – closer to production – and Shell's more downstream – closer to consumers.

BP seemed to have established a lead over its rival when it took a central role in the restructuring of the world oil industry in the 1990s. It consistently impressed the mind of the market with vigorous cost reduction and repeated earnings gains. Shell's standing with the public was diminished by environmental and political controversies, and its standing with investors diminished by its conservative business strategy and a scandal over misstatement of its oil reserves.

The sustainability of the competitive advantages of BP and Shell is demonstrated by the way in which these businesses have, for decades, been not just the leading European oil companies but among the leading European companies of any kind. It is hard to imagine that any firms outside the small group of established oil majors could replicate their integrated systems or ability to attract and develop strong teams of managers and engineers. The well-resourced national oil companies of major producing states like Norway and Saudi Arabia have not really tried, while Russia's predatory Gazprom continues to depend on Western expertise and distribution systems. The distinctive capabilities of these businesses extend from privileged access to oil reserves through their integrated production and distribution systems to their retail brands.

HSBC has an even longer history although its emergence as a major international bank is recent. As the Hong Kong and Shanghai Banking Corporation, the company facilitated trade and investment in the Far East in the heyday of the British empire. In 1980, with China still emerging from the rule of Mao and the status of Hong Kong uncertain, the future of the business seemed in doubt. But the company's fortunes have since been transformed by a programme of acquisitions around the world and the emergence of China as an economic power-house. Well-established banks have a series of competitive advantages: a name that others trust; a customer base of corporate and private accounts; and branch networks. The company has attempted to develop HSBC as a global retail brand, rebadging the local banks it has bought in many countries.

Glaxo was a small British drug company that discovered and developed an anti-ulcerant, Zantac, which became one of the most commercially successful products in the history of the pharmaceutical industry. By reinvesting these profits in research, and taking over two rivals, Wellcome and Smith Kline, the company became one of the world's leading pharmaceutical businesses. Today, its sales are heavily biased towards the United States, as is its management.

Glaxo's competitive advantage depends in significant part on the intellectual property it derives from drug patents. Even though these patents have limited life, drugs such as Zantac continue to have brand value in the face of the generic competition that emerges when such protection expires. As the leading British pharmaceutical company, Glaxo enjoys a privileged position in association with Britain's strong academic science base.

But original research in pharmacology is moving from large pharmaceutical businesses towards a mixture of publicly funded basic research and smaller specialist businesses financed by venture capital. The era of blockbuster drugs like Zantac, which alleviate but do not cure the chronic illnesses of the well-to-do, is coming to an end. Companies like Glaxo are organisations focused on marketing and the management of the complex processes of regulatory approval.

Vodafone came into existence only in 1985, when it secured one of the two initial licences to operate a mobile phone network in the UK. The company easily outperformed its rival, Cellnet, still subject to the influence of the newly privatised, but still bureaucratic, British Telecom. An ambitious chief executive, Chris Gent, bought mobile phone operators around the world, surrounding himself by the New Economy bubble. Vodafone's hostile acquisition of a German operator, Mannesmann, in 1999 was, at the time, the largest takeover bid ever undertaken. At the height of the boom, the company accounted for 15% of the value of all shares quoted in London and a higher percentage of turnover.

Vodafone's competitive advantage is based on its operating licences and ownership of the physical networks, which are hard to reproduce, and the customer base it has accumulated. Many of these assets – such as the Mannesmann acquisition and the 3G licences obtained in Britain and Germany – are worth much less than the company paid. Much shareholder wealth has been destroyed – in 2008, the company's shares are only one-third of the peak level they reached in 2000. But the company's competitive advantages remain, although less valuable than the business or its shareholders once supposed.

These companies illustrate common types of competitive advantage. Generally, the distinctive capabilities that create competitive advantages fall into four broad categories:

- *brands and reputation* – important for BP and Shell, both for the retail brands that serve their customers and the reputation that encourages governments to select these firms as partners in exploiting oil reserves. Brand and reputation are also important to HSBC;
- *strategic assets* – exclusive access to specific resources, such as Vodafone's licences and the reserves controlled by BP and Shell;
- *proprietary architecture* – systems and structures, such as those of the oil companies and banks;
- *innovation and intellectual property* – vital to Glaxo.

The value of competitive advantages depends on the extent to which they are appropriable and sustainable. A competitive advantage is appropriable only if the company can defend it against suppliers and customers. An asset is not appropriable if it can go down in the lift – much of the value created by City firms is paid out in bonuses to employees. A competitive advantage has continuing value only if it is hard to replicate.

Primark's brand of cheap retailing, for example, has recently been so attractive to customers that police had to be called to keep order when the company (a subsidiary of Associated British Foods) recently opened its Oxford Street store. But in retailing, almost every successful new formula, including Primark's, can be quickly reproduced. Other stores can see what is being done and can buy products from the same or similar suppliers. Competitive advantages based on market positioning – successfully identifying unfilled product niches – are rarely sustainable.

The competitive advantage created by a strong retail brand, such as those of Marks and Spencer or John Lewis (owned by an employee trust, and not available for investment), is much harder to reproduce. The same is true of the competitive advantage that Tesco and Sainsbury enjoy by controlling a network of well positioned out-of-town sites. Planning restrictions now ensure that, even if similar sites are identified, they are hard to develop.

In a slow-moving industry like soft drinks, a brand like Coca-Cola can be sustained, with appropriate management, indefinitely. If the market can be developed through geographic expansion – introducing Coke to China – or product extension – such as the sale of Diet Coke – the value of this competitive advantage may continue to grow.

In a fast-moving market, such as consumer electronic goods, a brand can only maintain its value if the name can be attached to a stream of innovative products. Apple and Sony have succeeded in this.

The chequered record of these companies is a reminder that innovation is a weaker source of competitive advantage than many people believe. Most innovation can be readily replicated. The financial services industry is endlessly innovative. But because most innovation can be immediately recognised and marketed by other firms, such innovations can rarely be a source of sustainable competitive advantage – although, as for Apple and Sony in their industries, a reputation for frequent innovation is often a source of competitive advantage in financial services.

Apple's easy-to-use MP3 players quickly found imitators. But the company's most important innovation came twenty years earlier. The graphical user interface with desktop, mouse and icons enables us to use computers without any knowledge of how they work. But the graphical user interface was successfully reproduced by Apple's more powerful competitor, Microsoft. While Glaxo's Zantac was a success that made the company's shares spectacular outperformers for twenty years, EMI's path-breaking CAT scanner – a more original innovation – proved bad news for EMI shareholders in the long run. America's General Electric was able to manufacture similar machines but brought enduring competitive advantages in marketing expertise and political networking to their sale.

Glaxo benefited because its innovation was supported by a patent. (Although there were numerous patents around EMI's scanner, the central breakthrough – the concept of computer assisted tomography – could not be protected.) Pharmaceuticals is one of relatively few industries in which intellectual property protection is sufficiently powerful to make innovation appropriable. Even here, the issue is more complex. Zantac was a me-too drug – the pharmacological principle was pioneered by SmithKline's similar Tagamet. Glaxo's real achievement was to market its product more effectively. Innovation – especially, but not uniquely, among sources of competitive advantage – is most effective when supported by complementary, but perhaps less distinctive capabilities.

Strategic assets like those of BP or Vodafone are powerful and valuable capabilities. But these depend on governments, and what governments give, they can also take away. As I write, the Russian government is expropriating part of BP's share in the Kovykta gas field. Western governments rarely expropriate, but can, and do, set and alter the terms on which monopoly franchises are offered, as demonstrated in the regular ad hoc modifications to North Sea oil taxation. Regulatory authorities can reduce the value of existing franchises by issuing more of them, as with airline liberalisation. More sustainable strategic assets are found where the monopoly is intrinsic rather than government-conferred, as with Heathrow and other London airports (owned by BAA, now a subsidiary of the Spanish company Ferrovial), or the *Financial Times* (owned by Pearson) which operates in a niche profitable for one newspaper but unlikely to be profitable for two.

Valuable competitive advantages are sustainable over time; appropriable for the firm that holds them; and defensible against pressure from competitors, suppliers and customers. Is it possible to use these principles to compute, numerically, the fundamental value of a business? It is certainly possible to sketch the outlines of a calculation. Such an exercise may have value as reality check – could these competitive advantages equal, or be much more or less than the value implied by the current market price? That calculation makes Google's valuation look surprising and BP's sustainable.

You should treat such calculations as illuminating rather than true. I'll discuss bogus quantification further in Chapter 8. The analytic framework described here, like many others, is better used as a set of questions. What are the sources of competitive advantage? Are they replicable, sustainable, defensible, appropriable? The calculations are a better guide to relative valuations – Google versus BP – than to absolute ones.

Value investing was once the purchase of tangible assets at levels below their market value. Value investing today is buying sustainable competitive advantages at a good price. The opportunity to do so arises most often because the mind of the market is distracted by essentially short-term considerations – a poor economic outlook for the industry, a strategic mistake by the business, weak management, or simply negative momentum.

These are the signals for the intelligent investor to make contrarian purchases. Buffett began his legendary run by purchasing a large stake in American Express when the share price was depressed by a large, but ultimately inconsequential, fraud involving salad oil.

CHAPTER 7

RISK AND REWARD

Risk and uncertainty

The first share I bought was in a small shipyard called Robb Caledon. The purchase was both a rewarding investment and a rewarding lesson in investment.

You might naturally begin to establish an investment portfolio with a selection of blue chip stocks, like BP, HSBC, Glaxo and Vodafone. Such a strategy sounds much less risky than a stake in Robb Caledon. But when I bought Robb Caledon, I was learning about the capital asset pricing model (CAPM) – the dominant theory of modern financial economics. That theory suggests the opposite conclusion.

Fast forward more than two decades. I am at a meeting of government economists and senior executives from major defence contractors. The largest defence contractor, BAE Systems, had recently suffered huge losses from cost overruns on a major project. Its business was in turmoil, its shares depressed, and loss of confidence and aversion to risk had affected the whole sector.

The government economists, who had recently learnt the CAPM at the best graduate schools, explained that the cost of capital to these companies was very low – on a par, in fact, with the government bond rate. They repeated themselves several times. They needed to – the business people reacted as they would have reacted to aliens describing life on another planet. The two sides meant completely different things when they talked about risk. In this chapter, I'll explain the CAPM and illustrate the different interpretations attached to the term 'risk' by business people and financial professionals.

During the New Economy bubble, stocks carried large risk for investors. Speculators hoped for – and sometimes made – large profits, and ultimately suffered very large losses. The principal risk faced by investment managers, confronting the same opportunities, was that they would lose the support of their customers by failing to match the performance of their rivals. The risk perceived by the fund manager was different from the risk faced by the customer.

Common sense tells us that flying is risky. Travelling in a metal tube at high speed and an altitude of 10,000 metres is intrinsically dangerous. But precisely because flying *is* potentially dangerous, planes are scrupulously maintained, pilots are rigorously trained, and safety precautions are extensive. In 2007, fewer than 600 people worldwide died in commercial plane crashes. More people died in England and Wales alone from falling down the stairs.

Fewer children are killed on the roads in Britain today than in the 1920s. The roads are more dangerous but, because parents recognise this, their children are safer. The statistics do not lie, nor do our assessments of risk. The figures that show that flying is safe, and the intuition that flying is risky, are both correct. It all depends on what you mean by risk.

Until recently, households found security in large families. In many parts of the world, they still do. Infant mortality was high and only in a big family was it probable that some children would live to become providers and homemakers. Few people in rich countries now think in this way. Large families are more exposed financially and run more serious risk of grief through accident or serious illness. What is risky in one context may be provident in a different context, and vice versa.

The government economists who thought some risks could be completely diversified used a different frame of thought from the business people who worried that a risky project might bankrupt their companies. The investor who worried about losing his shirt, and the fund manager who worried about losing his job, had different perceptions of risk. The nervous passenger and the student of accident statistics see flight risk differently. Some parents think it would be imprudent to have a large family, others think it would be imprudent not to.

The antithesis of risk is security. Much of the ambiguity in the meaning of risk results from different concepts of security. For the prudent investor, security means stability in the value of his or her portfolio; for the investment manager, security means earning a large bonus for outperforming the market or attracting new business, rather than being fired. All these perceptions are subjectively valid.

These multiple perspectives lead to confusion in the ways people describe and interpret risk, and to ambiguity in their use of the word 'risk'. These differences of definition mean that misunderstandings and errors are frequent. There are consequent opportunities to gain, and to lose, substantial amounts of money. Much financial services activity relies for its profitability on confusions and inconsistencies in attitudes to risk and interpretations of risk.

Yet amongst academics who teach students the theory of finance – and I have been both student and teacher – there is one, and only one, correct way of thinking about risk: the way of thinking about risk I had in mind when I bought Robb Caledon.

The system that I will call the theory of 'subjective expected utility' (SEU) is so universally accepted in financial economics that any other behaviour is described as irrational. SEU is the basis of virtually all the sophisticated models and quantitative techniques used in financial markets today. These models are both normative and positive – they claim that people should think about risk in SEU ways and derive conclusions about market behaviour from the assumption that they actually do.

Although this SEU approach dominates today, it was not always so. Early in the twentieth century two alternative ways of describing risk vied for supremacy. On each side was an urbane Englishman from Cambridge and an assertive American from Chicago. The winners were Frank Ramsey and Jimmie Savage.

Ramsey was a Cambridge philosopher who made important contributions to economics in his spare time. He died at the age of twenty-six but his brother, perhaps the less distinguished sibling, went on to become Archbishop of Canterbury. Savage was labelled

Jimmie by a nurse since his parents, not expecting him to live, did not bother to name him. (He survived another fifty-three years.) Ramsey and Savage, the founders of SEU, proposed a means of taking the mathematical tools of probability theory far beyond their initial field of application – the gaming saloon – into the boardroom and on to the trading floor. They are the founders of modern risk management techniques.

On the other side of the debate were Maynard Keynes and Frank Knight. Keynes' fellowship thesis – in effect, his doctorate – was not directly to do with economics. (Keynes, one of the great polymaths of the twentieth century, had taken a degree in mathematics.) His subject was probability theory, and his thesis was eventually published in 1921, long after its submission. In the same year, Frank Knight, a farmer's son from the American Midwest (who would come to loathe Keynes and all he represented), published a book, *Risk, Uncertainty and Profit*, in a different style but with a related argument. Keynes and Knight emphasised the uncertainty that arose from the necessarily imperfect nature of human knowledge. The future was not just unknown, but unknowable.

Donald Rumsfeld expressed the difference between risk and uncertainty with uncharacteristic clarity. Rumsfield famously distinguished 'known unknowns – the things we know we do not know' from 'unknown unknowns – the things we do not know we do not know'. This chapter will mainly be about risk – the things we know we do not know. The next chapter will deal with uncertainty – the things we do not know we do not know.

The claim made by the SEU school is that analytic tools can enable us to cut through much of this uncertainty with probabilistic reasoning and formal modelling. These approaches would provide the necessary underpinning for the growth in derivative markets after 1970 and the explosion of credit after 2000. They originate in the work of Ramsey and Savage, and received major extension in the modern portfolio theory of Markowitz and the capital asset-pricing model of Sharpe. In the remainder of this chapter, I'll give these arguments the best possible run for their money. Let's go back to Robb Caledon.

Think probabilities

Robb Caledon was bankrupt. The year was 1976, and a bill to nationalise British shipbuilding was going through Parliament. If the bill became law, the assets and liabilities of the yard would be assumed by the government and the shareholders would receive around 100p per share. If the bill failed, the shares would be worthless. They were selling in the market at around 40p.

I had to be persistent to buy these shares. The brokers I called told me that the Labour government was incompetent, and nationalising shipyards was a silly idea. They were right. They told me that the shipyard was on the point of financial collapse and yet the share price was twice what it had been two months before. They were right about that, too. They told me that I risked losing everything I invested. Again, they were right.

All these observations were justified, but none seemed relevant. With youthful enthusiasm, I was applying the lessons I had been taught. Think probabilities – plan for different scenarios, think about the consequences of each, and assess their likelihood. Be detached – don't be caught up in events and confuse what you want to happen with what you expect to happen. Mind your portfolio. The risk that is relevant to you is the overall risk of your whole investment portfolio, not the risk associated with the individual securities it contains.

Probabilities were central to my approach. Probabilities are essential to gamblers, though frequently ignored by them. The probability that a fair coin will show heads is one-half. This is a statement about frequency: if you throw a fair coin many times approximately half the calls will be heads. If you can be bothered to throw such a coin many times, you will confirm this statement.

The ancient Greeks laid the foundations of modern mathematics. Although they gambled, they never discovered the – elementary – mathematics of probability, which was not developed until the seventeenth and eighteenth centuries. Two elements of that framework are particularly important in understanding the principles of investment – statistical distributions, and expected values.

Statistical distributions describe the probabilities of different outcomes of repeated random events. If you throw a fair coin twice, the probability that you get one head and one tail is one-half, and the probability of each of two heads or two tails is one-quarter. After many throws, approximately half the calls will be heads, and the distribution of outcomes is described by the most famous of all statistical distributions – the normal distribution – with its familiar 'bell-shaped' curve. The normal distribution is ubiquitous – it describes a wide variety of both social and natural phenomena, from the distribution of voting intentions to the heights of the voters. The assumption that the normal distribution can be applied to the distribution of daily movements in securities prices is commonly made in financial economics. It is an assumption that is illuminating, but not true.

The second key concept from probability theory is expected value. The expected value of a gamble is measured by multiplying the values of the outcomes of a gamble by their probabilities. If a coin-tossing game will pay you £1 if you win, and nothing if you lose, then its expected value is 50p. Despite the name, the expected value is not what you should expect. You will definitely not get 50p from a single toss of that coin.

But the more repeated events there are, the more likely it is that the outcome will approach its expected value. If instead of gambling to win £1 on a single toss, you were to gamble to win 50p on each of two consecutive tosses, the distribution of outcomes is less extreme. There is now a one in four chance of winning £1, from two heads, and a one in four chance of winning nothing, from two tails. Half the time, one coin will come up heads and the other tails, and you will indeed receive the expected value of 50p. If you gamble for a penny on each of 100 throws of the coin, the expected value is still 50p, and you will probably win something close to this figure.

Comparing distributions

In investment matters, you will be concerned, not just with the expected value, but with the overall distribution of gains and losses. In particular, you will want to know what could go wrong. What is the worst that could happen?

The worst that can happen is that you will be convicted of a grave crime of which you are entirely innocent, or that you will be murdered by a passing psychopath. What you really want to know about is outcomes that are bad but not completely unlikely. Contemplate, for example, the worst 1% of outcomes, and then imagine the best of these conceivable outcomes. This is to take a gloomy view, but not so gloomy that you spend your life in bed. (Though note that, if the English statistics are any guide, more people die from falling out of bed than in aircraft accidents. Still, you would increase the probability of death dramatically by descending the stairs. There is no escape from risk and uncertainty.)

The best of the worst 1% is called the first percentile of the frequency distribution of outcomes. Similarly, the best of the worst 10% is the tenth percentile, and you might look at this if you don't want to be quite so pessimistic. Table 5 shows the first percentile of the cumulative frequency distribution of outcomes for the coin-tossing game. For a single toss of the coin, the first percentile of the distribution is zero – and indeed zero is the value of all percentiles up to the 50th. If you spread your bets across 100 tosses, however, the first percentile is 38p. On 99% of occasions you play the game, you will win at least that much.

The value-at-risk models used by most financial institutions today seek to measure and control risks by setting values for these low percentiles of the frequency distribution of outcomes. The bank asks How much could we lose on a bad (say, one in a hundred) day? The first percentile of the daily outcomes gives the answer to that question.

Table 5: The cumulative frequency distribution from tossing a coin

Winnings				
Percentile	1 toss	2 tosses	20 tosses	100 tosses
1st	o	o	26p	38p
10th	o	25p	36p	44p
49th	o	50p	49.7p	49.9p
51st	£1	50p	50.3p	50.1p
90th	£1	75p	66p	56p
Gain on each head obtained	£1	50p	5p	1p
Expected value of winnings	50p	50p	50p	50p

The same method can be used to describe the upper tail of the distribution. If you look at the worst 90% of outcomes, the 90th percentile is the best of these. The converse, and perhaps simpler way to look at it, is to say that you will do as well or better than the 90th percentile on only 10% of occasions. On a single toss of a coin, the 90th percentile is £1. In fact any percentile above the 50th is £1. For a gamble spread over 100 tosses, however, the 90th percentile is only 56p. You can expect to make more than 56p only 10% of the time.

To decide whether one distribution is preferable to another, it isn't really sufficient to make comparisons of a single percentile. The first percentile is a rather unlikely outcome. The prudent person, rather than the committed pessimist, might focus on the 10th percentile. You would have to be very gloomy to ignore altogether the good outcomes at higher percentiles. In banks, the traders tend to look only at the high percentiles, the risk managers only at the low ones. This creates tension between them which is sometimes constructive, often fatal.

The examples with a relatively small number of trials (one and two tosses) have lower payoffs at low percentiles, and higher payoffs at high percentiles. The worse outcomes are worse, and the better outcomes are better, in games of one or two tosses than those of games with 20 or 100 tosses. That is what we mean by saying a strategy is riskier. In the coin-tossing game, the crossover point at which both more and less risky distributions take the same value is at the 50th percentile.

There are two reasons why the crossover point of this game is at the 50th percentile and is the same for all distributions. Each distribution has the same expected value of 50p. A distribution that was generally more profitable, but was also riskier, might have worse outcomes for all probabilities up to, say, the 20th, but better outcomes for all higher percentiles. Most of the time, the riskier strategy would pay more, but the very worst outcomes would be worse.

But the expected value is only the median outcome, the 50th percentile, if the probability distributions are symmetric. In coin tossing, good and bad outcomes are equally likely. On 100 tosses, you suffer a 10% chance of falling more than 6p short of the expected value of 50p, and also a 10% chance of getting more than 6p above the expected value. Many risk distributions, however, are asymmetric. The tail-gating driver mostly gets to his destination a few seconds quicker, but occasionally dies in a car crash. The 10th and higher percentiles of these distributions are all good; the first percentile is terrible. The lottery ticket buyer usually loses, but might win the jackpot. The 50th percentile, even the 80th percentile of the outcomes of purchasing a single lottery ticket are lousy – you simply lose your stake – but the 99.9999th percentile makes you a millionaire.

This method of comparing distributions by comparing different percentiles of the risk distribution is quite general. One distribution is riskier than another if it yields worse returns at lower percentiles, and better returns at higher percentiles. There will be a crossing point. The lower the crossing point, the more attractive the riskier distribution. If one distribution has worse outcomes in its lowest five percentiles, and better returns at all other percentiles, it is more likely to be acceptable than one for which the crossing point is at the 50th percentile.

A common technique simplifies the comparison of its distributions with the aid of a mathematical trick. Many statistical distributions, including the normal distribution, are completely described by two parameters. One parameter is the mean or average, of the distribution – what is the average height of a population? The other is a measure of variability – how many people are over six feet or below five feet? If you know the average and the variability then you know every-thing about the normal distribution. If two distributions have the same expected value, then a comparison of a single percentile – any percentile – will be enough to tell you which is riskier.

The statistical measure of variability is the variance or standard deviation. The Greek letter *sigma* is commonly used for the standard deviation. This term has entered popular usage, so that 'a six *sigma* event' is an event that is, or should be, very improbable. The Sharpe ratio, which is the ratio of expected return (relative to a benchmark) to standard deviation, is widely used by quantitative investors.

If the analysts' distribution of returns were normal, or followed sufficiently closely another of the family of common statistical distributions – and if the parameters of these distributions were known – then techniques like value at risk and Sharpe ratios would be extremely valuable. The mathematics of probability, which opens the way to the application of powerful statistical tools, could be applied to the analysis of unique political and economic events, like the failure of legislation and the future of a shipyard. To see some of the possibilities, let's go back to Robb Caledon.

My ship came in

The fate of Robb Caledon was a risk – a known unknown. People sometimes make probability statements about known unknowns, as when they say 'The probability that Parliament will approve the shipbuilding nationalisation bill is one half'. Such a statement is called an expression of personal, or subjective, probability.

When I talked about tossing a coin, I used the terms probability and frequency interchangeably. But I can't do that for one-off political events. Someone who makes that statement about the shipbuilding bill is not saying 'If Parliament considers the bill one hundred times, the bill will be passed on fifty occasions'. They are making a statement of personal opinion. Or perhaps, in this case, an absence of opinion. It is common to say 'It's fifty-fifty', meaning 'I just don't know'. These expressions sound like statements about probabilities. But can they, should they, be interpreted in this way?

The idea that risk and uncertainty can be handled with the aid of personal probabilities is often called Bayesian, after the Reverend Thomas Bayes, an eighteenth-century clergyman who made important contributions to probability theory. Bayesians believe that each of us has a mental probability distribution of likely and unlikely outcomes, which we constantly revise as new information becomes available. Bayesians further believe that the mathematical rules for calculating compound probabilities (and hence statistical distributions) are universal. These rules can be applied to personal probabilities in the same way as they can be applied to frequentist probabilities.

There are some obvious difficulties in the use of rules that are based on the observation of repeated events – like tossing a coin – in the interpretation of one-off events – like shipbuilding nationalisation.

Coin tossing seems to be truly random. Whether the shipbuilding nationalisation bill will be passed is certainly not random. The fate of the bill will be the result of specific political developments which – if only we had enough information and insight – we might hope to explain and predict, and can certainly describe after they have happened.

However, both Bachelier's notion of the random walk and Samuelson's explanation of that notion through analysis of the ways markets handle information seem to provide a justification for the use of probability theory to describe the – unique – evolution of securities markets. Bachelier and Samuelson realised that the ways in which financial markets process information – the way expectations of tomorrow's events are incorporated into today's prices – will create patterns that have the appearance of randomness. This apparent randomness may allow us to 'think probabilities' even in situations where events are determined by deliberate human action rather than by chance.

Such apparent randomness of outcome doesn't mean or require that securities prices move for no reason, or that when the Monetary Policy Committee is in a locked room it makes a decision by tossing a coin. God does not play dice, Einstein said, and the remark is illuminating even though there is argument over whether its substance is true. There are underlying explanations of most physical and natural phenomena even if our understanding of these explanations remains imperfect. Randomness of outcome means that when you have analysed all that is known about the economic and monetary situation, and about the attitudes of the different members of the Monetary Policy Committee, it makes sense – or is at least conceivable – that the range of decisions available to the Committee can be described with a probability distribution.

But such a probability distribution is subjective. Different people may assess it differently. Many people do not find it easy to think probabilistically about what interest rates will be, whether Robb Caledon will be nationalised, or what they will be doing in retirement. They ask instead What is going to happen? A committed Bayesian believes that, however we express our attitudes to risk and uncertainty, personal probabilities govern our decisions. We can discover these buried probabilities by asking questions such as 'How much would you be willing to bet on interest rates being above 5% in twenty years' time?'

Securities markets elicit information by constantly offering such gambles. 'How much would you be willing to pay for a share in Robb Caledon which will pay 100p if the nationalisation bill goes through?' The market asks that question every day when it gives you the chance to buy, or sell, Robb Caledon shares. It asks you to bet on future interest rates every time it quotes a price on a bond.

To make this link from probabilities to market prices, we have to assume that personal probabilities can be used to calculate expected values. If my personal probability that the shipbuilding nationalisation bill would pass was 0.5, and the potential payout was 100p per share, my subjective expected value of a purchase was 50p. The implicit rule is to compare the expected value of 50p with the market price of 40p. Since the expected value – given my subjective probability – was above the market price, the stock was a good buy.

While the assertion that 'a fair coin falls heads with probability one half' seems to be an objective statement about the world, and can be verified by experiment, personal probabilities are unavoidably subjective. One day the dust will have settled, and Parliament will either have approved the nationalisation bill, or not. Even then no one can say whose subjective judgment, whose personal probability, was right and whose was wrong. The bill was passed and I received the payment of 100p per share. I was pleased with myself, but that doesn't mean my personal probability was right. Nor, if the bill had failed, would that necessarily mean my prior judgment of subjective probability had been wrong. A Bayesian would say that the stockbrokers I consulted had personal probabilities different from mine and that was why they had not recommended the shares.

Did the price of 40p, against a possible pay off of 100p, mean that 0.4 was the average of everyone's personal probability? No, it doesn't. Many people, like those stockbrokers, attached low personal probabilities to nationalisation – if they had ever thought in this Bayesian way, which is doubtful – and many more people had not considered the matter at all. The price of 40p indicates that the number of people who thought the bill was likely to pass was sufficient to hold all the available Robb Caledon shares. Since the shipyard was small, this number did not have to be large (the company never had more than a few hundred shareholders).

The metaphor of the market as voting machine is often used in this way to infer probabilities from market prices. On a Bloomberg screen, you can find implied probabilities that the Monetary Policy Committee will change interest rates. Commentators sometimes say '"The market" is assuming a 30% chance of an interest rate cut'. But such anthropomorphisation should be viewed here, as everywhere, with caution.

Still, there seems to be a profit opportunity if your subjective probability differs from that of Mr Market. That is what I was exploiting with Robb Caledon. With an expected value of 50p and a share price of 40p there was an expected profit of 10p. But, just as you will never receive the expected value of 50p when you toss a coin once, the expected value was not what I would receive from my Robb Caledon purchase. I would either have lost 40p or gained 60p. If I had lost, I would not even have had the consolation that if I had bought the share 100 times, I would almost certainly have made a profit. Coin tossing is a repeated event. The proposal to nationalise Robb Caledon was unique.

Still, if you always approach one-off risks in this probabilistic manner, while you will lose some and win others, over the long run you will probably come out ahead. That's a good argument, though not a conclusive argument, for the SEU approach. You will need to be sufficiently detached to ride both the swings and the roundabouts with equanimity. But it does not make the Bayesian approach to risk assessment objective or value-free. Frequentist probabilities and subjective probabilities are different. Frequentist probabilities are facts, personal probabilities are opinions. Subjective probabilities are not objectively right or wrong, even with hindsight. The passage of the nationalisation bill did not vindicate my decision to buy.

A decision that has a good outcome is not necessarily a good decision, and vice versa. When you can comfortably say to yourself

'Buying Robb Caledon shares was the right decision even though I lost my entire investment', you have learned to think probabilistically. You have also learned why most people – and especially most large organisations – find probabilistic thinking difficult. But you have also learned why individuals who have learned to think probabilistically – like Buffett and Soros – have an advantage over others who must be judged by superiors who will certainly exploit the benefit of hindsight.

Diminishing marginal utility

The principle that risky outcomes should be judged by their expected value was one of the earliest notions in probability. Daniel Bernoulli, an eighteenth-century mathematician, who played a major role in developing this theory, quickly identified a difficulty. Even if people who calculated subjective expected values would frequently end up better off, expected values were not what seemed to govern their attitudes to risk. Many people would prefer a 50% chance of £1m to a 10% chance of £5m, and the certainty of £500,000 in cash to either. But the expected value of all of the outcomes is £500,000. The example Bernoulli used to illustrate this problem became known as the 'St Petersburg paradox'.

In the St Petersburg game, a coin is tossed repeatedly. If the first toss of the coin is a head, the player receives £1. If the first toss is a tail, the prize is doubled to £2 and the coin is tossed again. If the prize is not won, it is doubled again, and so on until a head appears and the game ends. There is therefore a 50% probability that the game ends with a single throw and the player gains £1. There is a much lower probability of winning £4 on the third toss. Simple mathematics shows that the expected value of the game is infinitely large.

If you think this is not a very realistic game, you should know that two and a half centuries later investment bankers would invent 'payment in kind securities', loans on which payment would increase if the quality of the underlying credit deteriorated. In essence, these were St Petersburg games and like, St Petersburg games, not a good idea for either banker or player.

No one will pay more than a few pounds to play Bernoulli's St

Petersburg game. Its large expected value depends on multiplying large payoffs by their small probabilities. The game might run for forty throws, by which time you would be richer than Warren Buffett. But few people seem willing to pay much for that opportunity.

The resolution of the St Petersburg paradox that is most widely accepted today was known in Bernoulli's time. Jimmie Savage would articulate the reasoning most clearly, and in a manner that would have great influence on financial economics. The St Petersburg paradox, he suggested, is the result of what economists call 'diminishing marginal utility'. The first million is a lot better than the second million, or at least that is what people think before they've got their first million. By the time you have $50bn, as Warren does, the prospect of another million is of little consequence. So $50bn is valued at much less than 50 million times $1000, and the expected utility of the St Petersburg game is correspondingly low even if its expected value is high.

People who prefer a sure thing to a gamble with the same expected monetary value – people who prefer £500,000 in cash to a 50% chance of £1m and who are not impressed by the St Petersburg game – are described as risk averse. The standard hypothesis is that most people are risk averse when they invest. They are also risk averse when they insure – they accept a certain loss in return for giving up the gamble that their house will burn down or that they will have to pay unexpected medical bills. The insurance premium will generally be greater than the expected value of the claims, otherwise the insurance company would be unprofitable. Expected value is what the insurance company, which can use its portfolio of policies to think frequencies rather than subjective probabilities, will get.

Diminishing marginal utility can account for risk aversion. Such risk aversion can only be significant when the amounts you gain or lose are large relative to your wealth. Think of a gamble in which you can win, or lose, £1, and suppose you already have £14,265. If you refuse the bet you will still have £14,265, while if you accept it you will have either £14,264 or £14,266. Few people would think there was much difference between these outcomes. Fewer still would think 'I'd much rather see my wealth increase from £14,264 to £14,265 than see it increase from £14,265 to £14,266'. If the amount you are gambling is relatively small, then you should simply assess small bets by reference to their expected value.

This conclusion has major implications for intelligent investors who follow SEU. Since most individual investments will be small relative to your overall portfolio, far less your overall wealth, expected values are usually the right way to deal with risk. That leads to another, and perhaps the most significant implication of thinking SEU: always look at risk in the context of your portfolio as a whole, rather than its individual elements. Focus on the outcome, not the process. The 'mind your portfolio' principle is fundamental. To see its consequences I'll go back once more to Robb Caledon.

Mind your portfolio

In 1976, the Labour government promoting the shipbuilding nationalisation bill was struggling and unpopular. Margaret Thatcher had recently become Conservative leader and her party was gaining support. The government might lose a vote of confidence in the House of Commons and be forced to call an election, which the Conservatives would probably win. This happened in 1979 and Thatcher became Prime Minister.

A political development such as this was the main risk faced by holders of Robb Caledon shares, since a Conservative government would abandon plans to nationalise shipbuilding. While Labour's fall would have been bad news for Robb Caledon, it would have caused delight around the City, and the wider stock market would have risen immediately. Let's suppose that stocks would have been 5% higher as a result of Labour's defeat. And suppose that you had £5000 to invest. Consider three possible portfolios:

- put all the money into Robb Caledon;
- put all your money into blue chip shares; or
- buy 250 Robb Caledon shares for £100 and put the rest of your money into blue chips.

Here is the value of your portfolio if the bill is passed, and if the bill fails.

Table 6: Value of alternative portfolios depending on the fate of the shipbuilding nationalisation bill of 1976

	Robb Caledon only	Blue chips only	Mixed portfolio
Government survives	12,500	5000	5150
Government falls	0	5250	5145

Which portfolio would have been best? With hindsight, of course, you should have gone for the first, and dived into Robb Caledon's docks. But it is easy to be a successful investor with hindsight. If you felt sure the Labour government would fall, you should have gone for the portfolio of blue chips. The first portfolio is extremely risky, suitable only for the most hardened speculator. The paradox is that the least risky portfolio is not the second, which focuses on safe assets, but the third, which includes a small holding of Robb Caledon shares.

In this example, adding a small investment in a very risky asset reduces the overall risk of the portfolio. You are sure to end up with around £5150. The risk associated with a portfolio is not measured by adding up the risks of each individual element. A combination of risks may be less risky in whole than in part.

I thought Robb Caledon was an interesting speculation for two reasons. All three portfolios would have had the same expected value if the probability that the bill would be passed were slightly more than 0.4. My personal probability that the bill would pass was a good deal higher than Mr Market's. How much higher it would have had to be to have made the purchase worthwhile would seem to depend on how risk averse I was.

The 'mind your portfolio' principle transforms the way you approach this problem. If I had bought some blue chips, then however risk averse I was, Robb Caledon would have been worth buying because its shares would go down when other shares would go up and vice versa. An asset with this property is called a hedge, and adding a hedge to a portfolio reduces overall portfolio risk, even if the hedge is, in itself, a speculative investment – like Robb Caledon. So the ship-yard was doubly attractive.

Assets don't have to be hedges to reduce risk. It is sufficient that individual risks are not perfectly correlated with each other. If you bet £1 on a single toss of a coin, you win £1 or zero: if you bet 50p on each of two different throws, you win 50p half the time: if you bet 1p on each of a hundred throws, what you will win, as Table 5 shows, will be very close to 50p. This is the power of diversification. A small share in a large number of independent risks is much more certain than the outcome of any of the risks taken separately.

Hedging is the purchase of assets whose returns are negatively related to the returns on assets you already own. Diversification spreads risks across many securities whose individual risks – like the outcome of the toss of a coin – are unrelated to each other. The risk and reward of a portfolio, and the relationship between them, are determined not just by expected values and the variability of return. The portfolio risk also depends on the extent to which returns from different assets are related to each other. A risk-averse individual can build a low-risk portfolio from a collection of risky assets if the risky assets are appropriately selected. It is impossible to overstate the importance of this idea for intelligent investment.

The variability of a statistical distribution can be measured by its variance or standard deviation. A similar measure – called 'covariance' or 'correlation' – looks at how the variability of two different distributions is related. Similar assets have a high covariance, hedges a negative one. In a coin-tossing game, the covariance between the outcomes of successive trials is zero because successive trials are independent. The probability that the next toss is a head is not affected by whether the last was a head or a tail.

What does it mean to say that the returns from investments are independent of each other? Suppose one company is drilling for oil in Kazakhstan, and another has entered a new drug in clinical trials. These outcomes are independent – the dry hole in Kazakhstan does not influence the drug trial in the United States. The risks that a shareholder loses because an exploration does not find oil or that a drug trial fails are called specific risks, because their outcome is determined by factors that are specific to the company itself.

However, the returns to shareholders in Shell and in Glaxo are probably correlated. There is no direct connection between oil companies and pharmaceutical companies. But both businesses depend on economic prospects in the same countries and the share prices of both companies are influenced by the same vagaries of market sentiment. These common risks, which affect all businesses, are described as 'market risk'.

The relationship between the risk on an individual share and the market risk of a portfolio that follows the market as a whole is described by the parameter *beta*. Mathematically, *beta* is computed from a regression equation that estimates the effect of market movements on the security in question. A security will have a *beta* of one if a 1% market movement will change its price by 1%.

A share may have a low *beta* for one or both of two distinct reasons. Shares will have low *betas* if their risks are unrelated to the overall risk of the market. The prices of shares whose returns are derived from oil wells in Kazakhstan, or whose fortunes depend on the results of clinical trials, will have little correlation with the share prices of BP and Glaxo.

A share will also have a low *beta* if, although its returns *are* related to overall market risk, the company's activities *are* not very volatile. Companies such as food retailers or utilities, whose sales will be affected by economic recession have low *betas*. Conversely, shares whose performance is very sensitive to the general economic cycle – producers of steel or basic chemicals – might have *betas* which are greater than one.

An index, which by definition yields the average return on the market, will have a *beta* of one. For this reason, it is common to call the average return on that asset class 'the *beta*' of an asset class. '*Alpha*' is then a measure of the extent to which a fund manager beats that average return – the outperformance after adjusting for the risk of the manager's portfolio. Lovers of the Greek alphabet will find that derivatives markets extend the lexicon to *gamma, delta*, and beyond. But *beta* is key to the capital asset pricing model. This is the most influential economic theory in modern investment. It is important to understand its structure, its effect on investment thinking and practice – and its limitations.

The Capital Asset Pricing Model

Risk-averse investors will need to earn a premium over the yield on a safe benchmark such as 4.25% Treasury 2055 or indexed 1.25% Treasury 2055 if they are to buy less secure assets. The greater the risk, the greater the premium. But what is the relevant meaning of risk?

At the beginning of this chapter I described the gulf of incomprehension that emerged when economists explained to business people their approach to risk. The latter group did not recognise any operational value to the distinction between specific and market risk that the economists believed was so important. Most people, including those business people, would describe an investment like Robb Caledon as extremely risky. They would say the same of drilling for oil in Kazakhstan, or a clinical trial for a new drug, or accepting a fixed-price contract to develop new defence technology. They would think of a big holding in HSBC or BP, by contrast, as safe but boring.

The 'mind your portfolio' principle says that this view gets matters the wrong way round. Robb Caledon and the clinical trial are not really speculative, because the risk can be spread and diversified. So long as the risk of any of these individual stocks is only a small part of your portfolio you can employ diversification to sleep soundly at night. Conversely, stakes in HSBC or BP are risky because investors cannot hedge or diversify them much – the returns from these investments are likely to be broadly in line with those of the market.

Suppose everyone thought this way. Suppose everyone was a 'rational' investor, motivated by the principles of SEU. Then the general opinion would be that shares with specific risks were not very risky, but shares with market risk were. That general opinion, like all general opinions, would be 'in the price'. The implication is that what appear to be risky securities – shares in Robb Caledon or oil exploration in Kazakhstan – would offer lower yields than boring blue chips because the speculative shares have specific risks while the blue chips suffer market risks. This idea is the basis of the CAPM that won the Nobel Prize for its inventor, Bill Sharpe (of the Sharpe ratio).

In the CAPM, risk and reward are determined by the *beta* of a security. Robb Caledon had a *beta* around zero, because the risk was entirely specific (the company may even have had a negative *beta*, because its share price might have gone up when the market went down, and vice versa). Such an investment is almost as good as a risk-free asset, and will therefore yield very little more than a risk-free asset. An asset with a *beta* of one will have the same expected return as the market as a whole, and investors will demand a higher return still for an asset with a *beta* above one. In principle, this approach can be applied to all assets, not just shares. You can calculate *betas* for different kinds of property and for other asset classes. Commercial risk measurement services offer quantitatively-minded investors estimates of *beta* for the whole range of securities they might buy.

There is another customer base for these risk measurement services. The cost of equity capital to a firm is derived from the long-run expected rate of return on its shares. The expected return on equity is the combination of the *beta* of the individual firm and the equity risk premium for the market. For adherents of the CAPM this expected return is the return required by the market and, therefore, the basis of the cost of capital estimates needed for the DCF appraisal of business investment.

Companies such as Robb Caledon, or a small oil exploration company, the pharmaceutical business or the investor in emerging markets, should have a low cost of capital because the risk of investment in them, although large, is perfectly diversifiable. Companies such as HSBC and BP, with returns likely to be more in line with the overall market, should have a higher cost of capital. This is the argument that the government economists were presenting to the defence contractors, who did not believe it.

And empirical evidence is not very favourable to the economists. The CAPM follows directly from the notion that people both should, and do, follow SEU. It predicts that the returns on different securities will be determined by two factors: the overall return on the market, and the *beta* appropriate to that security. There are problems with both parts of this claim.

SEU explains the risk premium in terms of diminishing marginal utility. Investors do not judge risky ventures at their expected value because they value the second million of their wealth less highly than the first. But this factor doesn't seem to be nearly large enough to account for the size of the historic equity premium – the difference between the yield on shares and the yield on safe assets. Models based on risk aversion from diminishing marginal utility struggle to explain why the risks of equity investment would, in an SEU framework, justify a risk premium as high as 1%.

The data in Chapter 2 suggested that over the last twenty years the difference in return between safe assets and shares had been around 5%. The longer-term analyses of Dimson *et al* (2002) support figures of this magnitude with analysis from many markets over periods as long as a century. The inexplicably large difference between the predictions of SEU-based models and the observed equity premium is called the 'equity premium paradox'.

The second component of the CAPM is the use of *beta* to explain relative returns on different assets. The most exhaustive empirical study of the issue, by Gene Fama and Kenneth French (1992), concluded that estimates of *beta* contributed nothing to an explanation of the historic pattern of returns. These results have been disputed, but have not really been shaken.

Perhaps my business people, shaking their heads around the table, gave the answer. The CAPM describes what the world would be like if everyone behaved according to the principles of SEU. But its counter-intuitive predictions suggest a world in which people don't behave that way. If the cost of capital were significantly lower for firms such as defence contractors, speculative oil drillers, or small drugs companies, than for businesses with mainstream activities that followed closely the business cycle of major economies, then you might expect that people who had developed successful corporate careers would have noticed. I am sure those at that table were not dissimulating when they said that they had not. And nor had their bankers.

As SEU took hold in the 1950s, a French economist, Maurice Allais, developed a critique. Allais gave examples of common decisions that seemed to violate the principles of SEU (the Allais paradoxes). He wrote in French (no major economics journal would accept such an article today), and hinted that the whole exercise was an American plot. Although the power of his analysis created continuing nagging doubt, he failed to shake the consensus. Two decades later, two psychologists, Danny Kahnemann and Amos Tversky, would undertake experiments in which they offered their subjects choices among risks – they found frequent examples of behaviour inconsistent with SEU.

All these men would eventually receive the Nobel Prize for founding the subject now known as behavioural finance or behavioural economics. The motivation for behavioural finance is recognition that many people don't behave as SEU would seem to require.

Many real-life investors don't think probabilities, don't mind their portfolio and, above all, don't remain detached. They engage with the process, instead of focusing cold-bloodedly on the outcome. They look at their BlackBerrys several times a day, fixated by screens and clients. They feel upset when shares they own go down (even if you are Warren Buffett your shares will fall in value on almost half of all the days you own them). Some people need a premium to contemplate the risk of loss at all, even before they take specific account of what those losses might be.

SEU and CAPM suggest you need a premium much less than 5% to compensate you for equity risks. The evidence suggests you will nevertheless earn that 5%, because other investors, who don't think the SEU way, are wary of such investments. The CAPM says you have to pay a price for diversifying your portfolio. The empirical evidence says you probably don't.

SEU and CAPM are theories that are illuminating but, as explanations of actual behaviour in financial markets, are not true. They are illuminating, in part, because the investment strategies they suggest are more profitable if others don't adopt them. The equity premium paradox works in your favour, if you think SEU and others don't. As with EMH, the intelligent investor can gain by understanding these theories, but will lose by believing them. That is why this chapter is the longest and most complicated, but also the most potentially rewarding, in this book.

CHAPTER 8

A WORLD OF UNKNOWNS

Unknown unknowns

There were no derivatives markets in the savannahs, where our ancestors developed modern brains. Casinos (in which the highest value counters were the blue chips) came into being only at a late stage of evolution although an early stage of history. Hunters gambled in the evenings around the camp-fire and used animal bones as primitive dice. Human lives were always full of uncertainties, but pure risks – the well-defined problems found in games of chance that can be described using a frequentist approach to probabilities – were invented for popular amusement.

The fate of Robb Caledon was a risk – a known unknown. Either Robb Caledon would be nationalised, or not. Either its shares would be worth 100p, or not. Some issues in financial markets are of this kind. Interest rate risk and credit risk seem to be known unknowns. But there are also many uncertainties, unknown unknowns – events that cannot be sensibly described with probabilities, because we do not know what these events might be.

SEU works well for 'known unknowns'. If all potential states of the world are known (even if the one that will materialise is not); if the outcome of a gamble will be clearly and definitely recorded; if the processes that determine that outcome can be treated as random; then SEU is a sure guide to action. The gamble on Robb Caledon had all these characteristics. There seemed only two possible outcomes; the timescale was short and defined; the consequences of each appeared clear. But this case was exceptional. I have difficulty in thinking of another in my investment lifetime in which the issues were posed so sharply.

The Bayesian view is that any uncertainty can be described with the aid of personal probabilities. Keynes was sceptical. Between completion of his work on probability and its publication, the great economist had become famous for his polemical denunciation of the Versailles Treaty that ended the First World War. In a celebrated passage, he described the confidence of the pre-war mood. The English upper middle class viewed its comfortable, stable environment as a permanent condition. Consols reached an all-time high in 1897, as Queen Victoria celebrated her diamond jubilee and the British Empire extended round the world. Even in July 1914, with the end of dreams only weeks away, the bond market held steady.

If the world of the English middle class was transformed by the war that followed, the world of the central European middle class was shattered. Wealthy families whose lifestyle had seemed secure, lost everything in the default of Russian bonds, as a result of hyper-inflation in Germany and central Europe, and the expropriation of Jewish property.

The future has not become any more certain. The collapse of the Twin Towers was a major event for financial markets, as for international politics. No one , on 10 September, could sensibly have framed or answered the question 'What is the probability that the World Trade Center will be destroyed tomorrow by a terrorist attack?'

Keynes claimed that there could be no scientific basis for an assessment of probabilities in the face of uncertainty. The right response to the question 'What will interest rates be in twenty years' time?' was and is 'We simply do not know'. A question about the level of interest rates is one that might be answered probabilistically. But his uncertainty about interest rates twenty years after that statement appeared was prescient. A holder of British government bonds in 1941 could not have been certain whether he would be repaid in sterling, in reichsmarks, or at all.

Investors are vulnerable to defined, identifiable risks – interest rate risk, momentum and mean reversion in share prices. But investors are also vulnerable to fundamental uncertainty. Questions like 'What will be the outcome of the Iraq war?' 'What will be the economic consequences of China's rise?' or 'How will economic and political systems deal with climate change?' are open-ended. We cannot fully describe the range of outcomes, and decades from now there will still be disagreement over what the outcomes proved to be.

We may attempt to transform these open-ended questions into more narrowly defined ones like 'How many US troops will be in Iraq in 2010?' or 'What will be China's GDP, or the average world temperature, in 2025?' Even if it were possible to make such predictions – and it is not – the numbers would not tell people what they really want to know. Imagine a time traveller from the nineteenth century asking us what the world we live in is like. They would not understand enough about that world to be able to frame sensible questions. We suffer, not just from ignorance of the future, but from a limited capacity to imagine what the future might be. People who are today concerned about the Iraq war, China's rise, or climate change, would not have been worrying about these issues twenty years ago. They would have been worrying about the Cold War, Japan's economic pre-eminence, and the effects of AIDS.

These earlier uncertainties have largely been resolved, and in ways that few people expected. But the key point is not that we mostly fail to anticipate the answers, rather that we mostly fail to anticipate the relevant questions. No one predicted the catastrophes of the twentieth century – the stalemate of the First World War, the influenza pandemic, the murder of millions of people by deranged dictators. The same was true of transforming political and economic developments – the rise and fall of Communism in Russia, decolonisation, the development of information technology, the changed role of women in society.

Such failure of imagination is inevitable If you could anticipate the functions and uses of the personal computer, you would already have taken the main steps towards inventing it. To describe a future political movement or economic theory or line of philosophical thought is to bring it into existence.

Many great geopolitical events are unknown unknowns – the

First World War, the rise of Hitler, the attack on the Twin Towers. But unknown unknowns are also part of everyday life. Your journey home from work lends itself to description in frequentist terms. You have a rough mental probability distribution of outcomes in your mind, reflecting the schedule and reliability of trains, the variability of traffic conditions. But the outcome is also determined by events. You meet a long-lost acquaintance, you see an item in a shop window that attracts your attention, you slip on the pavement. You did not anticipate such events because you had not thought about them, and could not sensibly have attached a probability to them if you had.

More of these events will disrupt your journey than accelerate it, which is why your estimate of journey length will be below its expected value. Most people think of risk as an adverse event rather than a distribution about a mean (this was another source of the gap of comprehension at my meeting between the business people and the economists). For good reasons, our thinking about an uncertain world is partly probabilistic, partly not.

In this light, consider again the risk appraisal tools described in Chapter 7, which looked at the outcomes associated with various percentiles of the frequency distribution of outcomes. Your routine experience of how long it takes you to get home from work is likely to be described well by a standard statistical distribution. But your less routine experience is not – the occasional emergencies, the accidents, the days on which events at work make it impossible to go home at all. These events are rare, but the extremes of the frequency distribution of outcomes are the product of these out-of-the-ordinary events.

The same is true even in the banal, simple coin-tossing game. If you do in fact engage in repeated trials of a coin-tossing game, the extreme of your adverse experience – the first percentile – will probably not be the freak case in which only 38 of 100 tosses of a fair coin prove to be heads. It is much more likely that the worst outcomes will arise because the coin is not fair, the banker does not pay the amount he owes, or the game is disrupted before its completion. The limits of probabilistic reasoning are set by the limitations of the models on which they are based, and any model is an abstraction from a more complex context. The actual distribution of outcomes is the product of a combination of the risks that the model describes and the uncertainties associated with the applicability of the model. That is the fundamental reason why a model can often be illuminating but will almost never be true. We use different tools in the face of uncertainty. If I ask people what they think is going to happen, they will usually respond with a story rather than a probability distribution.

Narratives and patterns

Thinking probabilities does not come easily to the human mind. Telling stories and constructing narratives do. The stockbrokers I called in 1976 could not separate the question of whether shipbuilding *ought* to be nationalised from the question of whether shipbuilding *would* be nationalised. They told a story about what they thought *would* happen, heavily influenced by what they thought *should* happen. They pontificated about the market and complained about the government, as old-fashioned stockbrokers were prone to do.

We weave stories and fit events and expectations into them. There is evidence of halo effects – if we like something or someone, we interpret everything we know about them favourably; and for confirmation bias – people interpret new evidence in a manner consistent with the view they have already formed. The internet enthusiast at Davos who anticipated Wal-Mart's defeat at the hands of Webvan was a victim of halo effect and confirmation bias. So were the people at the Pentagon who thought that it was unnecessary to plan for post-war Iraq because troops would be greeted with garlands of flowers. Hopes and dreams had been confused with expectations.

Narratives and probabilistic thinking fit uncomfortably together because thinking probabilistically means thinking, at the same time, of two incompatible events – that Robb Caledon will go bankrupt, that Robb Caledon will be nationalised. It might have made sense to have bought Robb Caledon shares even if you had thought the bill was likely to fail. The issue for the probabilistic thinker was whether the expected value was above the market price. It may be appropriate to hold indexed bonds even if you do not think that inflation will rise, if you believe – and you should – there is a possibility that inflation might rise.

Many people find it hard to reason in these ways. If you ask the tail-gating driver what he thinks will happen, his answer will be that he will get home quickly and without incident; on the vast majority of occasions he will be right. The cautious driver, however, has in his or her mind an image of smashed cars at the side of the autoroute, hears the siren of an ambulance. Both think in terms of stories, neither in probabilities.

The most systematic way of trying to handle incompatible futures is scenario planning, a technique pioneered by Shell and widely used in business. Scenario planning demands multiple narratives. Work out two, three or four, internally consistent projections of the future, and plan for what you might do in each. My experience is that if you try to talk about the future in scenarios you will always be approached by someone who asks 'So what do you really think is going to happen?'

Our ability to tell stories is a valuable asset, the means by which we make sense of disconnected information. But in financial markets this skill often misleads. Bachelier and Samuelson discovered that, in securities markets, purposive and directed behaviour can produce outcomes with the appearance, and mathematical properties, of randomness. But we resist randomness. The search for patterns in randomly generated data warms the heart, as it hurts the wallet. Our abilities in pattern detection often lead us to observe systematic relationships that do not exist, or to confuse underlying causes with statistical noise. Such confusions help chartists stay in business.

Popular discussion, based on a poor understanding of probability, tells of a 'law of averages' – if there has been a run of heads, the next toss must be a tail. But the probability of head or tail remains at 50%. There is no law of averages, but there are many random walks. Chaos and randomness are rare in nature, but common in financial markets.

Hopeful investors and tipsters trail through historic series to find systems that would, in the past, have yielded substantial profits. There will always be some but that doesn't mean these systems will be profitable in any, far less all, future periods. Many 'anomalies' in efficient markets disappear when they have been identified. This would be true even if it were not also true that the very process of trading on the anomaly reduces or removes its profitability.

The 'hot hand' – an outstanding series of scores – is a well-known phenomenon. Careful statistical analysis of sporting records suggests that there is not much evidence for 'the hot hand'. Sequences of extraordinary performance are no more frequent than would be expected from chance alone. But long sequences of brilliant scores (or mistakes) stick in the mind.

Are there investment managers with the 'hot hand'? Even if investment returns were the result of pure chance, some managers would seem to have a record of success. But if returns are the result of chance, you cannot expect that these managers will perform any better in future than anyone else. And mostly they don't.

The persistence of performance of OEICS (mutual funds, unit trusts) has been the subject of extensive analysis – work done by the FSA contains both a survey of the evidence and some original research (FSA (1999), Rhodes (2001)). Table 7 is a representative illustration of the results. (Notice that each quintile contains 20% of all funds and that the average quintile is three.)

Table 7: OEIC performance, two years later

	Percentage in first quintile	Percentage in fifth quintile	Average quintile rank
	Performance in 1983 –4		
Funds in first quintile in 1981-2	30	35	3.0
Funds in fifth quintile in 1981-2	5	35	3.7
	Performance in 1993 –4		
Funds in first quintile in 1991-2	20	29	3.0
Funds in fifth quintile in 1991-2	39	8	2.6
	Performance in 1997 – 8		
Funds in first quintile in 1995-6	16	32	3.6
Funds in fifth quintile in 1995-6	16	28	3.2

Source: Rhodes, 2001

In these results, these first quintile performers, on average, do no better than average two years later; in the most recent period, they do slightly worse. Fifth quintile performers also do slightly worse than average two years later (although in the early 1990s they did better). One clear-cut result is that both good performers and bad performers are more than averagely likely to be either good or bad, rather than average, in subsequent periods. The probable reason is that both good and bad performers are often specialist, or idiosyncratic, funds, whose performance is not necessarily better but is likely to be different. Average performers, however, tend to remain average; and the results are consistent with the view that most differences in final outcomes are explained by chance rather than skill. The accumulation of evidence of this kind has led the FSA to require fund management groups to state that past performance is no guide to future performance. The intelligent investor should take heed.

There are a very few fund managers, like Buffett, whose record of outperformance is so persistent, and continues long after it has been widely identified, that the evidence of competence over chance seems irrefutable. The nearest equivalent in Britain to Buffett is Anthony Bolton, who managed the Fidelity Special Situations fund from 1979 until his retirement in 2007

The hot hand is frequently – and mistakenly – detected when what we see is the result of an asymmetric distribution that produces frequent small gains punctuated by occasional very large losses – an activity sometimes described as picking dimes in front of a steamroller. I call these Taleb distributions after a book in which Nicholas Nasim Taleb offers many illustrations (Taleb, 2001). Tail-gating drivers save a few seconds on most trips. Occasionally, you see their smashed cars on the side of the road. Participants dissociate the infrequent failures from the frequent successes. The early arrival is the result of skilful driving, the crash is caused by bad luck. The drivers' judgment is vindicated by their success so far.

The 'carry trade' is a Taleb process in financial markets. Interest rates vary across classes of borrower and across currencies. Riskier borrowers pay higher interest rates. If markets price credit risk correctly, then the premium from the higher interest rate will equal the expected value of the losses from default. For example, if a certain type of borrower will fail to repay with a frequency of 2% per year, then a bank with a portfolio of such loans will break even if it realises interest rates 2% higher than prime.

But the distribution of gains and losses is not symmetric. Most borrowers meet the principal and interest as they fall due, and the lender collects, year in, year out, the 2% premium. But when the loan fails, the loss is usually the full amount outstanding. As with the tail-gating driver, lenders win most of the time on risky loans, but when they lose, they lose big time. And when the credit bubble burst, they did.

Still, like the tail-gating driver, people who collect these regular profits congratulate themselves on their prowess, win the admiration of their bosses, and justify both their own bonuses and those of their superiors. Beneficiaries of Taleb distributions leave their more cautious competitors behind, so a process of rivalry forces others to follow, and to suppress any private doubts. From time to time, accidents happen. The losses are large, described as unpredictable, unanticipated, exceptional. One-time heroes are fired. The process begins again. The same financial follies are repeated.

You may wonder why many positions in large corporations are filled by people of apparently modest talent; find it inexplicable that dealers with so little knowledge or skill are applauded for their trading success; be surprised at the stupidity of drivers who take large risks for seemingly inconsequential gains. The answer to all of these paradoxes is the same: the people you see are on the upside of their Taleb distribution (and may remain there until they retire).

All political careers end in failure, goes an old saying, because politicians tend to continue until their luck runs out. The same phenomenon is common in the financial world. In any activity in which there is a random element in performance, the outperformers of one period, on average, will show subsequent deterioration and the underperformers will, on average, improve. Road accidents fall when speed cameras are installed, because speed cameras are installed where there have recently been accidents. The statistical result would be observed even if the camera had no effect on the behaviour of drivers. The data seem to show a pattern that may not be there. This is the regression fallacy.

And so it is with fund managers. Unsuccessful investment funds are much more likely to close, or be merged into other funds, than successful funds. The reported average performance of investment funds generally exaggerates the average performance of all investment funds because underperforming investment funds disappear – they are wound up or merged into more successful funds. This is particularly true of hedge funds. The same is true of management gurus and investment pundits.

Perhaps survivor bias is part of the resolution of the equity premium paradox. I'm writing this book about investing in shares in Britain and the United States, not about how to invest in Chinese bonds or South American utilities, both of which were popular choices a century ago. The markets we look at are the markets that have performed well. There were no books written in the 1920s on investment in Russia, but if there had been they would have had to acknowledge that recent performance did not justify an investment.

Sceptics and heretics sometimes observed that paintings of the devout who had survived tempests and floods after praying for salvation were not persuasive, because there were no paintings of the devout who had drowned after praying for salvation. Many heroes of the financial world are immortalised for similar reasons, and the many books about their successful investment strategies resemble those paintings of the devout.

As with managers, so with asset categories. Markets show short-term positive serial price correlation, but long-term negative serial price correlation. So don't be tempted by advertisements displaying how much money has been made recently in housing or commodities – that is more likely to be a signal to sell than a signal to buy. Assets that have recently done badly deserve attention – but not indiscriminate attention. The objective is always to exploit negative market sentiment to buy cheaply. Detect regression towards the mean; correct for survivor bias; beware data mining.

Models and their limits

Models are an indispensable part of modern finance, and all banks and fund managers use them. The professionalism and sophistication of models and modellers have increased steadily. Anyone equipped with school mathematics can do a discounted cash flow (DCF) calculation. The Markowitz model of portfolio selection, the basis of the CAPM, needs more complex mathematics. But even if Milton Friedman worried that Markowitz' work was outside the scope of the economics of the time, the techniques are quite simple (and today well within that scope). The Black Scholes model of option pricing, introduced in the 1970s, is both dynamic and stochastic (it involves differential equations and probability distributions).

These models are not rocket science (though they are often called such) but do require university-level training in maths or a maths-based subject. Today, an understanding of the frontiers of finance theory demands an advanced degree in maths or physics. Because the financial services sector is very profitable, financial institutions offer large salaries to able mathematicians, but the executives to whom they ultimately report have little understanding of what these employees do.

You don't have to understand what is under the bonnet of a car to drive it, and similarly you can be a competent manager of a pharmaceutical company or an electronics business without deep familiarity with the underlying chemical or physical characteristics of the product. But you cannot drive a car if you don't understand what a car does, and you cannot organise the marketing, manufacture or distribution of a product if you don't understand what the product can do – and what it can't.

Senior people in the financial sector – bank executives or fund managers – are not themselves able to build the models on which these activities depend. That is not the problem. The problem is that the techniques are so far outside their comprehension that they do not understand the limitations of the models. While professing scepticism, they take too seriously the conclusions that models generate. I'll call their attitude cynical naiveté. Executives seek 99% certainties from their risk management systems without appreciating that in an uncertain world there are never 99% certainties. 99% probabilities are derived from models whose applicability is never 100% certain (and rarely measurable). The first percentile in the distribution of outcomes is typically generated by events that were not incorporated into the structure of the model.

The attempt in Chapter 6 to apply DCF calculations to asset valuation illustrated a recurrent problem for all models in business and finance. Not only did we not know the numbers that the model required, but the outcome was very sensitive to the assumptions made in entering these numbers. This leads all too often to bogus quantification. People make up numbers they cannot know to derive supposedly scientific answers to questions whose answers are fundamentally unknowable.

If you have a well-trained financial adviser – one with a financial planning qualification or, better still, a CFA certification – then he or she will very likely build a model of your portfolio in the Markowitz tradition, emphasising the variance and covariances of different assets. That is what financial advisers are taught to do. Risk assessment models in large financial institutions have a similar structure. In line with the principles of SEU and CAPM these models have three critical inputs:

- what is the expected return on each asset you hold?
- what will be the volatility of that expected return?
- what will be the correlation between the volatility of the return on a particular asset and the volatility of your portfolio as a whole?

But neither you nor your adviser knows, or can know, the answer to these questions.

The difficulties fall into two main groups:

- the assumptions made about the statistical distributions that link the data to the model; and
- the reliance on history for that data.

I'll take each of these issues in turn.

A common assumption is that short-term movements in securities prices can be described through a normal distribution. If we look at day-to-day movements in share prices, it appears that the normal distribution fits them quite well. But there is a problem of 'fat tails' – there are many more extreme events than these statistical distributions would permit. If share price movements fitted the normal distribution, it is improbable that a market fall such as that of the US market on 19 October 1987 – a twenty *sigma* event – would occur even once in the entire history of the universe. But when several such 'once in a blue moon' incidents happen in the course of a few years – as in the last decade – it is time to rethink one's model.

Fat tails are a particularly troubling problem for people who are modelling risk in financial markets, because they suggest that these models fail in precisely the extreme situations in which they are most needed. Although the commonest reaction to the problem of fat tails is to note the problem and ignore it, there are two main groups of attempt to deal with the issue. One approach involves ad hoc modification to make the results of classical statistical distributions correspond better to reality. Examples are generalised auto-regressive conditional heteroscedasticity (don't ask) and a technique more attractively labelled 'robust statistics'. These approaches continue to assume that there is some correct description of the world enabling the properties of its prospective behaviour to be deduced from historic information – that we can find models that are not just illuminating but true, that we deal with risks not uncertainties.

The alternative, perhaps more interesting, critique developed by the mathematician Benoit Mandelbrot, rejects the assumptions of classical statistics altogether. Mandelbrot looked at charts of security prices and saw, not a random walk, but a beautiful process known as 'fractals'. You encounter fractal geometry when you look at a snowflake through a microscope and discover that, whatever magnification you set, the picture you see is the same.

Distributions that follow fractal processes show altogether different properties from those of classical statistics, with fatter tails, and average outcomes in which extreme events play a much larger role. The physical analogies are not the diffuse movements of solids in solution described by Brownian motion, but earthquakes and avalanches – constant small slips, often imperceptible, punctuated by large shifts. Those analogies correspond to many people's experience of financial markets.

Whether you use the distributions of classical statistics, or the different mathematical structures of Mandelbrot's approach, the information you must use to build a model comes from data on what these returns have been, and how they varied, in the past. For good reasons – this historic record is the only objective information available. Such figures may not be a good guide to the future. Investment allocation models based on recent experience will probably suggest a high proportion in equities. You may also be encouraged to invest more in alternative assets. That is because the returns from equities have in the immediate past been more than sufficient to compensate for their volatility. Alternative assets have also yielded high returns that were not strongly correlated, on a year-by-year basis, with other investment classes. But the model tells you these things only because someone has already told these things to the model.

No model can tell you what expected future returns on different asset classes, or the future correlation between these returns, will be. Robb Caledon was a hedge, whose price would move in the opposite direction to the main UK indices. But you would not have learned that by studying past covariances. Indeed, you would have found the opposite. Stocks subject to political risk tended to have high *betas*, moving with the general market by often violent amounts.

Only the peculiar circumstances of 1976, in which the government proposed to nationalise the company for more than it was worth, gave that share its particular risk profile. If broad economic conditions had improved, lifting the price of most stocks, there would probably have been little impact, in either direction, on the share price of the ship-yard. Neither in the past or present was there any stable correlation, positive or negative, between Robb Caledon and the general market.

Such observations illustrate why historic measures of *beta* have little value. Students of statistics are introduced to the alleged correlation between the stork population and the birth rate. The example illustrates that correlation does not imply causation – births are a function of population and dense populations attract storks. But almost all correlations between security prices have the property that gives rise to the stork fallacy. The correlation is the result of some common underlying factor that influences both variables rather than a direct causal relationship between them.

Since correlation and causation are not the same, only understanding of the underlying causal mechanism can make it possible to know whether a correlation will, or will not, persist in any particular time period. The correlation of stork population and birth rate would continue to hold if new families moved into the neighbourhood, but would not hold if illness or a predator struck the storks. One relationship between Robb Caledon's share price and general market movements held under a Conservative government, and a different one held under a Labour government. Only information outside statistical analysis can tell us that.

The antidote to errors of data interpretation is general knowledge, what many people call common sense: the disparate facts about the world that we apprehend but do not articulate systematically, and which inform every decision we make. Keynes was a successful investor, as well as a man who achieved success in many other fields, in part because he brought to all his activities a range of experience and knowledge of both ideas and affairs probably unparalleled in the twentieth century.

The requirement for general knowledge drawn from outside the model if the model is to be successfully applied, does not make the model useless. A model that makes assumptions about correlations between variables – even arbitrary ones – can illustrate ways in which careful diversification can improve the relationship between risk and return. But the quantitative precision claimed for the results of these exercises is generally spurious. I am a better investor for having learnt, and built, models of portfolio selection. I am a better investor partly because these models are illuminating. I understand the relationship between risk and return better as a result. But I am also a better investor because I understand the mistakes made by people who think these models are true.

Forecasts and their limits

If financial experts have limited ability to analyse the past, what of their ability to foresee the future? The commentators you hear on CNBC and other financial programmes make projections of general trends – the rise and fall of companies, industries and countries – and forecasts of specific economic variables – inflation, economic growth rate, exchange rates.

The record of the market pundits in anticipating events is poor. But this does not diminish the demand for their services. The power of conventional thinking strikes again. What is valued is not genuine knowledge of the future – to the very limited extent that such knowledge exists – but insight into the mind of the market. Keynes's analogy of the beauty contest is again relevant. The objective is not to predict what will happen, but to predict what others will themselves shortly predict.

The world in the 1990s experienced an unprecedented era of political and economic stability under American hegemony, following the end of the Cold War. The unthinking but contagious optimism of the era fuelled the conventional thinking of the New Economy bubble. Books and blogs proclaimed that the Dow Jones index would go to 36,000, or even 100,000, on the back of ever-soaring earnings and the disappearance of the risk premium. The beliefs were strikingly similar to those Keynes described for Britain exactly 100 years earlier.

Since we are ill-equipped to handle inevitable uncertainty, the future is seen through the terms of the near present. The opening of Russia and Eastern Europe, China and India to the market economy is genuinely momentous. But the main beneficiaries of this opening will be the populations of the countries concerned. While it is certain that much money will be made in China, that does not necessarily imply that there is much money to be made there by you and me. And the rise of China and India has not exactly passed unnoticed. The China effect is 'in the price'.

People who pronounce on geopolitical developments are mostly talking not about tomorrow, but today. They tend to project current trends to exaggerated extent and with exaggerated speed. As a result, they overestimate change in the short term while underestimating change in the long-term. They treat current events as more momentous than they really are – hence 'It's different this time' or the portentous talk of 'new paradigms'. Simultaneously, such commentators fail to anticipate the transformational effect of events that have not yet happened and of which they can know nothing – the unknown unknowns that shape our lives. The safe course is to talk about current preoccupations, and that is what successful pundits mostly do. We can all then agree in being astonished by the pace of change.

Economic forecasts of recession or recovery, of interest rates and exchange rates, are part of every investment conversation. Every fund manager delivers an assessment of general economic prospects to clients. The EMH should make you suspicious when people who profess special insight into the future reveal that insight to large audiences – the value of such information would surely depend on it not being widely available. Professional forecasters have little, or nothing, to add to public information – information that is printed every day in the newspapers, that can be ascertained every hour of the day on the internet, and that is available for free.

Such economists are valued, and rewarded by their employers, for their television manner rather than the accuracy of their predictions. It is a common perception that economists always disagree – two economists, three opinions. The facts are quite otherwise, at least as far as economic forecasters are concerned. There is typically far less divergence between forecasts than between forecasts and outcomes. For economic forecasters, as for other financial pundits, it is better to be conventionally wrong than unconventionally right. To see correctly what others have failed to see, or chosen to ignore, damages careers more often than it enhances them. Such prescience undermines the claim – so important to those who disclaim responsibility for what went wrong on their watch – that what happened could not have been foreseen. Ask the people who tried to warn their superiors before 9/11 (or the credit crunch). The weaknesses of forecasting are compounded by the difficulty of specifying how exactly changes in GDP, or interest rate changes, will translate into market prices.

Politicians, people in business and finance, and the public at large, display cynical naiveté in their attitudes to economic forecasts, as in their attitudes to models – the same mixture of scepticism and credulousness. They express disdain for economic forecasts as they lap them up. Most professional economists regard this forecasting activity as embarrassing and ridiculous, but it continues because the demand is insatiable. Because so many people want answers to questions that cannot be answered, they refuse to accept the limits of knowledge in the face of uncertainty. They justifiably deride those who profess knowledge of the future they do not have. 'Economic forecasters are always wrong'. Less justifiably, they also deride those who disclaim such knowledge, and emphasise that the future can only be described through many divergent, yet plausible, scenarios – 'Give me a one-handed economist'.

The economic environment is like the weather. We cannot forecast it accurately, but we know quite a lot about its broad properties – it won't snow in England in July, and it might rain on any day of the year. General knowledge of this latter kind is already 'in the price' and people who claim more specific knowledge of the future are mostly charlatans.

The common mistake is to believe that the uncertainty described by Keynes and Knight can, through diligent research or analytic sophistication, be transformed into the well-defined, quantifiable risk that responds to the techniques developed by the successors of Ramsey and Savage. Keynes correctly observed that the only justified answer to many questions about the future is 'We simply do not know', but no one is rewarded for saying that. Many people in the financial services sector profess knowledge of the future they do not have, and cannot have.In contrast, legendary investors, like Buffett and Soros, stand out for their readiness to acknowledge the limitations of their – and all – knowledge.

Here is Soros:

'My financial success stands in stark contrast with my ability to forecast events …. With regard to events in the real world, my record is downright dismal. The outstanding feature of my predictions is that I keep on expecting developments that do not materialise.'
Soros, 2003

And here Buffett:

'In many industries, of course, Charlie and I can't determine whether we
are dealing with a "pet rock" or a "Barbie". We wouldn't solve this problem,
moreover, even if we were to spend years intensely studying these industries
….. Did we foresee thirty years ago what would transpire in the television
manufacturing or computer industries? Of course not. (Nor did most of
the investors and corporate managers who enthusiastically entered these
industries.)'
Buffett, (in Cunningham, p.85, 2002)

Recall Keynes' 'There is no scientific basis on which to form any
calculable probability whatever. We simply do not know.' The intelligent investor knows that he or she does not know and (like Buffett,
Keynes and Soros) can enjoy the luxury of acknowledging that ignorance. Professional investment experts mostly cannot acknowledge
such ignorance – they are hired to provide answers to unanswerable
questions. Never mind, they are well paid for it. But not, if you are an
intelligent investor, by you.

Approaches to risk
In this and the previous chapters, I've described both the dominant
SEU theory and the more eclectic and pragmatic approaches to risk and
uncertainty favoured by Keynes and Knight. It is time to pull together
the strands and spell out their implications for intelligent investors.

In SEU theory, the term 'subjective' has a double significance. The
probabilities are subjective, and so are the valuations of outcomes.
Probabilities and values differ between people but, once established
for any individual, are held consistently. If the risks are the same, you
use the same probabilities whatever the payoffs; if the payoffs are the
same, you attach the same valuations, whatever the probabilities.

There is a powerful underlying logic to this approach. The reasons
the SEU school is today dominant in risk analysis in financial markets
can be traced, directly and indirectly, to a clever argument constructed
by Ramsey. If you don't adopt the SEU approach, people can devise
schemes that will make money at your expense. The process is called a
'Dutch book' (offended residents of the Netherlands have attempted,
without success, to track down the origins of the phrase). In a Dutch

book, you make a series of choices, each of which you believe is to your advantage, whose net effect leaves you worse off. The only sure means of preventing inconsistency in your choices is to follow the precepts of subjective expected utility. The Allais paradoxes described compellingly attractive Dutch books.

While SEU may appear a good way of thinking about risk, it is certainly not the only way of thinking about risk. Ramsey's argument was never as decisive as it appeared. In the uncertain, constantly changing world that Keynes and Knight correctly perceived, it is impossible to be sure if behaviour is consistent or simply stubborn. You are steadfast. I am pragmatic. There is no objective basis for the claim that two similar situations are indeed identical.

The findings of behavioural economists are often interpreted as evidence of irrational behaviour. This interpretation is simplistic. The demonstration of supposedly irrational behaviour in the principal Allais paradox rests on the human tendency to value certainties much more highly than extremely probable events. There are good reasons for this trait. There is no such thing in everyday life as an event with a calculable 99% probability. The first percentile of a distribution is generally encountered as a result of uncertainties outside the model.

A common feature of these behavioural experiments is that the subject applies a rule which makes sense in everyday life, that is full of uncertainty, in an abstract experimental situation in which problems can be reduced to risks that are precisely defined and described. There are choices in which rigorous application of the principles of SEU seems to make sense – Robb Caledon – but mostly calculations have to be tempered with the more qualitative judgment that enables us to handle uncertainty. It is not easy to draw a clear line between situations for which SEU is relevant, and situations for which it is not. There is tension between people who are wired to 'think SEU' and those who are not.

These conflicts are as old as history. Throwing dice is one of the oldest forms of gambling – bones shaped like cubes were used for this purpose thousands of years ago. Games of dice and other forms of gambling were invented precisely because they create conditions in which a probability-based SEU approach is valuable. The modern casino similarly allows people who 'think SEU' – the operators – to make money at the expense of people who do not think SEU. The casino, like the insurance company, is concerned with expected values. The motivations of the customers of both groups of institution are more complex.

The ability to 'think probabilities', to apply the premises of SEU, is one that will save you from costly mistakes at the casino. But in an uncertain world in which risks cannot be clearly identified, we don't approach all questions probabilistically because the probabilistic approach often isn't useful. If people turn out not to have consistent personal probabilities, it may be that the reason is that a scheme of personal probabilities is incapable of fully describing the way they think about the First World War, the Twin Towers, or even their daily journey home from work.

Detachment means that you focus single-mindedly on the outcome of a risky activity, and ignore those aspects of the process that you cannot control. This is also difficult. There is evidence that we worry more about risks we cannot control than about those we can. This may be why so many people are nervous about flying, but far fewer are nervous about driving, even though it is more dangerous.

Sometimes involvement gives pleasure, as when we cheer the horses we have backed at the races. Some people experience a rush of adrenalin as lights flash on the fruit machine or as the roulette wheel spins. Sometimes involvement in events we cannot influence causes anxiety, as when I turned on the news to hear the progress of the shipbuilding nationalisation bill through Parliament.

Whether pleasurable or painful, the experience of engagement is costly. The thrill of the race and the excitement of the casino are paid for by the majority of punters who lose. Sleepless nights worrying about which way Members of Parliament will vote bring no benefit – this attention is not going to affect the outcome. But the prospect of those sleepless nights dissuades most people from undertaking investments, like buying shares in Robb Caledon, even if the odds are attractive. If you are detached you will pay no special attention to the prices of shares you have sold, or decided not to buy. But you will!

In a world of unknowns, engagement is part of the process of managing uncertainty. To be detached about mountain climbing or buying a lottery ticket is to miss the point of these activities. Regret for our mistakes is part of the process by which we learn from them. Compartmentalising our decisions and the information relevant to them – a process known as mental accounting – is the only way we can cope with a complex world.

But training yourself to think in line with the principles of SEU will give you a technique that will serve you well in investment decisions. We don't naturally or easily think probabilistically, achieve detachment, or always make decisions in the light of the totality of our circumstances. But if you want to make money in financial markets, there are substantial rewards to training yourself to think in that way. That is why this chapter and the preceding one, which are the most difficult in the book, may also be the most profitable.

If you don't practise SEU, you will be Dutch booked – sold products that will be financially rewarding for the promoter, but not for you. For years, I taught that people would behave in line with SEU precepts since others would make money at their expense if they didn't. The logic was correct but the conclusion was wrong. People often don't behave in line with SEU precepts, and others do make money at their expense, and that is a large part of what financial markets are about. Conversely, if you can learn to 'think SEU', then you will often make money at the expense of people who don't.

It isn't always a mistake to be Dutch booked. The enjoyment of the daydream some people feel as the national lottery draw approaches, the excitement of watching the roulette wheel spin, the worry that is removed by buying an insurance policy – these feelings are real. But they are also expensive, and the other side of the Dutch book is the profits of the lottery and of insurance companies. If you can successfully suppress emotions of excitement and regret, you will be financially better off. You may prefer to enjoy these experiences, and I'm certainly not going to label you irrational in consequence. But this is a book about how to be a successful financial adviser to yourself. And one of the best pieces of financial advice you can give yourself is to familiarise yourself with the principles of SEU.

But people who think SEU are not necessarily more successful in life than people who do not think SEU, only more successful in not losing money at the casino. In casinos, the house wins and the punters lose. But perhaps the punters have the money to stake, and the attractive women on their arms, because they are over-confident. They tend to view life in terms of lively stories and vivid narratives rather than the abstract world of Bayes' theorem inhabited by nerdy economists. Who would you rather date?

So the evolutionary argument, popular with these economists, that SEU will drive out other methods of thinking is wrong. Around the camp-fires of those savannahs, *bon viveurs* and entertainers brought together groups that contained many different personality types – the enthusiastic, energetic hunters who killed the game and the more analytic tribesmen who focused on dividing it out. All these groups cooperated and prospered, as they do in modern financial markets. The world accommodates different approaches to risk and uncertainty, and so must you.

CHAPTER 9

MODERN DEVELOPMENTS IN FINANCIAL MARKETS

Derivatives

In September 2000, Jim Chanos read the notes to the accounts of Enron. Enron's filings with the Securities and Exchange Commission ran to thousands of pages, including many notes printed in small type. The notes were ignored by the many Wall Street analysts who promoted Enron shares, and didn't know, or didn't care, about the detail of the accounts. (The only Wall Street analyst to have been consistently critical of Enron, John Olson, left Merrill Lynch in 1998. His departure followed a complaint by the firm's investment bankers, who feared being excluded from Enron transactions.) The notes described the complex relationships between Enron and associated companies. Chanos was not impressed by what he read.

If you like a security, and you own it, you are 'long' of that security. If you don't like a security, and you own it, you can sell it; if you don't own it, you can refrain from buying it. But Chanos and the fund he managed, Kynikos, took such a negative view of Enron that they wanted to sell it even though they didn't own it. Selling a share you don't own is called 'establishing a short position', and the market for derivatives enables such trades to be made.

Derivatives are securities whose value is derived from the value of other securities. However complex the contract, almost all derivatives are based on shares, bonds, property, commodities or currencies.

Someone who is long in a security profits when its value rises. A short seller profits when the shares fall. When Enron shares plummeted, Chanos and other short sellers made substantial profits. Vanco also received attention from short sellers, the collapsing share price anticipating the collapse of the business.

The usual method of short selling today is to take out a 'contract for difference' (CFD). Suppose the share price today is 100p. A contract for difference is an agreement that can be terminated at any time, either to pay, or receive, the difference between 100p and the market price. The value of the contract for difference varies from day to day in line with the market price. Such contracts are a means of speculating on price movements. Not much upfront cash is required. When Enron's market price fell to zero, the holder of a suitable contract for difference could close the transaction and receive what the market price of Enron shares had been on the day he made the agreement.

A contract for difference, like all derivatives contracts, is made with a counterparty – typically an investment bank. The bank may, but need not, hedge its side of the contract by itself buying, selling or 'borrowing' the shares. That decision will be part of the bank's management of its own portfolio of risks. A retail investor can engage in spread betting as an alternative to a contract for difference. The substantive transaction is the same but, under UK tax law, gains on CFDs are subject to tax (and losses are deductible) but gambling winnings (including the proceeds of spreadbets) are not.

Another common derivative contract is a 'swap'. Swaps were first widely used when exchange control made it difficult to buy foreign currency. British investors who wanted to hold American stocks were not allowed to change pounds into dollars. But an American company wanting to set up a plant in the UK would need sterling. The UK investor could lend pounds and the US company would make a matching quantity of dollars available to the investor.

This market for currency swaps vanished when exchange controls did, but the underlying idea caught on, and today you can swap almost anything. Interest rate swaps are the most common. You exchange an interest rate which varies from day to day for an interest rate that is fixed for a period of years. Mortgage lenders use swaps to offer retail investors a choice of fixed and variable rate products. People who take out mortgages often trade in derivative markets even though they don't know it. When retail investors buy structured products, such as enhanced bonds or protected equities, they are often buying derivatives.

A futures contract is an agreement to buy or sell something in the future at a price that is fixed today. Futures have a long history. A merchant might have to wait three months till a ship reached port, and would be vulnerable to price changes while his cargo was at sea. A farmer might wish to establish, now, how much he will get for his crop. The earliest futures contracts brought such producers together with users who were concerned about how much they might have to pay for the raw materials they would need. Such contracts enabled both parties to meet their requirements with greater certainty – to hedge. But you can buy a futures contract without any need, or intention, of hedging. You can buy it to speculate, and that is what most purchasers of futures contracts do.

The price of buying a future is governed by the present price of the asset. If a commodity does not deteriorate physically, its price three months from now can't be more than the price today, plus the cost of storing it for three months. But if there is a physical shortage of the commodity today. the current price could be higher than the futures price. As I write, this is true in the oil market, and in some other commodities.

Storage costs influence the relationship between futures prices and current prices. There is a financing cost. Money that has been borrowed, or could otherwise be invested, is tied up in the purchase. A physical commodity needs to be warehoused and insured. For securities, there is only the financing cost, and this cost will be reduced if there is a dividend on the share, or interest on a bond. Interest rates differ in different currencies – generally there will be one interest rate at which banks borrow and lend dollars, and different interest rates at which they borrow and lend euros or pounds. The cost of owning a currency is the difference between the interest rate on that currency and the interest rate in your home country.

A futures contract is a firm agreement to buy and sell at a pre-agreed price at a future date. An option confers the right, but not the obligation, to buy or sell at a specified price, known as the 'strike price'. Some options have a fixed exercise date, others can be exercised at any time until they expire, but since you usually won't want to exercise an option before expiry the difference isn't great. Since the option confers right but not obligation, an option seems preferable to a futures contract. If the option were free, it would be preferable. But, while you can usually buy a futures contract in a commodity or a security for something close to the current price, you have to pay a premium for an option. The right to buy is known as a 'call option' while the right to sell is called a 'put'. What are these options worth?

Two influences on value are obvious. The longer the life of an option, the greater its value. The value of a call option diminishes, and the value of a put option increases, the higher is the strike price relative to the current price.

There is another, less obvious, principle of option pricing. The value of an option increases with the volatility of the underlying asset. The riskier a security, the more valuable are options in it. This may seem paradoxical, but note that the riskier the asset, the more likely it is that you will be glad you own an option rather than the security itself. Until the 1970s, assessments of option value were guesses. Then the Black-Scholes model of derivative pricing, which analysed that relationship between the option price and the security price, appeared. That apparently scientific basis for assessing the value of derivatives was essential to the subsequent explosion of derivatives markets.

The value of the option therefore depends on its exercise price, its expiry date, and the volatility of the price of the underlying security. Given these parameters, the standard model calculates an option value on the basis that successive price changes are independent of each other (follow a random walk) and follow the normal distribution.

That is fine if these assumptions of independence and normality hold. But there are strong reasons for querying both. Deviations from a random walk arise from momentum or positive short-term serial correlation. The 'fat tail problem' – extreme events happen more often than the normal distribution allows – is especially troubling. These valuation models seem to work well in relatively placid times but it's not so clear that they work well when markets are unsettled. That's a major problem, because it is in unsettled markets that options are most useful, most profitable and most dangerous, and the need for measures of what they are worth is most urgent.

'Mind your portfolio' – look at your investment portfolio as a whole. Most derivatives are, in themselves, risky investments – the return on an individual transaction is very uncertain. But adding derivatives to an existing portfolio can reduce the risk or improve the expected return on the portfolio without additional risk. A futures contract can hedge a portfolio against a market fall; a put option will limit the maximum loss. Derivatives can lock in profits or anticipate future needs, or allow you to benefit from a market rise while limiting risks. But hedging and insurance aren't the main reasons why people buy derivatives and related products based on them. They buy them because they think they are a good bet.

The normal experience of gamblers is that only the house makes money in the long run. This is as true of speculation in derivative markets as elsewhere. Valuing derivatives is complex and there are no correct answers. But the financial institutions that sell derivative products have access to sophisticated computer programs, extensive databases, Black-Scholes and other models, and roomfuls of maths and physics PhDs. They are better at derivative valuation than the fund managers and treasurers of big companies and public authorities who buy them. Buying derivatives because you think they are cheap, rather than as hedges in a programme of portfolio diversification, is almost certainly a mug's game. The risks are in the price, and if you think the risks are not in the price, the most likely reason is that you are wrong. Why do I want to buy what they want to sell?

Trade in derivative markets has grown steadily, and the products have become more opaque. Some people – notably Alan Greenspan, former chairman of the Federal Reserve Board – explained this growth in trade terms of an ever more sophisticated risk allocation. Perhaps the German regional banks that invested in asset-backed securities related to the value of sub-prime mortgages in American inner cities did so because they were particularly knowledgeable about these loans, or believed they hedged or diversified other assets in their portfolios. More likely, victims of information asymmetry, they did not understand what they were doing.

When assets are difficult to value, they will be owned by people who overestimate that value. Most derivatives are bought by people who are making a mistake, and the proliferation of ever more complex financial instruments, hard to assess even with sophisticated models, encourages these mistakes.

There is a history of spectacular crises in derivatives markets. Sometimes credulous individuals in public agencies or large corporations fall for a sales pitch. In the 1990s, many embarked on programmes of trading in derivatives or structured products whose nature they at best dimly understood. The municipality of Orange County went bust after trades made by the appropriately named Robert Citron came unstuck. The London borough of Hammersmith and Fulham was spared similar embarrassment when the courts ruled the council had no authority to gamble with local residents' money and the banks could get lost.

Naïve incompetence is not confined to local authorities. Major US companies, such as Gibson Cards and even the mighty consumer group Procter and Gamble, suffered large losses from speculative derivative trading programmes. A second line investment bank, Bankers Trust, was particularly aggressive in marketing these programmes to its clients. Ultimately, the angry reaction of clients and threats of litigation destroyed the reputation of the bank.

Financial institutions themselves are frequently victims as well as perpetrators. Managers of profitable trading divisions within banks receive large bonuses and may not be inclined to question closely how the profits are made. Traders who begin with honest losses may turn to fraud to conceal these losses. Nick Leeson achieved notoriety as the rogue trader whose speculations at Barings destroyed one of Britain's oldest investment banks, but in 2008 Jérôme Kerviel surpassed Leeson's record by helping his employer, the French bank Société Générale, lose €5bn.

The most famous of all failures was the demise of Long-Term Capital Management in 1998. This collapse received particular attention – and caused particular joy in some quarters – because of the personalities involved. Founded by John Meriwether, a legendary Salomon trader, the management team included two Nobel Prize winners, Bob Merton and Myron Scholes (of the Black-Scholes model).

LTCM relied on arbitrage trades based on fundamental value – reversion to the mean in relationships between similar but different securities. But momentum may drive prices sufficiently far away from fundamental value for sufficiently long to exhaust the patience, and the resources, of investors – 'markets can be wrong for longer than you can be solvent'. Apparently unrelated bets proved to be correlated in the widespread panic that followed the Asian financial crisis and Russian debt repudiation of 1997-8. The scale of LTCM's borrowings – the magic of leverage meant that this relatively small fund had liabilities of trillions of dollars – was such that the Federal Reserve orchestrated a rescue operation.

Many derivatives in modern securities markets are complex. However elaborate, they are mostly based on combinations of the four basic mechanisms I have described above: shorts, swaps, futures and options. Most retail investors will not trade in derivatives directly. But they may do so through hedge funds and structured products, or through funds that invest in hedge funds or structured products.

Alternative assets

Keynes was an active speculator, famously trading from bed in the mornings, managing his own money and that of King's College, Cambridge, shorting securities and dealing in a wide range of assets. He seems to have been successful in the long run, though not extraordinarily so. He died in 1946 with assets of around £½m, a wealthy man by the standards of the time but not rich on the scale of Soros or Buffett. Benjamin Graham, the legendary value investor, would establish short positions in businesses he did not like as well as having long positions in those he did.

These styles of investing were the precursors of the modern hedge fund. The first investor to attract that label seems to have been Alfred Jones, who traded aggressively through the 1950s. Hedge funds attracted wide popular attention with the famous bet against sterling by the Quantum Fund of George Soros in 1991 and came into the spotlight again with the failure of Long-term Capital Management in 1998.

Until 2000, hedge funds were used only by rich individuals and a few sophisticated institutions. Academic endowments, notably those of Harvard and Yale, were early and successful supporters. After the end of the New Economy bubble, investors searched for new ways of generating the high returns that had seemed to come so easily in the 1990s. They turned to hedge funds. Exceptional individuals such as Soros had been able to command high fee levels for their serv- ices and newer funds set their charges at the same level. The prospect of such fees proved irresistible to many people in investment banks. As newcomers rushed through the door, Soros made for the exit. So did another legend, Julian Robertson. While the long-term perform- ance of his Tiger Fund rivalled that of Soros, Robertson may have lost more money in his last year than he had made throughout his career.

Different hedge funds pursue different strategies. A long/short fund, like Graham's, will deploy the stock-picking skills of its managers to select losers as well as winners. Jim Chanos, who helped expose Enron, specialised in taking short positions. A market-neutral fund will hedge its exposure to general market movements. It will focus on *alpha* and eliminate *beta*. A macroeconomic event fund in the style of Keynes or Soros aspires to predict major financial and political developments in the world economy – such as Britain's EMS failure – and trades on the basis of these forecasts.

Arbitrage strategies, such as those deployed at LTCM, rely on stable relationships between the prices of related, but different, securities. Such pairs might be currencies within a region, or the debt and equity of the same company, or the shares of an acquiring company and its potential target. As at LTCM, arbitrage strategies are often based on complex modelling. Relying on history in this way is dangerous, as it proved for the LTCM partners.

Distressed debt funds buy bonds of businesses or countries in financial difficulty. These funds may hope to profit from buying below fundamental value, or to increase that fundamental value through liti- gation or the threat to block proposals for financial reconstruction.

Investment banks established proprietary trading operations – their own hedge funds – in the 1980s. LTCM emerged from what was for years the most successful of these, at Salomon. But Salomon's proprietary trading activities were curtailed after Warren Buffett took control, and finally closed when Citigroup acquired the business. Proprietary trading is nevertheless a major activity for most large banks (including Citigroup). These 'prop desks' benefit from the information that flows continuously through the bank but, despite Chinese walls, the conflicts of interest between these trading activities and the interests of clients are obvious.

Although most hedge funds are based in London or the United States, for legal and regulatory purposes they are normally registered offshore. While the City of London (and its increasingly important annex at Canary Wharf) remains the centre of London's financial services business, hedge fund managers emphasise differentiation and exclusivity by clustering in St James's (and, in the US, in Connecticut). Charging typical fees of 2% of funds under management and 20% of profits, the managers can afford West End rents.

The fee structure, in effect, shares profits but not losses. Investors look for reliable month-by-month appreciation in the value of their funds, and hedge fund managers are closely monitored month by month. Both these incentives and this supervision encourage the adoption of strategies with Taleb characteristics – frequent small profits, occasional large losses. Hedge funds make extensive use of the 'carry trade', which relies on interest rate differentials between good and bad credits, or strong and weak currencies.

Retail investors cannot easily access major hedge funds, as a result of regulatory restrictions and high minimum investments, and many of the most highly regarded funds are closed to new investors. Retail investors have the opportunity to invest in more conventionally open – or closed-ended funds which themselves invest in hedge funds. Since many hedge fund managers reveal only limited information about what they do, intermediaries may be helpful. These funds of funds can diversify across funds with different strategies. The returns on, say, a long/short fund should not be correlated with the returns on, say, a distressed debt fund. Historical analysis supports this claim.

But do not count on the stability of historic correlations in times of extreme financial strain. Funds learnt this lesson in 2007–8.

The shift from mainstream to alternative investments also favoured private equity. Private equity is a means by which investment institutions, either directly or through managed funds, invest in unquoted businesses. Before the late 1990s, private equity used to be more or less synonymous with venture capital – the provision of funds for startup and early stage businesses.

Not all private equity deals were of this kind. As large corporations restructured, unwanted 'non-core' divisions were often sold to consortia led by their managers and funded by private equity. The newly established business was often refinanced or the subject of a fresh IPO within a few years. Many individual managers became very rich through these transactions, a development that helped to raise the pay aspirations of all executives.

The development of junk bond financing in the 1980s made it possible to use debt to buy even very large companies. That boom ended with the collapse of Drexel Burnham Lambert, the imprisonment of Michael Milken, and the relatively unsuccessful outcome of the massive acquisition of RJR Nabisco by KKR. Still, the search for new investment avenues after 2000 led to explosive growth in the funds available for private equity, and the scale of the typical transaction grew rapidly. Private equity funds would buy an established business from the existing owners. These owners might be other companies, family and founding shareholders or, increasingly, the shareholders of public companies quoted on the stock exchange.

The largest private equity deal in the UK was the takeover of Boots, the high street chemists, for £11bn, including more than £8bn of debt. In such a transaction, private equity has come a long way from its roots in the provision of funds to small growing businesses. Private equity investment became an indirect, expensive and exclusive method of buying shares in medium and large companies similar to those in the main index. The returns from such investment will therefore be correlated with the returns from other equity investments but, given the leverage involved, the *beta* associated with such equity is well above one.

The concentrated share ownership of private equity deals allows more effective monitoring of company management. Such concentrated ownership has been common for many years in continental Europe. Public companies find their ability to focus on fundamental value inhibited by the management of quarterly earnings forecasts and reports. Some patient private equity investors are willing to hold their financial investments for many years, encouraging more long-term strategic thinking and productive investment. But the major private equity firms, and the investors who back them, are generally in search of a rapid exit. The objective is normally to sell the company or float it on the stock market within three to five years, returning the money obtained to the investors in that particular fund.

I described in Chapter 6 the numerous ways in which businesses can enhance earnings in the short term. Private equity, and the threat of takeover by private equity, has increased pressure to use these strategies. During a recent stay in a hotel, looking at the frayed carpet and overpriced extras, I thought 'This hotel has been bought out in a private equity transaction'. It had been. It is easy to enhance the earnings of most businesses if your time horizon is three years.

Both the citizen and the investor should be concerned about the difficulty modern management finds in taking a long-term view of the growth and development of the business. The public company encounters the blight of quarterly earnings reporting; the private equity owned business must accommodate the time-scale of investors seeking a quick profit. This short termism is reinforced by the incentive schemes offered to managers – even, or perhaps especially, the so-called long-term incentive schemes that now constitute a large part of executive remuneration. Even if you are concerned with the fundamental value of the business in which you own shares, the managers may not be.

It is difficult for the investor to judge the historic success of private equity, far less its prospective future returns. Some private equity houses may have been able to supervise management teams more effectively than public markets. Some may possess skills that add value through financial engineering. Private equity houses have recently (but no longer) had access to debt financing whose pricing did not reflect the risk involved. The reporting of historic perform-

ance is confounded by survivor bias – it is the more successful investors who are raising new funds – and by the capacity of leverage to
produce very high returns to equity investors in a period of rising
share prices (with the opposite effect when share prices are falling).

Against these potential advantages must be set the certainty of
charges. 'Two and twenty' is a common charging basis for both hedge
funds and private equity investments. The private equity house takes
a management fee of 2% of the fund per year, and 20% of the profits,
known in private equity as the 'carried interest'. Like other investment
managers, they may also arrange for many of their own costs to be
directly or indirectly charged to their funds. When these percentages are applied to large transactions – such as those of Boots –
the numbers become eye-watering. Many hedge funds and private
equity managers have become very rich very quickly.

But what of the customers' yachts? 'Two and twenty' reduces a
10% underlying return to 6%. A retail investor will normally make
an investment in a hedge fund or private equity fund through a fund
of funds or a feeder fund, for which a charge of 1.5% of assets for
management and 10% of profit is common. The addition of these
charges means that a 10% return on the underlying investment might
be no more than 3.5% in the hands of the investors. Even if the fund
secured a 20% yield, the net return to the investor might be only half
of that, with 6% going to the underlying fund and 3% to the fund of
funds. Tax and inflation take a further bite of the return.

Such figures make no sense. Returns on financial investment are
ultimately governed by returns on productive investment. While
some investors in hedge funds and private equity will make excellent
returns from a mixture of skill and luck on the part of their managers,
most stand no chance of earning profits commensurate with the risks.

Hedge funds and private equity are not the only alternative assets.
Other options include commodities such as oil, gold, other metals;
undeveloped land such as farms, forests, building plots; collectables
such as wine, art, jewels, furniture.

Commodity exchanges, large and active, meet the needs of people
who produce or use the physical commodities. Commodities have
always been a fertile field for speculation by those who believe they

can anticipate 'the mind of the market'. If this is you, then good luck and good fortune; you will need good luck to preserve good fortune. If you simply want to invest, there are funds whose value is linked to commodity prices, which I will describe in the next chapter. In the last five years, the search for new asset categories and real increases in fundamental demand have produced large rises in commodity prices.

But over the long run, commodity investment has not been very profitable. Despite continuing worries about forthcoming resource scarcity, new technology and new discoveries have more than offset the exploitation of existing reserves. It is cheaper to own commodities in the ground than in a warehouse, and mining companies are generally better investments than the commodities themselves, and are good portfolio diversifiers. The aphorism that a small minerals company is a hole in the ground with a crook at the top is, however, often true. London's Alternative Investment Market has become a magnet for small resource companies from around the world.

Other alternative assets are marketed to private investors either as hot tips, or as additions to a diversified portfolio. The general rule is to avoid these areas unless you have specialist knowledge. Timber offers attractive tax concessions – and is therefore not very attractive to those who do not benefit from these concessions – and is in over supply in Britain as a result of excessive tax advantages and subsidies in the past. Land with remote prospects of future planning permission for building has recently been widely marketed by 'advisers', i.e. salespeople.

Buy wine, art, jewels or furniture if you like wine, art, jewels, or furniture. While it is certainly possible to make money in these investments, the differences between buying and selling prices are wide and there is none of the regulatory apparatus that protects small investors in securities markets. If you are expert, and even more if you are not, buy only collectable items you like.

Structured products

A structured product is a security whose risk and return characteristics have been created by financial engineering. Such engineering can take the form of packaging one security with others: splitting the risk and return from an asset into several components; combining a security with a derivative based on the same or another security; or, frequently, a combination of all these methods. A synthetic investment resembles a fund, but the issuer does not hold the underlying assets to which its value is related; the risks may be hedged through derivatives (but need not be).

Financial engineering sounds complicated, and the legal and economic structure of these instruments is indeed complicated. But good financial engineering is like watch making. Its objective is to create products whose properties appear simple, even if the underlying mechanisms are not. Much financial engineering, however, is more like the skills of the illusionist: what the audience sees is not the reality.

The aim of financial engineering is either to increase the yield on bonds with little addition to risk or to reduce the risk in equity investment with little loss of return. I'll call these two basic types of security 'enhanced bonds' and 'protected equities'.

Protected equities came into vogue in the 1980s. The use of a derivative would reduce the risk of a share portfolio. A variant called 'portfolio insurance' involved a rolling programme of computerised trade known as 'dynamic hedging'. This mechanism came unstuck on 19 October 1987 when the US market fell sharply. Dynamic hedging triggered many sell orders. These led to further price falls and many of the transactions that the trading strategies required simply could not be made. Portfolio insurance aggravated market volatility and often failed to provide the 'insurance' its customers sought.

Government bonds offer virtually no credit risk. Enhanced bonds add some return and credit risk. Such bonds were usually issued by large corporations. But in the 1990s, banks issued increasing quantities of asset-backed securities. The business model followed by Northern Rock placed packages of mortgages into a special purpose vehicle (Granite). In turn Granite created asset-backed securities sold to investors on the security of these mortgages.

Most readers will have experienced the detailed and careful assessment of both the borrower and the house that is undertaken by a bank or building society before agreeing a mortgage. They may wonder why other people would want to take on these loans without equivalent, or often any, inquiry. This is a good question, and I am not sure that it has a good answer. One partial answer is regulatory arbitrage – regulators treated bonds and mortgages differently, even if the bonds were, in reality, simply collections of mortgages. This created the absurd situation where banks and building societies sold portfolios of mortgages they had themselves assessed, and used the proceeds to buy bonds based on portfolios of mortgages about which they knew nothing. Whatever the reasons, demand for these and similar asset backed securities grew rapidly and the supply of mortgages grew to meet it.

Banks widened the range of structured products by issuing bonds whose security depended on successive tranches of the same underlying loans. Senior debt would be repaid before junior debt, and would therefore receive a lower interest rate – the senior debt might qualify for a coveted triple A rating. The junior debt would be more risky but the interest rate would be enhanced. Rating agencies would assess the quality of each tranche.

Collateralised debt obligations required the issuing bank to support the bond with assets of a quality acceptable to rating agencies. Credit insurers might guarantee payment of interest or principal on corporate bonds, or on these more complex products, and doubtful bonds might acquire a higher rating as a result of the insurer's guarantee. The largest insurers were Freddie Mac – an agency established by the US government to underwrite mortgages for house buyers – and AIG, a general insurance company, which guaranteed a wide range of bonds. The connection between the security which investors bought and sold and the underlying debts became more and more remote, and impossible to analyse. The objective was always to make a silk purse from a sow's ear – to secure a good credit rating for a bond whose underlying value was derived from borrowers with lower credit ratings.

None of this matters directly to retail investors, who do not hold these bonds themselves, but the consequences have mattered a great deal. Institutional investors held – and hold – many such bonds. By 2007 the volume of flaky credit had reached proportions that threatened the future stability of the banking and financial system. Structured credit had succeeded the New Economy bubble as the new market madness. At the beginning of 2007, the first cracks emerged when default rates on 'sub-prime' mortgages – mortgages to borrowers with poor credit histories, on properties in rundown areas – rose steeply. Mortgages had been offered freely to meet the hitherto insatiable demand for mortgage-backed securities.

Investors had been blind for years to the conflict of interest inherent in the rating agencies' practice of charging the borrower, not the investor, for the assessment of the bond he hoped to sell. Suddenly, these investors were reluctant to buy structured products – or to lend to institutions that held them. Fear spread throughout the banking sector. The result was the most extensive series of banking failures since the Great Depression. Fannie Mae and AIG were both taken over by the US government.

If sophisticated investors have done badly with structured products, retail investors have also suffered from their repeated failures. The enhanced bonds most frequently offered to retail investors are usually, and misleadingly, called 'guaranteed bonds', which are aggressively marketed by financial advisers. The guarantee applies to the income from the bond, but not to the capital. The small print explains that you will usually get your capital back, but that you might not. In the trade, these securities are known as 'precipice bonds'.

Avoid these offers. The issuer of these bonds writes a complex derivative contract with an investment bank. The bank makes a payment but is entitled to receive a much larger sum if the complex combination of events described in the small print materialises (the 'punt'). The premium pays for the higher interest rate you are guaranteed (and for the marketing expenses of the bond, which will be substantial).

The investment bank has done its own modelling and considers that the punt is a good deal. But if the punt is a good deal for the bank, it is a bad deal for you. It is very unlikely that you would buy this kind of complex gamble with negative expected value as a stand-alone product. Once again, you can apply the 'mind your portfolio' principle to the structured product by analysing its components. You will get to the same answer quickly and simply through two other principles: Why do I want to buy what they want to sell? and Keep it simple. Both these maxims are good guides in the world of structured products and they tell you not to go there.

For several decades, the main protected equity products available to the retail investor were the 'with profits' funds of insurance companies. These policies sought to provide retail investors with a diversified portfolio – including equities, bonds and property – in a single purchase, but also to insulate the returns from short-term fluctuations in the value of investments. The company's actuaries would hold back profits in good times to support returns when markets fell.[1] But in the market setback of 2000 the smoothing process failed. The traditional with profits model, no longer attractive to either savers or providers, has no long-term future.

Innovative new protected equity products are now widely marketed. Such a product might promise that your portfolio will never fall by, say, more than 5% in a quarter. Another might give you a proportion of the upside (but not the downside) in the FTSE index over the life of the product. All of these instruments are constructed from packages of derivatives and can be divided into the underlying components. The first is an index fund combined with a put option, the second is a deposit combined with a call option.

Few retail products now offer, as life policies once did, a portfolio diversified across all asset categories. A new development is the lifecycle fund, which varies the asset composition of a portfolio according to the age of the holder. The mechanism assumes that most people want to reduce volatility (and will accept a lower return in consequence) as they get older. I'll discuss that proposition further in Chapter 11. Both protected equity and lifecycle products are worth considering by lazy and timid investors. But you will always find it

1 This scheme can work only if the companies involved maintain large reserves. As this type of investment is wound down, ownership of the reserves companies built up from their with profits funds – 'orphan assets' – is controversial. But competition forced companies hungry for new business to pay an increasing proportion of their investment returns. (In 1999-2000 Equitable Life, perhaps the best regarded provider of these products, came close to collapse. The trigger was a legal case over guaranteed annuities but the basic problem was that the company's reserves were inadequate for its business model.) The need to maintain regulating solvency margins in the stock market downturn forced Standard Life, the largest issuer of with profits policies, to sell large quantities of shares from its portfolio, raise new capital and demutualise.

cheaper to achieve the same balance of risk and reward from your own diversified portfolio.

If you adhere to the 'mind your portfolio' principle you will not want to buy structured products. The structured product alters the risk/return characteristics of individual investments. What matters to you is the risk/return characteristics of your overall portfolio. You can and should achieve the overall objectives – the balance of risk and return – by balancing your overall mix of investments. Mind your portfolio! You do not need funds or companies to gear or diversify on your behalf because you can do these things yourself. The best and cheapest way of limiting the risk in shares is to hold a lower proportion of your assets in shares.

But rigorous application of the 'mind your portfolio' principle is hard. Many intelligent investors will feel better if they limit the risk on the individual components of their portfolio as well as on the aggregate. Others like the risk and return combination offered by particular structured products. One of the very first structured products, and still the one with most appeal to retail investors, is an enhanced bond from the British government. The premium bond was introduced in 1956 with a showman's style by the future Prime Minister Harold Macmillan. The bond offers no income, only the chance to participate in a monthly prize draw. The premium bond is a combination of a deposit account and a lottery, and since the deposit rate is competitive and the lottery is fair, the combination is an attractive proposition for people who are interested in both holding bonds and entering lotteries.

This method of analysing a structured product unravels the financial engineering of the product's designers. The technique can also be applied to any structured product, and should be applied by anyone who adheres to the 'mind your portfolio' principle. Split the package into its component parts, and ask whether each component is something you would want to add to your profits.

A bond issued by a large company will offer a higher return than a British government stock, but at a higher risk. There is a greater possibility (though still not a very large one) that the company will default. Seen in this way, a corporate bond – say a ten-year bond for

British Telecom that yields 100p per annum per £100 invested more than a similar British government stock – is like buying a completely safe bond and offering to insure the credit risk associated with BT. You promise to pay out £100 if British Telecom defaults in return for a premium of 100p per annum.

Put this way, the deal doesn't sound very attractive. There are companies that sell credit insurance (in 2008 they were rapidly disappearing). You do not have the information needed to assess the risk on these policies. Credit insurance is an activity whose returns are strongly correlated with your overall portfolio (a situation in which BT defaults on its bonds is likely to be one in which there is mayhem in other financial markets). The additional risk and return that the corporate bond implies relative to the government bond is probably not a risk you would add to your portfolio if it were offered on a stand-alone basis.

Many markets offer bundled products. Buy one, get the second half price. Television programmes are sold as packages of channels. Buy coffee and croissant together. Eat a *prix fixe* menu. The cost of the menu is typically less than the cost of the separate components.

Not so in financial markets, where the cost of the structured product is generally *higher* than the cost of the components and the premium is the source of the financial engineer's profit. No one would buy a *table d'hôte* menu at a price higher than the sum of the items on the *à la carte* menu. The premium also indicates that structured products are often bought (in my view, mostly bought) by people who misunderstand them. The analogy of the illusionist is more relevant than the analogy of the watchmaker.

The market for structured products illustrates all the issues of information asymmetry. Asking 'Would I choose to buy each of the separate components of this package?' is an important discipline in both the restaurant and in financial markets, but especially in financial markets. Because structured products are often bought by people who are making mistakes, they are usually better bought second-hand.

Michael Milken used data on the past performance of bonds with high credit risk to create the junk bond market in the 1980s. But there was a difference between bonds that became junk – the distressed securities of good companies that had fallen on hard times – and those that were intended to be junk from the beginning. The fallen idols were often cheap because unwilling holders needed to be rid of their unsuccessful investments at almost any price. The sale might stave off embarrassing questions from bosses or trustees. Or it might be necessary because many investors are not allowed to hold low-quality bonds by regulatory constraint or internally imposed rule. The newly minted junk bonds were in a different category. The potential holder always needs to ask the question Why do I want to buy what they want to sell?

Split-level investment trusts were, for a time, a popular structured product for retail investors. Companies offered zero dividend preference shares. These securities rolled up the interest due and repaid a capital sum at maturity – provided that the portfolio had sufficient value. Typically, the company borrowed to increase its overall size, and invested in securities of similar companies. If the overall market fell, the loss would be magnified by leverage.

These shares failed the component test. The design of the gamble was unattractive. There was a small probability of large loss and that loss correlated with a general market slide. The odds offered were poor, for the usual reason – the costs and fees of setting up the arrangements.

When the fundamental value of these shares collapsed, the reputation of this share class became toxic. Financial advisers risked being sued for having recommended these securities to clients for whom they were unsuitable. There were few if any clients for whom they had ever been suitable. The market value fell well below the fundamental value. As the market recovered, such shares became low-risk, high-return investments. Similar opportunities may arise as investors flee from the enhanced bonds of the credit boom.

If you are going to hold bonds, hold bonds. Complex financial engineering is expensive, and the expense is likely to be yours. If you have an offset mortgage, then putting your money in the associated savings account offers a rate of return, tax-free, that easily exceeds any other completely safe option available. You are lending to the most reliable borrower you can find: yourself.

CHAPTER 10

THE CONVENTIONAL INVESTOR

Establish your portfolio

Every financial adviser is trained to begin by asking you to define your investment objectives and your attitude to risk. As your own financial adviser, you need to pose these questions to yourself. The professional adviser must tick boxes to complete the 'fact find' so he can get on and sell you products. You really want to know the answers.

Are you a net saver, or a net spender? Are you building up assets or managing existing assets to support your standard of living? Most people before retirement are, or should be, net savers. Many people, after retirement, will be net spenders. People before retirement need to consider how much saving they should do. People after retirement need to consider how much they can afford to spend.

If you gathered nuts for twenty-five years, and planned to retire for twenty-five years, you would need to set aside half your nuts for your old age. If you can earn a return on your investment, you can save much less. Table 8 shows how much less. If you meet the 10% target rate of return, 8.5% of income will grow to a cache large enough to meet your needs. You can now eat more than 90% of the nuts you collect.

Table 8: Save now, spend later

% of income needed to maintain the same spending power in retirement with a saving/spending period each of 25 years

Realised rate of return (p.a.)	10%	8%	6%	4%	2%	0
% of income required to save	8.5	12.7	19.0	27.3	37.9	50.0
% of income available to spend	91.5	87.3	81.0	72.7	62.1	50.0

Every 2% that you gain or lose in investment return will make a big difference. You can sacrifice more than 2% through poor investment performance, bad timing of sales and purchases, or unsuitable allocation across investment categories. You might lose 2% in tax, and another 2% by paying more than you need in fees and charges. And you can lose 2%, or more, by making large allocations to assets that advisers describe as low-risk investments which offer lower but more predictable returns.

In this and following chapters, I will describe how you can minimise the leakage of return under each of these headings. I'll suggest how to turn the timing of investments to your advantage, and how to approach asset allocation and stock selection. I'll direct you to the most tax-efficient forms of investment. I'll stress the importance of keeping down costs and charges, and explain how to do it. And I will offer practical guidance on how to think about risk and uncertainty based on the principles outlined in Chapters 7 and 8. The lesson of that discussion is that you don't necessarily have to accept low returns to achieve low risk.

Chapter 2 described the essential preliminaries – listing assets and liabilities, reviewing your banking arrangements and your mortgage. Now you need a stockbroker. Most people still have an image of the stockbroker derived from the days before players replaced gentlemen: grand, but seedy; with good social skills and connections; streetwise but not clever; well-off but not hard-working. These people still exist, mostly outside London, but are a dying breed. They will levy annual management charges, or substantial commissions on purchases and sales, or both. They are expensive.

Your stockbroker should be an online share dealing service. Such facilities are provided by major banks – Barclays is market leader. There are also monoliners, such as Selftrade. Some traditional stockbrokers and financial advisers offer online share-dealing services. What you need is an execution-only service, in which you make decisions and give instructions yourself. These services are very cheap, because computers do most of the work, so cheap that price should not be a major factor in your choice. The securities that you buy will be held electronically in the nominee account of a bank or other financial institution. You can obtain paper certificates but there are no advantages and several disadvantages.

When you set up this account, you will want to take advantage of the substantial tax exemptions available to retail investors. An ISA (Individual Savings Account) is free of tax on income or capital gains. A SIPP (Self-Invested Personal Pension) allows you to roll forward the money you invest in it free of income or capital gains tax, and additionally gives you tax relief on the whole of your contribution.

These tax concessions carry snags. The maximum investment in an ISA is £7200 a year. With returns reinvested this allows a couple to build up, over five years, a portfolio of £100,000 or so. The limits for investment in a SIPP are much higher, but normally you cannot take any money out until you are fifty (rising to fifty-five). You can then cash in a quarter of the fund but the rest can only be withdrawn in annual instalments calculated by reference to an actuarial formula and is subject to income tax. Although irksome and complex, these restrictions are not very constraining for someone planning to build up savings for retirement (their purpose is to encourage the use of SIPPs for retirement savings).

All internet stockbrokers offer self-select ISAs at low or no cost. These are simply broking accounts in which you choose your own investments and qualify for the tax-favoured regime. Many internet brokers also offer self-select SIPPs. If you have a substantial amount to invest, you may prefer to take out a SIPP from a specialist provider, who will charge you a bit more but will allow you a wider range of investments, such as property, and greater flexibility.

ISAs and SIPPs both enhance returns and simplify administration, and the two schemes complement each other. Someone anticipating an investment portfolio of £100,000 or so should usually focus on building up their savings in an ISA. Anyone planning a larger port-folio should begin with an ISA, but expect to place a significant frac-tion into a SIPP. The tax concessions on these forms of investment mean that savers in Britain need pay little or no tax on an investment portfolio until it exceeds several hundred thousand pounds.

On savings outside the scope of ISAs and SIPPS, you will have to pay tax. If you are a 40% taxpayer, you will pay tax on dividends at about 25% and capital gains on realisation at 18% (with a £9600 exemption). On a deposit account, or a government or corporate bond, you will pay tax at 40%. These differences in effective tax rates can have a substantial effect on returns (although you should bear in mind that tax paid by companies may create a wedge between the underlying returns on productive investment and the returns on your financial investment).

While securities will be the main component of your investment portfolio, the 'mind your portfolio' principle implies that you should consider insurance at the same time as you contemplate investment. You should think probabilities when you take out insurance. But so does the insurance company, and the company knows probabilities well. That is its business.

You should be detached. While it is vexing to have your television stolen, or to lose your bag on holiday, insurance will not bring back either your television or your bag. The financial loss from a stolen television or lost bag is probably less than you will incur on a bad day on the stock market. Much of the premium on policies that insure against these minor contingencies goes not to pay policyholders but in the administrative costs of small claims.

So anyone who is truly minding their portfolio, and recognises that the insurance company has calculated the expected value of their policy, will insure only things they cannot afford to lose. You need insurance against your house burning down, but not for replacing the bedroom carpet; you need insurance against being hospitalised in the United States, but not for the cost of an extra night's hotel accommodation because your plane is delayed.

Many people find this advice difficult to accept. Insurers observe that their customers have little appetite for policies that rarely pay out, even though low-probability risks are precisely those that are appropriate for insurance. Policyholders like the reassurance of occasional small cheques even if such cheques add up to much less than their premiums. Regret is a powerful human emotion, even if often an unproductive one.

You will be financially better off if you can be detached and learn to control these emotions, but it is difficult, even for people educated in intelligent investment, to exercise such control. If, when an uninsured television set is stolen, you can't refrain from kicking yourself, or your spouse can't refrain from kicking you, then you should take out the policy. This strategy is, however, likely to cost you money – even after taking account of the insurance companies' cheques.

Pay less

Over the forty-two years that Warren Buffett has been in charge of Berkshire Hathaway, the company has earned an average compound rate of return of 20% per year. For himself. But also for his investors. The lucky people who have been his fellow shareholders through all that time have enjoyed just the same rate of return as he has. The fortune he has accumulated is the result of the rise in the value of his share of the collective fund.

Suppose that Buffett had deducted from the returns on his own investment – his own, not that of his fellow shareholders – a notional investment management fee, based on the standard 2% annual charge and 20% of gains formula of the hedge fund and private equity business. There would then be two pots: one created by reinvestment of the fees Buffett was charging himself; and one created by the growth in the value of Buffett's own original investment. Call the first pot the wealth of Buffett Investment Management, the second pot the wealth of the Buffett Foundation.

How much of Buffett's $62bn would be the property of Buffett Investment Management and how much the property of the Buffett Foundation? The – completely astonishing – answer is that Buffett Investment Management would have $57bn and the Buffett Foundation $5bn. The cumulative effect of 'two and twenty' over forty-two years is so large that the earnings of the investment manager completely overshadow the earnings of the investor. That sum tells you why it was the giants of the financial services industry, not the customers, who owned the yachts.

The least risky way to increase the returns from your financial investments is to minimise agency costs – to ensure that the return on the underlying investments goes into your pocket rather than someone else's. The effect of charges on investments is so large that it is as important to understand the structure of charges as the principles of investment analysis.

The first charge that hits you when you invest is the spread between the buying price and the selling price. For government bonds and for blue chip shares, like BP, this spread will be extremely small, and you can deal at any time in any quantity you like. The only other dealing costs are commission (you should expect to pay less than £20 for an internet deal) and government stamp duty on shares, which is 0.5%. There is no stamp duty on an exchange traded fund (ETF), which you can buy and sell as easily as any other share. ETFs carry a small spread and a brokerage commission. The total cost of making and realising an investment of £10,000 in a FTSE 100 company should be less than £100 (1%).

Small companies are different. The spread between buying and selling prices may be 3% or 4%. Even a purchase of £10,000 may require a telephone call rather than a mouse click, and telephone orders will entail higher commission. The difference between what it will cost you to buy and what you will get if you sell could be as much as 5%.

The effect of these costs on returns depends on the frequency with which you deal. Online trading is so inexpensive and easy that you may be tempted to trade often. Only one thing eats up investment returns faster than fees and commissions, and that is frequent trading. Do not succumb. Do not accept the invitation to subscribe to level two platforms or direct market access. The total costs of running your own portfolio should be less than 1% per year.

Investing in actively managed funds will cost you more. The choice of funds available, both open and closed-end, is unbelievably wide. There are more funds investing in shares than there are shares to invest in. This situation doesn't make sense, and is both cause and effect of the high charges. Costs need to be high to recover the expenses of running so many different, mainly small, funds that all do much the same thing. At the same time, the high level of charges encourages financial services companies to set up even more funds.

Table 9: Available UK retail investment funds, 2008

Asset class	No of funds	Av size (£m)	Median TER (%)
Sterling bonds	179	120	0.8
Global bonds	167	78	1.1
UK equities	554	181	1.5
Global equities	601	124	1.6
Japanese equities	209	87	1.7
North American equities	366	121	1.7

Source: Lipper

The proliferation of funds means that choosing a fund may be no easier than choosing individual investments. You can hire an adviser to recommend funds. There are also many advisers. The problem seems to multiply itself, as do the fees. The fees attract more advisers, and so on. This plethora of choice would be less confusing if all funds, managers and advisers were excellent, but most are not.

The underlying problem is one of information asymmetry. The marketing of financial services emphasises quality, not price, and for good reasons. It would be worth paying more – a lot more – to get a good fund manager. But since it is hard to identify a good fund manager, good and bad managers all charge high fees, with the consequences described above. It is hard to escape the dilemma posed by this market inefficiency.

If you own a mainstream British unit trust for five years, it is likely that the direct and indirect costs and charges you incur in buying, holding and selling that investment will total 3% a year. Other investment funds may cost you more. The total charges on a fund of hedge funds are such that it might yield less than a government bond even if the underlying investments returned more than 10% per year.

Costs and charges for funds fall into three broad categories:

- annual costs of managing and administering the investment. Regulated investment funds must quote this figure, which is called the total expense ratio (TER).
- costs and charges incurred in buying and selling the investment,

which include initial fees, commission charges, and any difference between the quoted buying and selling price. The effect of these charges on your annual return depends on the length of time for which you hold the investment.

The estimated reduction in yield (ERY) is the sum of the first and second of these costs, under a specified assumption about the holding period. The ERY may also include some part of the third cost heading:

- costs incurred by the fund manager and charged against the value of the fund (e.g. commission on transactions and the difference between the buying and selling prices of the underlying securities).

Annual management charges range from 0.1% or 0.2% for some indexed funds and ETFs to 2% or more for an insurance policy linked fund or a hedge fund. Other administrative costs will usually be between 0.2% and 0.4%. If you buy a fund of funds that invests in other funds, you may have to pay more than one level of these charges. Some funds also charge a performance fee, which gives the managers a share of any profit, or of outperformance relative to a benchmark.

A typical initial charge on an open-ended investment company (unit trust) is around 5%. You should never pay this. Most of it goes in commission to intermediaries. You cannot avoid the charge when buying directly from the fund manager. The management company wants to keep the goodwill of intermediaries, and will charge you the full whack and keep the money. You can reduce the initial charge by buying through a fund supermarket or via a discount broker, who will rebate much of his commission to you. Do not weep for him. The discount broker will still be receiving part of the annual charge as a back-hander (trail commission) from the fund manager.

You will, however, still have to pay the annual charge (a very few intermediaries will rebate part of their trail commission to you). If you buy one of the funds recommended to neophyte investors, you will probably end up in an open-ended fund, or life insurance bond, linked to a selection of mainstream UK shares. Most such funds are closet indexed – although they are actively managed, their composition is very close to the makeup of the UK index. That minimises the risk – to the manager – that the fund will significantly underperform the market. If the largest holdings are BP, Shell, HSBC, Vodafone and Glaxo, the fund is closet indexed. You can achieve a similar result much more cheaply yourself, and you should.

Table 10 shows the median performance of UK retail open-ended funds. The figures, compiled by Lipper from the funds identified in Table 9, are probably rather favourable to the funds. They reflect the manager's own chosen benchmark (generally an index related to the investment category), they are subject to survivor bias – only funds which have a ten-year record can be included in the ten-year figures, and they normally exclude the costs of buying and selling. Even so, the record is poor, and that of property funds downright disgraceful.

You may be tempted to think that, even if you can manage your UK investments yourself, you need to find a manager to invest overseas. The thought is wise, the conclusion not. If UK investors struggle in other markets, so do UK fund managers. Table 11 shows that the underperformance in foreign markets is considerably greater than in the UK. The clear lesson is that the representative UK retail open-ended fund does not provide performance to justify its charges and that most fund managers have little or no investment skill.

Table 10: Relative performance of UK retail investment funds, 1998-2008

Median cumulative outperformance (%) relative to manager's own defined benchmark to 31 July 2008		
	5 years	10 years
Sterling bonds	-4.7	-1.2
UK equities	- 6.0	-3.0
Global equities	1.2	-3.3
UK real estate	-16.0	-39.8

Source: Lipper

Table 11: Relative performance of UK retail investment funds in non- UK asset categories, 1998-2008

Median cumulative outperformance (%) relative to manager's own defined benchmark to 31 July 2008		
	5 years	10 years
Global bonds	-7.1	-17.7
North American equities	-5.6	-11.3
Japanese equities	-12.7	-8.6

Source: Lipper

There may be hope of better value from funds. In the United States, the Vanguard Group, a not-for-profit company with a messianic founder, John Bogle, has become market leader in retail fund management with charges substantially lower than the US, or UK, norm. Today the largest providers of retail funds in the US are monoliners. These businesses do not suffer the conflicts of interest inherent in the cross-selling of retail products or the provision of investment banking services to companies in which the funds invest. The UK remains far behind. Vanguard does not operate in Europe (although retail investors with substantial sums can access their Irish funds) and banks have a large share of the funds market. However, the worst US fund managers are greedier, and probably more corrupt, than their British counterparts.

The most attractive equity-based funds for small investors are generally indexed funds, exchange traded funds, and investment trusts (closed-end funds) with low charges and significant discounts to underlying asset value. I'll discuss these options in more detail later, and also the – necessarily more expensive – options available for property investment. These funds provide more than sufficient choice for normal purposes. All of them can be accessed through your online execution-only share-dealing account.

The conventional investor's portfolio

Where to begin? Many people will sensibly start the job of being their own investment manager as conventional investors. The conventional investor is hesitant to trust his or her own judgment, and prefers to rely on the consensus of professional opinion. The conventional investor is probably hesitant to 'think SEU' and is still not quite convinced that a share such as Robb Caledon is part of a low-risk investment strategy. I shall describe a strategy for the conventional investor and then suggest how that strategy might be developed by those who are more ready to use their own judgment.

Even twenty or thirty years ago, the commonest form of long-term saving was through the investment funds of life insurance companies, which managed a complete range of investments – shares, bonds and property. In this way, the conventional investor could hand over investment allocation decisions to a fund manager. But recent returns on with profits policies have been poor, the basis on which returns are determined opaque, and these are no longer attractive investments (except to those who sell them). Even conventional investors must now make their own asset allocation decisions.

Large institutions that are conventional investors get advice on asset allocation from consultants, such as Mercer or Watson Wyatt. Most of these firms originated as actuarial practices (actuaries measure the liabilities of insurance companies or pension funds) and have broadened their business activities. Consultants will usually base their advice on portfolio models and on their knowledge of what other similarly placed investors are doing. The activities of consultants are a means of disseminating conventional thinking.

Reports such as those compiled by WM show what these conventional investors do. As a result of the decisions of its managers and trustees, with their consultants in 2007, the average local authority pension fund held around 70% of its portfolio in shares. Slightly more than half of these shares were in UK companies, the balance in foreign equities. The typical pension fund held 15% – 20% in bonds, 5%-10% in property, and around 5% in cash and other assets.

The conventional investor can, simply and cheaply, replicate the portfolio of these institutions with a sum as small as £10,000. The UK share component can be purchased through either an index-tracking unit trust or an exchange traded fund. The Fidelity and F&C index tracker funds have total expense ratios of around 0.3% per year.

Avoid index funds with charges little below those of active managers. The popular Virgin Money index fund charges 1% per year while the Halifax index tracker imposes an astonishing management fee of 1.5% per annum. Ensure that the TER (which funds must disclose) is below 0.5%. There is not much to choose between the Fidelity or F&C funds and an exchange traded fund such as Barclays iShare or Lyxor linked to a UK index. Put £4000 of your £10,000 in one of these investments.

For the foreign component you also have the choice of an index-tracking trust, such as that from Norwich Union, or an exchange traded fund linked to the MSCI World Index. The Norwich Union tracker excludes the UK, so you might put £3000 in that. If you buy the MSCI ETF, about 15% of the world index that it replicates is the UK, so that your international component includes about £500 worth of British shares anyway. So if you opt for the ETF, lower the component of your portfolio to £3500 and increase the world component to £3500.

£2000 is earmarked for bonds. You may be able to hold bonds in your internet stockbroker's account, but some basic dealing services do not offer this option. You can buy British government stock online through the Debt Management Office. However – and absurdly – you may find it cheaper to buy bonds through an exchange traded fund. Moreover, an ETF such as the iShare all British Government Bond Index Fund saves the conventional investor the worry of deciding which British government bond to buy.

Finally, there is £1000 for property. You are not going to buy a property of your own for £1000, so your choice is between funds. The simplest way is to buy shares in a closed-end fund. When I started writing this book, these funds were at a premium, but as the book was completed they were at substantial discounts. The two largest British property companies, Land Securities and British Land, each own a diversified range of prime properties, mostly in the UK. The shares of these companies are mostly held by institutional investors. The dismal performance of retail property funds described in Table 10 gives reason for concern that fund managers have favoured institutional clients over retail investors in their allocation of properties.

You can avoid this problem by choosing a suitable closed-end fund. Put £1000 into one of these – or perhaps a bit less, since these companies use gearing to enable you to own more underlying property than the value of the investment.

And that is it. With four clicks of a mouse you have a diversified portfolio similar to that adopted by a well-advised large investment fund with long-term aspirations to total return. And you have constructed it at low initial and ongoing cost. You can safely forget about this portfolio for a long time – years if you like. Your investments may or may not do well, but their performance will most likely be similar to, but better than, the balanced portfolio a consultant or adviser would construct on your behalf. Similar to, because it reproduces the balanced portfolio of the conventional institutional investor; better than, because you have greatly reduced the costs of establishment and management.

You should have aspirations to do better still. The conventional investor should consider separating a part of his or her portfolio in order to test his or her own judgment. As experience and confidence grow, the plan is to devote more and more funds to intelligent investment.

CHAPTER 11

THE INTELLIGENT INVESTOR

Matching assets and liabilities

As a conventional investor, you don't really have to give much thought to your investment objectives. Historically most conventional investors didn't; they simply did what others did. In the last decade, however, consultants have encouraged large institutional investors to adopt liability-driven strategies that match portfolios to investment objectives. This principle is right for both institutions and individuals. The risk that is relevant is the risk of failure to achieve your realistic investment objectives. Your investment objectives are personal and so must be your concept of risk.

Some people save to make a specific purchase. But most plans for future expenditure are less well defined, and full of unknown unknowns as well as known unknowns. The same is true of income, and personal circumstances. Most investors want to secure their consumption in the medium and long-term, without very specific notions of the items of expenditure or the times when that will be incurred. They save for retirement, or a rainy day.

Retirement saving should take priority. At the beginning of the last chapter I raised the question of whether you were a net saver or a net spender and offered an illustrative calculation of what you might need to save. You might want to make a similar calculation based on your own circumstances. You will want to tweak the figures in many ways. You will probably need less in retirement than in your working lifetime. You are likely to spend less, you will pay less tax, and you will have some other sources of pension income. At age sixty-five, life expectancy for men is today seventeen years and twenty years for women. Readers of this book are, on average, healthier than average[1] so your plan should cover at least twenty-five years. But – if you can – you should also plan to save for more than twenty-five years. Your capacity to save may increase over time, along with your income. You will already have some assets. Your calculation needs to be tailored to your particular circumstances.

This is the sort of problem that a model helps to solve. Remember that no such calculation will be true – there are too many unknown unknowns for that. But the sum can be illuminating and help illustrate whether your hopes and plans are feasible. There are some useful programmes on the internet. But with simple arithmetic you – or your children or grandchildren – should be able to construct a spreadsheet to illuminate it.

While your own circumstances will be particular, the meaning of financial security for most readers of this book is certainty about their future standard of living. There are several threats to the achievement of such security through an investment portfolio. The portfolio may decline in monetary value through market risk or credit risk. The monetary value of the portfolio may lose its purchasing power through inflation risk.

But the world is also uncertain. There are many historical instances of people who thought they had secured their financial future, but who were proved wrong. Wealthy Central Europeans, who had never expected to work for a living, discovered in the economic turbulence of the 1920s that they had lost all they had, because banks failed or because hyperinflation made their savings worthless. Prosperous Jews thought that owning their own houses gave them security, but discovered when Nazi persecution made it impossible for them to enjoy their German property, that they would have been better off with assets overseas.

It is disconcerting to realise that there is no such thing as security

1 Seriously. If you are reading this book, you are likely to have educational, income and occupational characteristics that are associated with above-average longevity.

in an investment portfolio. There is no security because there is no certainty. Do not confuse the control of risk with certainty. Certainty is knowing what is going to happen, but perhaps what is going to happen is not very satisfactory. The man who knows he is going to be executed tomorrow has certainty but not security. More generally, low aspirations give a degree of certainty but rarely security.

People who crave certainty typically frequently achieve the appearance of certainty by relinquishing control over their lives, only to find there are no certainties. People who sought careers they thought offered lifetime employment only to have their employers reneging on the promise. People who thought that giving most of their retirement savings to Equitable Life offered safety and diversification. People who make career and retirement plans and are suddenly diagnosed with a grave illness. The lowest percentiles of the risk distribution are generally the consequence of wholly unanticipated events.

The citizens of East Germany operated in a predictable environment at the price of a dull life and a modest standard of living. Many of them were willing to accept that deal, only to witness the collapse of the regime which had made the offer. To take control of one's own life or financial affairs may seem to create uncertainty, but it is a prerequisite of security in a world that is inescapably uncertain The most attractive financial goal for most people is to have enough money not to worry about money.

But it is impossible to eliminate such worries altogether, as those twentieth-century European households discovered. A few investment gurus, harbingers of the apocalypse, recommend gold bars, or the equivalent, which can be cashed in the event of financial collapse. Barton Biggs, Morgan Stanley's long-term naysayer, has urged everyone to have 'a farm or a ranch somewhat far off the beaten track but which you can get to quickly and easily'. This is not a realistic recommendation for most people. But there are episodes in history in which coins or jewellery have literally been lifesavers. An insurance policy like this is sometimes described as a real option. A financial option pays off if the market price is above (or below) the strike price. The uncertain world offers, and requires, many real options, which pay off in unlikely contingencies.

If your investment goal is a specific purchase, the lowest risk method of achieving that objective may be to buy it now, even if you have to borrow. If you accept that risk is failure to achieve your realistic investment objectives, then both the financial difficulty that follows excessive ambition and the inability to achieve your financial goals are risks. You will have to balance the risk that servicing the borrowing will prove difficult against the risk that you will not be able to afford to make the purchase in future. We are taught to regard the former, but not the latter, as a risk – to shun failure, but to accept disappointment. Both are causes of unhappiness and regret.

If you cannot, or do not want to, achieve your goal immediately, then you may be able to hedge it in whole or part. A secondary property is the most common specific investment objective. The clearer you are about its characteristics, the better placed you are to hedge. If it is a UK property, and your time horizon is reasonably long, then buy-to-let property may be relevant. If you are determined to buy a house in France, then you can bias your portfolio towards property and assets denominated in euros.

Diversification adds to security because combining uncorrelated risky assets reduces the average risk in a portfolio but not the average return. Diversification also adds to security because diversification gives you a range of options. Neither you, nor anyone else, can know what will pay off in contingencies that have not been anticipated. If you don't know which tool you will need, have as many as possible in your bag.

The illusory security of cash and bonds

Cash, and short-dated bonds are often described as low-risk investments. But they are not low-risk investments for those who want to protect their future real living standards. Many people find that statement difficult. Part of the problem is confusion between the minimisation of risk and the search for certainty. With cash and short-dated bonds you know – in a sense – what is going to happen. But if security is confidence in your long-term standard of living – the ability to be relaxed about retirement, the confidence that you can one day buy the property you have dreamed about – then cash does not provide it. The inflation protection provided by index-linked bonds offers greater security. Even then it is difficult to match the bonds exactly to your personal objectives. You are exposed to personal inflation risk as well as interest rate risk and the return is extremely low. Currently most maturities offer a real yield below 1%.

Consider the likely outcomes of, say, a twenty-five-year investment in bonds with a twenty-five-year investment in equities within the framework I described in Chapter 7. This is a thought experiment – we cannot actually build a model that describes these distributions, because of fundamental uncertainty, although there are actuaries and consultants who pretend they can. If we are being pessimistic, we will focus our attention on the lowest percentiles of these distributions.

If the return you earn on your shares is in the lowest percentile of the distribution of equity returns, then you will certainly wish you had been in cash. That does not establish that cash is safer than equities. After all, if you experienced the lowest percentile of the distribution of cash returns, you will wish you had been in equities. In fact, if you experience the 50th, or perhaps even the 80th, percentile of the distribution of cash returns, you will wish you had been in equities. The relevant question – and the distinction here is crucial – is whether the first percentile of the distribution of outcomes of holding cash is better or worse than the first percentile of the distribution of outcomes of holding equities. The answer to that question is not obvious.

The difficulty of making such comparisons is particularly acute for these extreme percentiles, which are typically generated not by risks but from uncertainties. Extreme events are sometimes the result of identified, but very low probability, risks which had been identified. But extreme investment outcomes are most often a consequence of the large-scale breakdown of social, political and economic institutions. In Britain, such breakdown was within sight on three occasions in the last century: in 1931, when the Great Depression threatened political stability; in 1940, when Britain faced the real prospect of hostile invasion; and in 1974, when markets collapsed as a weak government presided over inflation that seemed out of control. The United States survived the political and economic crisis that had closed the nation's banks as Franklin Roosevelt was inaugurated President in 1933.

In all these cases, breakdown was averted. But in none was the margin so wide as to suggest that such breakdown was inconceivable. In Germany, extensive institutional collapse occurred twice in the twentieth century: first, as a result of defeat in the First World War and its political and economic consequences; and then as a result of the seizure of power by the Nazis in 1933. In both the German experiences, holders of real assets generally did better than holders of cash or bonds (although in the Russian revolution, for example, only overseas assets left holders with anything at all).

The extreme percentiles of the risk distributions are the result of these apocalyptic outcomes. The financial failures with which we are more recently familiar – the oil stock market meltdown and hyperinflation of the 1970s, or the credit bubble of 2007-2008 – represent bad, but not extreme, percentiles of the risk distribution. Milder crises – the Asian collapse of 1997-8 or the bursting of the New Economy bubble – are adverse outcomes, but only moderately so. All these events, however, are sufficiently abnormal to have fallen outside the scope of most conventional modelling.

The greater certainty that cash appears to provide is perhaps only that exceptionally favourable outcomes are unlikely, since nothing can provide certainty that exceptionally unfavourable outcomes are unlikely. A portfolio of bonds offers little security, even the relatively stable political and economic environment in Britain. Investors in consols lost more or less their entire wealth in the course of the twentieth century. A portfolio of indexed bonds would perform better, although this is a modern asset category that has never been tested in extreme conditions. Risks can never be eliminated, and uncertainties are inescapable.

I don't think cash or conventional fixed interest bonds normally have a role in an intelligent investor's portfolio. You will want to keep enough cash on hand for impulse and emergency purchases. Many, probably most, of the investments in the intelligent investor's portfolio are as good as cash for these purposes. You can turn an investment in a blue chip share into money in the bank within a week.

But we employ mental accounting. We don't think of our liquid securities as cash. Like me, you will probably keep more money in a deposit account than you need. If you have an offset mortgage, you can at least reduce the cost of this habit.

These conclusions represent a very different approach to risk from that of the conventional investor. Most financial advisers will recommend a mix of safe and risky assets, assuming that the meaning of safety is both obvious and universal, and that investors need to be paid a premium to relinquish that safety.

That conventional view, which is illuminating but no more than partly true, is that there is a tradeoff between risk and return. But there is a critical difference, as the tale of Robb Caledon illustrated, between the volatility of an individual asset and the risks and uncertainties in your portfolio. The conventional investor – and the conventional investor's adviser – is often confused between the two. Even if high risks and high expected returns were indissolubly associated at the level of the individual security, it does not follow that high risks and high returns would be associated in a portfolio. You cannot measure the risk of a portfolio by simply aggregating the risks of individual investments. A portfolio that consists of a collection of conventional but individually risky investments, like Robb Caledon, can be a low-risk portfolio. Such a portfolio may carry a lower risk, in fact, than a collection of blue chips – individually safe, but with returns that are likely to be strongly correlated with each other. This is the illuminating insight of the capital asset pricing model, and that insight remains valid even though the CAPM is not true.

In fact, the insight is more profitable for investors precisely because the capital asset pricing model is not true. The pattern of returns on different assets is the result of the market as voting machine – it reflects other people's views of risk, uncertainty and security. Paradoxically, although the equity risk premium is at the heart of the capital asset pricing model, the CAPM framework struggles to explain the size of the premium. In common with the returns on other risky assets it is much larger than could be justified by the risk aversion associated with diminishing marginal utility. The return to risk is governed by the average of other people's attitudes to risk. Other people's attitudes to risk are different from yours. They avoid mistakes for which they might be criticised. They are wedded to benchmarks. They do not 'think SEU'. They focus on individual assets, rather than the risk of their overall portfolio. Their mistakes provide your opportunities.

The prudent spending rate

Intelligent investors think 'total return' and so, nowadays, do most conventional investors. The trustees of charitable endowments, once limited to spending their annual income, are today encouraged to think total return. But, faced with year-to-year volatility of total return, they have to make a decision about how much it is prudent to spend. So will you. An individual who has retired, and owns a portfolio of assets must decide how much he or she can safely withdraw.

The definition of income given by the economist John Hicks provides the starting point. Hicks argued that income is what a man can spend and still expect to be as well off at the end of the year as at the beginning. (The sexism is remarkable since Hicks's formidable wife was a much better practical manager than her husband.) So if you plan for a 10% total return, and achieve it, you could spend 10% of the value of your portfolio each year and still meet Hicks's test.

Well, not quite. First, 10% is a target, not money in the bank. Prudence suggests you should plan for less. Second, taxes will eat into your total return. I've suggested you might allow 2% for that, giving a realistic target of 8%. Third, inflation will erode the value of your assets. Even if prices rise at only 2% per annum, you will need to earn a 2% total return simply to stand still. Taking these factors of prudence, tax and inflation together, you might conclude that spending 4% – 5% of assets each year would be consistent with Hicks's test. This is the sort of figure – call it the prudent spending rate – widely used by sophisticated charitable funds such as university endowments. The prudent spending rate should be a little less than your target rate real post-tax of return, and revised from time to time in line with experience.

As an individual, you might choose a prudent spending rate a little higher than 4% to 5%. Trustees must be more conservative than individuals. Universities hope to exist for ever. St John's College has already clocked up over 450 years. You, however, are mortal. Ben Franklin famously remarked that only two things were inevitable:

death and taxes. For individuals, both are inevitable; for institutions, neither applies. In setting a target rate of return, you might plausibly conclude that one offsets the other.

Older people might be a little less conservative. Buying an annuity was a traditional method of providing for security in old age. In the modern world, these investments are not attractive. Annuity rates are poor, because of high charges and investment strategies that focus on individually low-risk assets. There is also the problem of moral hazard created by information asymmetry. Annuities are bought by people in excellent health, not people with low life expectancies. Purchasers are more long lived than the population as a whole. That is why compulsory purchase annuities, which people may be obliged to buy on the maturity of their pension funds, offer better returns.

A man aged sixty-five can expect to live another seventeen years, but an annuity for him will yield only 7.5% and, if linked to inflation, less than 5%. The indexed annuity will give you some security – the conventional annuity less – but not security against the costs of long-term care, which may be substantial for the very old. You will generally do better to aim for a high target rate of return through intelligent investment; be conservative in your assessment of Hicksian income; and aim to live for ever.

If you are managing investments for total return, you may well find that annual interest and dividends are less than your prudent spending rate. If so, you will need to sell assets from time to time if your expenditure matches your prudent spending.

It requires discipline to resist mental accounting. The notion that a prudent person spends no more than his or her income is firmly ingrained in our culture, and for good reasons. A wise farmer would divide the crop into the amount that should feed his family – the income – and the amount – the capital – that should be planted for next year's crop. But principles that worked well on the land do not necessarily serve as well in a world of swaps and derivatives. Habits honed by evolution can be costly. One mechanism for challenging this mental accounting is to set up an automatic transfer from your savings or stockbroker's account to your current account.

Contrary thinking

The conventional investor avoids judgments wherever possible. The intelligent investor is willing to make judgments. Most retail investors show bad judgment. The average investor does much worse than the market average mutual fund. An American company, Dalbar, has for many years monitored the actual return earned by investors in mutual funds. Their extraordinary finding is that the average actual annual return over the last twenty years has been 7% points worse than the market index and far below the return earned by the average fund.

Why? The average mutual fund investor, with encouragement from the financial services industry, gets timing badly wrong. Momentum effects are picked up most quickly by proprietary traders, next by professional fund managers, and finally by the marketing departments of financial services businesses. Their salespeople, naturally, promote the funds that have recently done best. So money floods into fashionable sectors. Retail investors bought technology in 1999-2000, and were encouraged to buy bond funds after equity markets had collapsed. Most recently, property funds were strongly promoted. In each case, investors bought at the top and quickly incurred losses.

Retail investors, towards the back of the crowd, tend to suffer from mean reversion rather than benefit from momentum. They enter the market when short-term positive serial correlation turns into long-term negative serial correlation. Jaded investors later sell the funds that promised much but delivered little. They get it wrong both when they buy and when they sell. I suspect that more than a few readers of this book recognise their own experience.

Timing peaks and troughs in the market is as hopeless as looking for hot tips. Professional doomsters continually predict market crashes and are, like stopped clocks, occasionally right. Chartists detect patterns or investment indicators that provide buy and sell signals in randomly generated data. There is little evidence of anyone, amateur or professional, generating superior returns from systematic identification of the tops and bottoms of market cycles.

George Soros and Warren Buffett understood well that the 1999-2000 New Economy bubble would burst and that markets would crash. But they didn't know the date, and so they didn't profit. Even if you know that long-term mean reversion will eventually lead prices back towards fundamental values, you can't tell when. If Soros and Buffett can't – and no longer try – nor can you.

Once you have accepted that you can't time the market, there is a great deal you can still do. The dismal record of mutual fund investors suggests a place to start. Watch what these people do, and do the opposite. Their underperformance will be your outperformance. Look at the sectors promoted in the advertisements in the Saturday papers. These are the sectors to avoid. When the promotions favour technology and emerging markets, think infrastructure and property. When they show photographs of roads and offices, think technology and emerging markets. Be contrarian. Your aim is to avoid following in the rear of the crowd, and to be travelling in a different – even the opposite – direction.

Modern financial markets are dominated by the power of conventional thinking. City folk share superficial views with each other and project current trends too far and too fast. Social and commercial pressures, reinforced by ubiquitous benchmarking, encourage professional fund managers to act on these widely shared opinions regardless of private reservations.

There is, almost always, an underlying element of truth in conventional thinking. The internet was an important commercial and social development. The economic progress of China and India does have a major impact on the global economy. This information is 'in the price'. More than that – the herd behaviour of professional investors means that these conventional opinions are more than fully in the price. That is part of the reason why prices display positive serial correlation in the short run and negative serial correlation in the long run. In the short run, momentum drives prices as fashion spreads; in the long run, mean reversion drives prices as fashion fades.

There are two possible ways of exploiting this behaviour. One is to ride momentum. But this is like riding a tiger. The experience will certainly be stressful and exciting and it may be rewarding for a time, but the difficulty of timing accurately when you get on and when you get off is so great that, sooner or later, it is probable that you will be mauled (as happened to Julian Robertson). There is not much evidence that anyone can do it successfully over a long period. If anyone can do it successfully, it will almost certainly be someone very close to the market, who can detect shifts in sentiment in that brief interval when it is still possible to act but before these shifts are incorporated in prices. It is very unlikely that you will be that person.

In the second strategy – defying the fashion – the retail investor potentially has an advantage over the professional. Not being close to the market means that you are not subject to the pressures the professionals experience. You don't have to talk to trustees or clients who want to act on the news they have read in the newspaper that morning (and which everyone else has also read) – that China is growing rapidly or that the housing market is entering the doldrums.

The converse of the power of conventional thinking is the power of contrarian investment. There is something paradoxical in the idea that the best way to use the expertise of the financial services industry is to do the opposite of what it recommends. This is not because that expertise is no good. It is because that expertise is 'in the price' and characteristically more 'in the price' than is objectively justified.

Some of the biggest mistakes in my own investment history have been following the crowd when the crowd was going in the right direction – for example, buying European property in 2006 when the mind of the market identified it as an undervalued asset class. Even if the crowd is right about fundamental value (and in that case I think it was), the fashion is 'in the price'. When the fashion fades, so will some of the money you have paid (and within two years, it had).

Being contrarian should not be interpreted as perversity, or counter-suggestibility. Begin by limiting your contrarian strategy to broad asset categories and to funds. Be much more hesitant about taking a contrarian view of individual shares. There is a real likelihood that a share price has fallen because someone knows something you don't. It is a common mistake to believe that if a share once sold for 500p it will reach that value again. Most railway stocks, like most dot.com stocks, finally vanished from the scene at values far below their issue price. Often that value was zero. A stock which has fallen by 95% from its high had earlier fallen by 90% – and then halved in value.

A contrarian investor will, however, see cases where a stock has fallen for a specific reason but by an amount far larger than that specific reason would justify. The opportunity that first established Warren Buffett's reputation was provided when a fraud over cooking oil dented the reputation and, even more, the share price, of American Express. Buffett bought heavily. The scandal was soon forgotten by both customer and market, and the stock prices rose steadily. If, however, the fall had affected all housebuilders, or most Japanese stocks, then it is likely that the explanation of the price fall is to be found in general knowledge exaggerated in conventional thinking than in inside knowledge not yet available to the markets.

Contrarianism is equally relevant to your purchase of funds. Buy the funds that aren't promoted rather than the ones that are. Closed-end funds move to large discounts to asset value when the sector in which they specialise falls out of favour. This is an additional reason to favour investment trusts on discounts of 15% or more.

Market timing

Here is a scheme for beating the market that really works. Imagine a volatile share that sells for 50p in odd years and 100p in even years. If you invest £100 every year in this share, over a ten-year period you will have accumulated 1500 shares at an average price of 66.7p, well below the average market price, which is 75p.

This system will, on average, outperform the market and the more volatile the markets, the greater the gains. The method is known as pound (or dollar) cost averaging. It works through its built-in mechanism for buying more when prices are relatively low and less when prices are relatively high. No judgment is required by the investor that prices are relatively low or relatively high.

Many individuals do, and more should, make regular savings to build up an investment portfolio. Some investment managers use the benefits of pound-cost averaging and extol the benefits of a regular savings scheme in their marketing literature. On this occasion, believe them. The benefits are real. But keep an eye, as usual, on their charges. Regular saving is a practice you can organise for yourself. You do not need to pay someone a commission to take direct debits from your account. (Halifax Sharedealing offers a very inexpensive scheme for regular investment.)

The effectiveness of pound-cost averaging illustrates how low share prices are an opportunity rather than a problem for the intelligent investor. Conventional investors are usually excited when they hear that the market is going up, disappointed when they learn that it has fallen. As Buffett has occasionally pointed out, this is odd. We are pleased when we hear that a favourite shop has a sale, or car dealers have reduced their prices. We want high prices when we are sellers, but low prices when we are buyers. We are usually only buyers of clothes or durable goods. However, for shares – as perhaps for cars and houses – we may be both buyers and sellers at different times.

People under the age of forty-five are probably better off with lower than higher house prices. As householders age, they may see the question differently. When we are fifty, we have probably bought the most expensive house we will ever buy. Young people are more likely to trade up to a more expensive house than down to a cheaper one. People in middle age may intend to move to a smaller property when their children leave the nest. Retirees may use equity release schemes to realise some of the value in their house.

For similar reasons, the investor should probably want share prices to be low when he or she is young, and high when he or she is old. It is facile, and often wrong, to think that investors benefit from market rises and suffer in declines. There are always as many purchases as sales.

When should the intelligent investor sell? The simple answer is 'Not very often'. Frequent trading endangers returns. But sometimes the mind of the market will take a security to a price well in excess of any reasonable estimate of its fundamental value. Money is a means to an end, not an end in itself, and you will sometimes sell investments in order to spend, especially if most of your total return is capital gains. In recent years, the rate at which small companies have been acquired has ensured that portfolios have a regular inflow of cash from acquisitions. This will not be true if you invest mainly in funds rather than individual securities. But if you invest in well-chosen funds, you have even less reason to wish to trade.

Pound-cost averaging makes sense for both conventional and intelligent investors. Conventional investors can feel relieved that their approach yields profits without requiring judgment. Intelligent investors know that market timing is unlikely to make money and can feel happy with an approach that is inherently contrarian. The reasoning that makes pound-cost averaging attractive applies to decisions about asset classes as well as to decisions about market timing. Let's see how.

Asset allocation

Investment funds submit data to the WM Company because both the consultants and the funds follow each other closely. Trustees or managers are required to set benchmarks for asset allocations, and deviations from the norm require considered justification. The easy and safe course for them is to do what other people are doing.

When an asset category rises in value, the proportion of that asset class in the benchmark increases. Individual investors may choose to follow the market allocation; institutional investors feel obliged to follow it. Such benchmarking has led to a steady increase in the share of equities, the best performing asset class, in conventional portfolios.

The consequences can be perverse. At the peak of the Japanese stock market bubble of the 1980s, Japanese shares accounted for almost half of the value of all shares – American, European, Brazilian, Australian – in the world. American and European investors, who had thought they were brave if 10% of their assets were in Japan, felt under pressure to acquire more securities in Japan. Fifteen years later, Japanese share prices had fallen, while those in other countries had risen. Today, Japan accounts for less than 10% of the market value of world indices.

Common sense suggests that an allocation of half your portfolio to Japan in the late 1980s was far too much, given that Japan never accounted for more than 10% of world output. Most investors did, at least intuitively, understand this. While few people fell comprehensively into this Japanese trap, many investors have been victims of milder versions of the error, buying technology shares, bonds, infrastructure and property at the wrong times. Looking at market weightings when deciding asset allocation leads institutions and fund managers to buy high and sell low. They purchase overpriced assets in order to achieve desired portfolio weightings.

The attempt to give precision to this common sense has led to a search for 'fundamental indices'. The idea behind a fundamental index is that asset-class weightings should be based, not on market value, but on some underlying measure of economic contribution. Intelligent investors look behind the financial assets they buy to the value of the productive assets that underpin them. A benchmark for allocation to Japan might, therefore, be Japanese national income as a percentage of world national income, implying a range of 5% – 10% that would remain unchanged by the vagaries of the Japanese stock markets.

From this perspective, the model pension fund portfolio contains a heavy concentration of oil companies, pharmaceutical businesses and banks, relative to the economic importance of these activities. The investor who has thought in terms of fundamental indices is bound to wonder why the standard local authority pension fund portfolio allocates ten times as much to shares as to property. Very large economic sectors, such as agriculture, education and health care, and legal and accounting services, are not represented at all in the model pension fund portfolio or only in very limited ways.

You can change that. There are few quoted securities in agriculture, education or health, but there are some. Although there are (as yet) no stock market prices for law firms or accountancy practices there are other businesses, such as recruitment agencies and public relations firms, whose fortunes are closely related. The conventional investor's assets are much less diversified than they might be.

The numbers that emerge from analysis based on fundamental indices may be illuminating but not true – certainly no one should regard them as more than qualitative grounds. The illuminating insight is that investors should be wary of allowing fluctuations in market prices to influence their target allocations to different asset classes. If the price of property rises relative to the price of your other assets, consider reducing the proportion of your assets you hold in property, and vice versa. Many people find this paradoxical. Should we really sell securities just because they have done well? In a world characterised by momentum and mean reversion, you should. That way you can realise the benefits of pound-cost averaging in asset allocation as well as market timing.

But what is the right asset allocation? How should an intelligent investor's portfolio be divided between shares, bonds and property? I'm not sure that this is the right way to pose the asset allocation question. To do so supposes that all shares are much more like each other than they are like any of the assets in the other categories, such as property and bonds, and that the same is in turn true of these asset categories.

For the assets that local authority pension funds typically hold, this may well be true. Their share portfolio will mainly contain large, global companies, whose prices tend to go up and down together; the bonds will mainly be medium- and long-dated British government securities; the properties will mainly be well located city centre office blocks with similar prospective growth in both rental levels and capital values. These pension funds will have followed the conventional investor's strategy of minimising the risks on individual investments rather than the intelligent investor's strategy of looking at the risk of their portfolio as a whole. So when they buy property, they buy whichever category of property their advisers currently tout as the best mixture of return and reward, and they buy several such properties. They fail to diversify effectively.

The 'mind your portfolio' principle implies that you should look at the expected return from individual assets and their correlation with your overall portfolio. Your objective is that every single investment you buy should significantly diversify your portfolio. You don't need, and probably shouldn't have, an intermediate process of asset allocation. Asset allocation percentages will be the result, not the preliminary, of diversifying investment decisions about individual securities. In the next chapter I'll discuss how these securities should be selected.

CHAPTER 12

INTELLIGENT INVESTMENT

Diversify

Most financial advisers will tell you that the conventional investor uses a low-risk strategy. I disagree. Between 2000 and 2002 the conventional investor's portfolio would have fallen in value by around 30%. Many pension funds, insurance companies and charities suffered badly during that period. Nor was that fall unprecedented. The loss in 1973-4 would have been greater and there would have been other significant dips in value in the meantime.

The issue, once again, is the different meanings different people attach to the term risk. Conventional investors like local authority pension funds focus on large, widely held, stocks. They interpret low risk as meaning avoidance of investments that involve the possibility of loss. Each individual stock in their portfolio is low risk.

From the perspective of the pension fund trustees and their investment managers, such a perspective is understandable. As I have emphasised, the major risk a financial adviser runs is not the risk that his clients do badly but the risk that his clients do worse than other people. Every committee and large organisation is crowded with people who will say 'I told you so' when things go wrong. The conventional investor will be reluctant ever to hold an asset which he or she can be criticised for having bought. I can take more individual stock risks with my personal investment portfolio because I don't have to justify decisions, before or after the event. I can do that even though my personal style is to maintain a low portfolio risk. I am free to 'mind my portfolio', and so are you. The typical institutional investor is not. Robb Caledon would be a risky purchase for anyone managing someone else's funds, because there is a substantial probability of total loss.

A portfolio indexed to the FTSE 100 or all-share index contains a lot of shares. That is not the same as diversification. Look behind the index and the broad allocations to asset categories and see the disposition of the conventional investor's £10,000. You will have large holdings in the oil majors – Exxon, Shell and BP, and in General Electric, Glaxo, Vodafone and Microsoft. There will be a substantial chunk in the major international banks – HSBC, Citigroup, JP Morgan Chase, Royal Bank of Scotland, Barclays. All these companies sell mainly to the advanced economies of the United States and Western Europe. Their fortunes wax and wane with the world economy, and so does market sentiment towards them. All bank shares have fallen over the last year. Returns from all these stocks are strongly correlated with each other and stocks like these make up most of the 70% of the portfolio that the conventional investor holds in equities. The conventional investor's portfolio is not well diversified.

An emphasis on diversification implies a different approach to the selection of stocks and funds. Almost everyone, thinking about investment opportunities, begins by asking the question 'What is likely to go up?' But the general knowledge about companies, industries and countries is knowledge that you share with everyone else and is already 'in the price'. The record of most investment professionals in knowing what will go up is poor. You don't know what is going to go up. That is why you may have been tempted to take advice. But those who offer to advise you have little or no more valuable knowledge than you, and different interests.

The construction of a diversified portfolio requires as much attention to correlation as expected return. Such an approach means rejecting investments for which there is a plausible case because the returns from these investments are correlated with investments you already have. This will happen often, since the reasons that made the earlier purchase seem attractive may also apply to the new one. An indexed portfolio is more diversified than a portfolio in which you keep using similar arguments to buy more assets of the same kind. An indexed portfolio is neither diversified nor contrarian, because the weights in the index are driven by the power of conventional thinking. A more diversified portfolio should offer you expected returns similar to those of an indexed portfolio with lower volatility. (I need to enter again the health warning that if you accept the conclusions of the CAPM, as most finance academics though few practical people do, then the diversified strategy will be so popular that it will force down the average return from adopting it. Perhaps that should be true, but I don't think it is.)

Increasing diversification means less in banks, pharmaceuticals and oil companies, and more in sectors whose performance is less strongly correlated with the investments you already hold. General insurance companies and housebuilders, for example, experience cycles of their own that are not necessarily in sync with the general economic cycle.

Think about activities like gold mining and timber, whose performance is likely to be very different from that of the general stock market. Diversify internationally. But there is no point in reducing your holding in Glaxo in order to increase your holding in Pfizer – these companies have very similar businesses. A small pharmaceutical company – whether British or American – whose fortunes will probably rise or fall with the success of individual drugs, will offer returns with lower correlation. Look to Japan, or Russia or Taiwan, but real diversification from these investments will come from companies oriented to their domestic economies, rather than businesses with which you are more familiar. Sony, Gazprom and Lenovo sell to the same people as Microsoft, Shell and Vodafone.

Fund selection

Most investors will, and should, begin with funds rather than individual stocks. Funds may be distinguished by investment style or by sectoral or geographic specialisation. Choose funds whose returns are not strongly correlated with each other – be diversified. Choose funds which are out of favour rather than fashionable – be contrarian.

A website like Morningstar or Trustnet will give you a wide – far too wide – selection. In every category, there are many similar funds doing similar things. I am not going to recommend specific funds, but the criteria I will describe will narrow the range very considerably.

The list of exchange traded funds (which you will not find on these sites) is a good place to begin. Issuers of ETFs – such as Barclays iShares and Lyxor – offer a variety of country options. You can invest not just in the US and US indices, but in Brazil, Taiwan and other small and emerging markets. In the larger markets, you can choose to focus on smaller or larger companies, or on a particular sector, like utilities or real estate. Plan to build up a diversified portfolio of such funds, emphasising sectors that are unfashionable.

Then consider an allocation to actively managed funds. Pick two or three idiosyncratic funds with widely different styles and approaches. This gives a better balance of risk and return. But keep a close eye on charges. A company that charges 1% or more for a closet index fund is ripping you off. Buying a closed-end fund with a low TER and a large discount to asset value gives you a chance of earning the return generated by the underlying productive investments. Most funds go to a discount of 15% or more from time to time if you are content to wait. The widening of the discount is a good contrarian signal when the result of the unfashionability of the sector rather than the poor performance of the fund. If the TER is above 1%, the fund must justify these charges by its distinctive style (low correlation with market indices) and proven success.

How to distinguish proven success from the 'hot hand'? Favour funds that are strongly identified with an individual. Good fund managers are people rather than corporations although, on occasion good processes are the creation of innovative founders. Idiosyncratic funds with a strong record are typically provided by boutiques, but there are exceptions – Anthony Bolton ran funds for Fidelity as did the legendary US manager, Peter Lynch.

Buy funds that have a history of good performance, but look for a long history and, above all, ensure that the track record was good both before and after the fund manager became famous. Do not follow names that are famous for reasons other than their investment performance, such as supermum Nicola Horlick or the ubiquitous Richard Branson. Most good track records are the product of lucky streaks, and are then aggressively marketed, only to disappear. There is some evidence of investment skill but it is rare.

Property

While most equity funds are open ended, most property funds are closed end. Such funds may, since 2007, be real estate investment trusts (REITs). Companies with REIT status are tax exempt so that shareholders are taxed broadly as if they owned a share of the properties of the fund. Land Securities and British Land, the largest UK property funds, are REITs. Some other property funds, such as F & C Commercial Property Fund, achieve a similar effect by registering the company offshore while being listed in London. There are also many closed-end property funds that do not qualify as REITs, typically those with large development programmes, extensive borrowings, or that are invested largely overseas.

Closed-end property funds generally have substantial leverage – much more so than closed-end funds that invest in shares. You need to be careful about this leverage. Your £1000 investment in a fund might correspond to £3000 of property and £2000 of borrowings. If you hold geared assets, you should remember the 'mind your portfolio' principle. An investment of £1000 in such a fund, with the balance of £2000 in bonds, would give you the same property exposure as £1000 in a leveraged open-ended fund.

These open-ended property funds mostly do not use leverage. Some, such as Morley and New Star, are invested directly in property, and they sell and redeem units at a price that reflects the value of the underlying assets. When the property market fell in 2007 some open-ended funds suspended redemption. Some open-ended property funds, such as Aberdeen, invest only in REITs and other property shares. While some property funds cover a wide spectrum of properties, most have a bias towards particular geographical areas or sectors. As in other areas of investment, closed-end funds are attractive when you can buy them at significant discounts to their asset value (which, at the moment of writing, you can); again, do not buy closed-end funds at a premium. You should expect to pay higher management charges for a property fund than for an equity fund, because the costs of looking after buildings are greater than the costs of looking after paper.

Following the boom in UK property over the last decade, British investors have been increasingly interested in property in continental Europe, including Eastern Europe, and many small companies have been established to meet this demand. The proliferation of these new investment vehicles in the property market has meant the entry of promoters who levy high charges but who may have limited expertise. You do not have to buy foreign property through UK based funds. You can easily buy REITs or property companies domiciled in American or European markets, such as Vornado (the largest US REIT) or Unibail (a French company, the largest quoted property business in continental Europe).

With such a range of possibilities, it is easy with two or three purchases to construct a portfolio of property assets diversified across different kinds of property – offices, shops, industrial, residential – and across geographical locations – Britain, the rest of Europe, North America.

Stock picking

As your experience of intelligent investment grows, you will wish to consider individual stocks. Even if you have a large, diversified portfolio, you will probably not own more than 99% of the stocks you could buy. That means you can, and should, be extremely selective. It is as though you were speed dating thousands of potential partners. You are fortunate in being spoilt for choice and one good reason for rejection is enough.

The basic principles of stock picking follow from Chapters 5 through 8. You are concerned with fundamental value, not momentum in the share price; with the characteristics of the company, not the stock price history. Conventional investors are unduly averse to specific risk which affects one company alone and which can and should be diversified. You do not mind that an individual stock is risky, so long as it does not add greatly to the risk of your portfolio as a whole. That implies, of course, that you can understand what the risks are.

If conventional investors are sometimes too prone to avoid risk – the known unknowns – they are also too prone to accept uncertainties – the unknown unknowns. Use probabilities to assess risk; be detached; and minimise uncertainties by knowing when you don't know.

Everywhere and always in financial markets, you are vulnerable to information asymmetry. The company and its executives know more – or are at least capable of knowing more – than you do. The greater the information asymmetry, the more likely it is that you are being offered a lemon. If you don't understand something, or the affairs of the company or the strategy or construction of the fund appear unnecessarily difficult to understand, do not buy. If the share price is falling for inexplicable reasons, do not buy.

Institutional investors will have access to the research on companies that banks circulate to their clients. You will find it difficult to obtain much of this, although you can see similar material in magazines such as *Investor's Chronicle* or in newsletters (tip sheets). These reports are more useful for the information they obtain than the recommendations (though you probably will have readier access to the latter). You should understand a little of what these analysts do, not in order to reproduce their conclusions, but because their approach and conclusions are 'in the price'.

An analyst will provide 'coverage' of a group of companies with similar activities. If these businesses are very large, the analyst will be responsible for only a very few stocks, though an analyst of smaller companies may cover twenty or more. The bank that employs the analyst frequently hopes to obtain corporate finance business from the companies on which it undertakes research (or has already done so); for small companies, the bank that managed the IPO will often provide the only coverage. This limits objectivity.

An analyst is rewarded for 'good calls'. (The results of Thomson/Extel ratings, based on opinion polls of institutions, have a major influence on the reputation and remuneration of analysts.) A good call is a successful prediction of a sharp upward or downward movement in the share price. But the time-scale on which the call is judged will rarely exceed six months. Although many research reports appear to be concerned with fundamental value, a good call will often anticipate a news announcement relevant to the company (generally either merger and acquisition activity or a substantial revision to earnings expectations). Or, in the manner of Keynes' beauty contest, an analyst may make good calls by being quick to assess the changing mood of other analysts.

The favoured analyst will be close to the companies he follows, able to infer from nudges and winks whether announcements will be behind, or ahead of, market expectations. The less favoured analyst – one whose reporting has a critical tone – will be shut out. Analysts who take a negative view of a company frequently receive abuse from chief executives and complaints to the senior management of the banks that employ them.

As I described in Chapter 5, the effect of Big Bang was to transform analysts into a sales force for investment banks. Following the New Economy bubble, the damage to the reputations of the firms concerned, and pressure from regulators, forced investment bankers to concede greater independence to analysts. Recommendations still have a strongly positive bias, but the institutions at which they are aimed are able, at least in part, to discount this bias. Analysts' research is focused on short-term earnings announcements and projections.

Most analysts simply project current earnings in a mechanical fashion. Even if they are trying to assess fundamental value, they typically do the calculation by making estimates of earnings and translating them into a DCF model. These analysts' valuations are what is 'in the price'. Estimates of fundamental value play a relatively minor role.

Stock selection

A basic checklist for any company you consider investing in should contain the following points: the company should be clear and transparent in the presentation of its affairs and accounts; and the background and remuneration of its senior executives should suggest that they are experienced in and interested in the business, rather than people whose primary concerns are self-aggrandisement or self-enrichment. These are necessary precautions against information asymmetry, and necessary preliminaries to judging risks. If you wouldn't buy a used car from the directors, then you shouldn't buy a share in the company, and for essentially the same reasons.

There should also be a clear, comprehensible business model, based on a distinctive capability that has the potential to create sustainable and appropriable competitive advantage. The only sources of fundamental value are tangible assets and competitive advantage. If you cannot identify tangible assets from the accounts that support the valuation, or don't understand the source of the competitive advantage of the business, then you cannot judge either its fundamental value or the risks associated with it. Avoid unnecessary uncertainty.

You will normally look for companies that are soundly financed. Borrowings should be less than readily realisable assets and the business should generate cash. Operational risk in a company is inescapable. But when an established business compounds operational risk with financial risk, and becomes dependent on the indulgence of its bank or the vagaries of interest rates, and vulnerable to modest economic or business setbacks, it adds uncertainty to risk. Usually this vulnerability in profit and loss accounts or balance sheets is the product of debt-financed acquisitions or of financial engineering. Both large-scale acquisition and financial engineering generally give negative signals about the preoccupations of the company's management.

Where the weak balance sheet is the result of recent poor trading, the position may be more interesting. Most players in financial markets tell stories rather than think probabilities. They believe the company is going bust, or that it is not – rarely that there is a probability of 0.4 that it might. Analysts, brokers and fund managers are not often detached. They may still be in love with the purchase they made at a much higher price, or worried by the criticism they might receive from bosses or trustees who possess the benefit of hindsight. As at Robb Caledon, the market price of a risk investment may be a poor guide to the expected value.

Be wary of companies with growing profits and negative cash flow. A new, rapidly expanding business or a firm with a large investment programme may have transparent reasons for these. The difficulty of explaining the discrepancy between profits and cash should have steered intelligent investors away from both Enron and Vanco.

You can reduce uncertainties by focusing on stable businesses. There are fewer uncertainties in the markets for water – a monopoly whose basic technology was developed millennia ago – than in more competitive and exciting activities, like computers or biotechnology. Even companies in relatively stable markets can create uncertainty by programmes of acquisitions and disposals. Most of the fundamental value of any company derives from the cash it will generate five and more years into the future. If you don't know what the company will be doing five years from now, how can you assess its value? Such uncertainty is unnecessary and avoidable.

Look for clarity and transparency in the company's account of its affairs: a simple business model based on distinctive capability that offers sustainable competitive advantage; and a strong balance sheet with cash flow generation and a stable business. A stock that meets all of these criteria is unlikely to be a ten or twenty bagger, but you are looking for a reliable 10% of annual target return, not ten or twenty baggers. Most companies will fail at least one of these criteria. But there are many more fish in the sea. Your aim is to buy good companies on a contrarian basis, probably when their sector is out of fashion.

If investors generally applied these criteria in selecting stocks, their decisions would transform the behaviour of British corporations. And overwhelmingly for the better. There would be less financial engineering, fewer acquisitions, simpler and more modest executive remuneration. And, above all, less emphasis on investor relations activities to influence the mind of the market and more on the creation of fundamental value through the identification and development of competitive advantage in operating businesses.

The preoccupations of most professionals are elsewhere. They are focused on earnings guidance and their quarterly performance figures. They are fixated on 'corporate activity'; a term that is often simply a euphemism for mergers and acquisitions, and more generally means an announcement that may have a material effect on share prices. Such activity is the basis of market gossip, and keeps market turnover high.

The intelligent investor isn't, and doesn't want to be, party to that market gossip. The intelligent investor isn't seeking votes in the Thomson/Extel survey. Your reward comes from good investment returns, not from the bonuses you receive for the business you attract.

CHAPTER 13

THE CUSTOMERS' YACHTS

'Why do I want to buy what they want to sell?' This question is fundamental to investment. Both buyers and sellers own securities in the hope of income and capital gains. But the returns the buyer will obtain are exactly the returns the seller could have obtained. Why should you buy what they want to sell?

In any market in which there is wide and unresolvable uncertainty, in any market where participants have different information and beliefs, many trades will be the result of mistakes. In financial markets, uncertainty and differential information are endemic. When you trade you need to be confident that it is not you who are making the mistake. Bear in mind the old gambler's maxim: if you don't know who is the patsy in the room, you are.

Keep it simple. If you don't understand a financial product, don't buy it. We purchase cars and computers and many other things without understanding how they work – it is enough to understand their purpose. We rely on the reputation of Mercedes or Microsoft for our belief that their products will actually deliver what they promise. Many people dislike thinking about money, and would like to hand over their financial affairs to someone they can trust. Unfortunately, such trust isn't enough to deal with product complexity in modern financial markets. The nature of trade in financial services, and the ethics and behaviour of financial services businesses, are different. Good reputations seem to survive bad behaviour. Many of the suckers who were ripped off in the New Economy bubble came back to be victims of the credit bubble.

Scepticism is appropriate. If it sounds too good to be true, it usually is. In most markets, you tend to get what you pay for. The greater the extent of differential information, the less likely it is that costs and charges represent value. The most certain way of increasing returns on your investments is to pay less in fees and commissions.

You are on your own but, in the modern world, you are never alone with a computer. The contents of the last chapters are startlingly different from those I would have included even a decade ago. The internet gives cheap and easy access to financial products for everyone, and immediate access to information that only a decade ago required diligent research. Innovation in financial markets – such as the growth of exchange traded funds and property vehicles – have transformed the opportunities available to retail investors to build for themselves a portfolio that achieves low risk through wide diversification. The intelligent investor today is in greater danger of trading too much because it is easy, than of being deprived of opportunities because access is too difficult.

The market is a process that mediates among differential information. The activity of trading assimilates uncertainty and disagreement to establish 'the mind of the market'. The market is often described as a voting machine, weighing and evaluating different assessments to arrive at a market view. This line of thought leads to the efficient market hypothesis. All available information about securities, economic developments, the success and failure of business strategies, and our political and technological futures, is already in the price.

There is something in this argument, although it is a mistake to take it too seriously. The efficient market hypothesis is illuminating, but not true. There are investment lessons and profit opportunities both in what is illuminating, and in what is not true. Across the market as a whole, the profits on financial investment must ultimately depend on the profits on productive investment. For all the intricacies of modern finance, the yield of securities depends on the ability of trading businesses to find profitable ways of serving their customers; on the willingness of tenants to pay rents on shops, offices, houses and factories; and on the ability of companies, consumers and governments to service and repay loans that finance their recent investment or current consumption.

The value of companies depends on their ability to establish competitive advantages over their rivals and such sustainable competitive advantages are the only enduring source of superior returns. The value of a property depends on the rents derived from it. The value of a bond depends on the interest it yields and the principal it repays. These determinants of fundamental value necessarily drive securities prices in the long run.

The notion that market prices are the result of a plebiscite on competing estimates of fundamental value is far removed from the reality of frenzied trading in modern financial markets. Most participants are preoccupied, not with long-term economic trends and the competitive advantage of companies, but with evolving market opinion and the ephemeral news that passes across the Bloomberg screen.

In an efficient market what is 'in the price' is an average of divergent views. But often what is in the price is the manifestation of a common City view, generally held within the Square Mile, but not necessarily well-founded. The New Economy bubble was an extreme instance of widely held perceptions that were also widely at variance with reality. Prices that are going up tend to continue going up – markets are characterised in the short term by short-term serial price correlation, or momentum. In the long run, prices that have gone up by a lot tend to go down – there is mean reversion to fundamental value. If only we knew when the short run becomes the long!

It is possible, though unusual, to make money out of observing and anticipating market momentum. Some people, though not many, are close to the market and have an intuitive feel for, or perhaps an analytic understanding of, its determinants. Whatever the books on trading will tell you, the chances that the person who makes money out of observing and anticipating these fluctuations will be you, the retail investor, are very small.

The only basis on which the intelligent investor can hope to keep up with, far less beat, the market is by attention to fundamental value. Through attention to fundamental value, the intelligent investor gains a big advantage over investment professionals who are judged on their performance quarterly, or even more frequently. There is no way in which an investor, amateur or professional, who is focused on fundamental value can reliably outperform the market on a monthly or quarterly basis – the noise is far too loud. But, over the long run, mean reversion works in your favour.

Not being part of the conventional wisdom of these professionals gives you an opportunity to be contrarian. Contrarianism requires scepticism but is not perversity. The opportunity for contrarianism arises when the question 'Why do I want to buy what they want to sell?' can attract the answer 'Because they have bad reasons for wanting to sell it'. The investment community cannot afford to ignore the noise but you can. Patience pays. Assets are worth more to a long-term investor than to a trader.

The principal risk investment professionals run is the risk of underperformance relative to their peers. Most investment institutions benchmark their performance against their competitors and market averages. There are good reasons for this, but also malign consequences. In any event, what interests the intelligent investor is how much money he makes, not how much money he makes relative to other people. Relative performance doesn't pay bills.

Relative performance has no spending power, but money has equal spending power whether it comes as income or capital gain. Think 'total return'. Treat both income and capital gain as part of the yield on your investment. Set a prudent spending rate by reference to your expected total return over a period of years. If your underlying investment objective is capital growth, then reinvestment of dividends will contribute substantially to capital appreciation in the long run. If your underlying investment objective is to obtain a steady income from investments, then an 'income' can be generated, if necessary, through occasional sales from a growing portfolio. A 'think total return' strategy is equally relevant to investors who are accumulating wealth and investors who are using their assets to support their standard of living.

The return on productive investments provides the basis for realistic expectations of what an investment portfolio can yield. If you earn higher returns than the yield on productive investments, these returns can only be obtained at the expense of other people who are obtaining lower returns than the yield on productive investment. This may be because you are willing to take risks that they are not, or because you have a superior investment strategy. But you cannot expect consistently to derive more than a modest premium to market returns from these sources.

Your objectives colour your strategy. One justification for the substantial fees the financial services industry take from retail investors is that such investors need individually tailored advice. While there are some honest and conscientious independent financial advisers, the majority of people who make contact with small savers do not have the capacity or knowledge to give such advice, even if they had the inclination and the financial motivation. If you still doubt this, test them with some questions about the meanings of terms defined in the glossary.

I am not convinced that much tailoring of investment strategy to particular needs is required anyway. The most important issue is the stage of your working and investing life. Are you a net saver or a net spender? Most people have broadly similar investment objectives – to support their future standard of living, without more precise definition. For the vast majority of investors, risk is uncertainty about their future standard of living. These objectives define both the meaning of risk and your approach to risk.

I've given a lot of space in this book to different ways of thinking about risk, and described at length in Chapter 7 the theory I have called SEU. Treated both prescriptively and descriptively, this theory completely dominates quantitative approaches to investment today. Intelligent investors should learn to 'think SEU' – to understand its principles but not to follow them blindly. That means learning to think probabilities and expected values. Such an approach recognises that many different outcomes are possible, and assesses, even quantifies, the likelihood of attractive and unattractive outcomes.

SEU implies detachment in investment decisions. If you are a gambler by temperament, you may enjoy the search for a ten bagger, but the expected value of the search is likely to be negative. If you are concerned principally to minimise the regret that you will feel (or your bosses will make you feel) with hindsight then the expected value of your strategy is also likely to be negative. These losses of expected value are the costs of emotional involvement in your investments.

The most important implication of SEU is the 'mind your portfolio' principle. Every investment decision should be judged, not just by the character of the individual investment, but by its contribution it makes to your overall portfolio. An incidental, but large, benefit of being your own investment manager is that you are the only person who knows everything you are doing.

Like the efficient market hypothesis, SEU is an illuminating theory so long as you do not make the mistake of believing that it is true: true either as a prescriptive theory – What should I do? – or as a descriptive theory – How do market participants respond to risks and uncertainties? The conventional view is that you, the typical dumb investor, doesn't think SEU but markets do. This view is mistaken. Markets don't generally think this way, but you often, though by no means always, should. SEU is a powerful tool for thinking about well-defined risks, the things we know we don't know. SEU can describe the risks you encounter when you play roulette, or wonder what the Monetary Policy Committee will decide about interest rates at its next meeting. But SEU helps little when we contemplate uncertainties. The things we don't know we don't know.

The prevalence of uncertainty explains why SEU thinking doesn't come naturally. We didn't experience the complexities of modern financial markets in the long process of evolution that hardwired our brains, or in the schools and playgrounds where we were taught to cope with life. Many, though by no means all, situations we face in financial markets are ones for which SEU methods are relevant. We make mistakes. Sometimes the mistake is not to use SEU principles when they might help us – as with the stockbrokers who could not take a detached view of Robb Caledon. More sophisticated investors sometimes make the error of using SEU principles where they don't help us – as in the banks whose risk modelling failed to describe the events that brought them to their knees.

The sophisticated world of modern finance relies on models and forecasts in its assessment of both risks and fundamental values.

Most people who are not professionally engaged in building models or producing forecasts respond to models and forecasts with cynical naiveté – a curious mixture of disdain and credulousness. At a visceral level such people know that no model can capture the complexity of the world of finance, business and politics, yet they treat the output of models with the utmost seriousness. They believe that economic forecasts convey little useful information and yet they pay almost obsessive attention to them.

Financial analysis without models is impossible. But investment managers and executives of financial services firms who rely on the output of models they don't understand have relinquished decision-making to a black box. Such individuals profess adherence to science, but their behaviour is identical to that of earlier generations of decision makers who consulted the oracles or employed soothsayers to read the entrails. You don't have to be able to build models yourself, but you do have to understand a little of what the models can do to understand and make best use of the limited but real insights they can provide. Numbers can illuminate, but can also blind.

You need analysis and models more than you need forecasts. If you were able to see the future, profitable investment would be easy, but you can't. Nor can anyone else. The only useful information that people who predict the level of the stock market a year from now give you when they speak is that you should pay very little attention to anything they say. General knowledge about the future is 'in the price'. Specific knowledge about the future is vouchsafed to very few, and the people who have it are mostly prohibited from trading on it.

Instead of devoting time to speculation about what the future holds, recognise that the future is inescapably uncertain. Equip yourself with options that will be robust to many different contingencies. Options and diversification are the most effective responses to cope with a complex world. Knowing what you don't know gives you a considerable advantage over those, amateurs and professionals alike, who don't know what they don't know or do know what isn't so.

A broadly diversified portfolio based on real assets will give you considerable protection against risk and uncertainty with little compromise on return. In a 100% efficient market, there would be a tradeoff between risk and return, but in a partly efficient market, there is not. New investment technology using internet dealing means that the retail investor can achieve a diversified portfolio with relatively modest sums.

Three simple rules – pay less, diversify more, and be contrarian – will serve almost everyone well. If you have an established investment portfolio based on advice you will almost certainly find that a substantial part of your total assets is in open-ended managed funds that are closet indexed. This costs you too much and is inadequately diversified. You can transfer this money into a group of exchange traded funds, closed-end funds and real estate investment trusts on substantial discounts. That strategy will give you exposure to a range of countries, types of security, and styles of management. Such a strategy will give you lower charges, and less risk in your overall portfolio. An emphasis on market sectors at a discount will automatically imply a contrarian stance. You will lose what you have already paid in initial charges to set up your investments, but that money has gone anyway. If you are at an earlier stage of your investment career, you can structure your portfolio on these lines from the beginning.

Modern financial markets are complex, but much of the complexity is for the benefit of providers rather than consumers of financial services. If you don't understand it, don't do it. That simple maxim would have saved both amateurs and professionals billions of pounds over the years. The more recent the years, the larger the savings.

CHAPTER 14

THE LAST WALTZ

In July 2007, Chuck Prince, chief executive of Citigroup, told the *Financial Times* that 'As long as the music is playing, you've got to get up and dance. We're still dancing.' He was talking about his bank's role in the credit bubble. Prince understood that the music would stop. The party ended a month later, when the credit bubble burst on 9 August. Before the end of 2007, Prince had been sacked (with a very large payoff) and his bank had written off $10bn.

The power of conventional thinking explains why Prince was 'still dancing' even though he was probably well able to see the inevitable denouement. If Prince, or any other Citigroup CEO, had tried to impose serious restraint on Citigroup's activities, he would have been ousted – by bankers anxious for bonuses, shareholders demanding earnings growth, non-executive directors steeped in conventional thinking.

His options were to dance or be expelled from the party as a killjoy. Prince chose to wait till the music stopped. Most people in the same situation would make the same choice. Some might even persuade themselves that the evening would end happily. Although Prince occupied the most powerful position in the financial world, he was the prisoner of his own employees.

So are we all. The credit bubble damaged the financial security of millions of people who were persuaded to take out loans they could not repay. It damaged the wealth of investors who had entrusted their savings to intermediaries who bought structured credit products they did not understand. The credit bubble threatened economic stability both by its direct effects and by inducing panic reactions from public officials who thought it their duty to save the financial world from itself. Yet, at the beginning of 2008, the New York banking controller announced that the top seven banks in the state – the major international investment banks – had paid out $33bn in bonuses for 2007. A figure of £7bn was reported for bonuses in the City of London.

No one should doubt that a vibrant and professional financial services industry is essential to a prosperous economy. Experience has shown that only market economies can provide citizens with the standards of living that the people of Western Europe and North America have come to expect. A market economy needs to direct investment to the most productive uses and needs to monitor the performance of large businesses. A market economy finances the operations of governments and requires active secondary markets that enable borrowers and lenders to operate on different time-scales. A market economy must serve the individual financial needs of its citizens. It should allow them to save and to borrow to meet changing financial needs across their lifetimes. A market economy should protect citizens, or enable them to protect themselves, against the risks they encounter in daily life.

The liberal capital markets of Britain and the United States achieve all these things. They do not achieve them particularly well, but they achieve them better than any other system. They achieve them much better than the state-controlled economic systems that used to prevail in Communist Eastern Europe. But the scale of activities needed to allocate capital efficiently to industries and companies is a small fraction of the resources that the financial services sector employs today. We have created a monster that is out of control. The scale of resources the sector demands, the size of the personal financial rewards it offers, and the political influence that financial institutions wield are all excessive. The wealth of the individuals employed in financial services affects every aspect of economic and political life, sucks in talent that would be better employed elsewhere, and distorts the values of whole societies.

The modern financial services industry is a casino attached to a utility. The utility is the payments system, which enables individuals and non-financial companies to manage their daily affairs. The utility allows them to borrow and lend for their routine activities, and allocates finance in line with the fundamental value of business activities. In the casino, traders make profits from arbitrage and short-term price movements. The users of the utility look to fundamental values. The occupants of the casino are preoccupied with the mind of the market.

Modest levels of speculative activity may improve the operation of the utility. By exploiting arbitrage opportunities, they can bring the mind of the market back in line with fundamental values. But as trading levels increase, the mind of the market, determined by the power of conventional thinking, is itself the main influence on prices.

The analytic tools which were developed in markets in recent decades added little to the exposition of the determinants of fundamental value provided by Ben Graham. Financial economists, looking to market efficiency, assumed that Graham's problem had essentially been solved. The data relevant to market prices was already in the market. And so the activities of the casino came to dominate the utility.

In the summer of 2007, the handsomely remunerated leaders of the financial services industry announced that if the governments of the world did not provide emergency funds to keep casino players at the tables they would bring the utility to a halt. The US Federal Reserve and European Central Bank came quickly to the rescue. The Bank of England arrived somewhat more slowly, arguing that the players must learn a lesson. Britain's regulators allowed Northern Rock to fail.

As gamblers everywhere were forced to acknowledge the scale of their losses, they became increasingly mistrustful and reluctant to play with each other. They pleaded that governments should take the role of 'the house', and ensure all debts were settled. In the US government intervention of October 2008, the US government acknowledged that role. European governments followed suit. The British government provided the most extensive funding, but on the most demanding terms.

There is universal agreement that 'more effective regulation' must be the price of the bailout. There is less agreement – in fact almost no specificity – about what that 'more effective regulation' might mean.

The professionalisation of financial services has changed regulation as it has changed markets. The focus of regulation is now on principles and rules, not character.

Central bankers and financial regulators were once City grandees, weighty figures distinguished by experience and connections. Alan Greenspan, who acquired near saintly status as America's central banker for almost two decades, marked a transition. Greenspan was certainly heavyweight and well connected, but he was also a professional economist, if not a particularly distinguished one. Now, people versed in modern financial economics have taken over. When Greenspan retired in 2007, both the Chairman of the US Federal Reserve Board and the Governor of the Bank of England were people who had enjoyed careers as respected academics, with significant articles in scholarly journals. The financial economics described in this book, based on the efficient market hypothesis and subjective expected utility, is a major influence on the structure of financial market regulation.

This is not the book in which to review the way in which technical issues in economics have become bound up with ideological belief in the superiority of American capitalism. I have considered that question more extensively in *The Truth about Markets*. (Kay, 2003). But the application of economic theory to financial markets is often naïve, and often has political motivation, or political implication, or both.

Efficient market theorists asserted that the New Economy bubble was a distillation of the wisdom of thousands of market participants. Devotees of SEU claimed that the credit bubble was a new and more sophisticated system of allocating risk where it would be most effectively managed. Financial market professionals, and the politicians who represented their interests, stood ready to applaud these supposed insights and flatter those who delivered them.

The models bore little relation to the tawdry reality. No one can have lived through the New Economy and credit bubbles and still seriously believe that market prices are a balanced representation of well-considered assessments of fundamental values of securities. An understanding of information asymmetry and the winner's curse is more important to an appreciation of modern financial markets than the efficient market hypothesis. Subjective expected utility does not explain how traders think.

Whenever consumers find product quality difficult to assess, those who buy tend to overpay. Goods and services are bought by those who overestimate their value, not by those who underestimate them. When investment banks hire traders, when small savers purchase funds, when corporate executives select advisers, when treasurers invest in structured credit, the winner's curse comes into play. The difficulties of distinguishing skill from luck, of penetrating complexity, of determining fundamental value, all work towards encouraging people to pay too much.

And that gives a clue to the question which most people outside the City of London – and some inside it – often ask: 'Why are people in the financial services industry paid so much?' The simple arithmetic of compounding gives a basic insight into the answer. Small percentages of large amounts, levied on many occasions and accumulated over time, add up to very large sums.

But why, an economist will ask, are these returns not competed away? To some extent, they are. Much of the revenue of the City goes into the pockets of employees, and into lavish offices and expenditures, as well as into the profits of City firms. That is why there are so many investment funds vying for your attention. But the profitability of the City is mainly the result of information asymmetry. Where information is imperfect, markets and market outcomes are imperfect. The financial services industry exists – and is needed – because of imperfections of information.

Arbitrage, the product of market imperfection and the mainstay of the financial services industry, is absurdly rewarding. Seeing something is worth £2 when it is priced at £1 is as profitable as making something priced at £1 into something that is worth £2, although the social value of correctly assessing wealth is very much less than the social value of creating that wealth.

Most trade in financial markets occurs because of differences of information and understanding, and financial instruments are constructed to take advantage of these differences. Traders are overconfident and do not hold attitudes to risk or expectations about the world that are coherent or consistent. They cannot achieve detachment; they become obsessed by the processes of financial markets; and they constantly monitor markets, inventing causal explanations for statistical noise.

It is impossible to explain the extraordinary volume of trading that takes place in modern financial markets, or how people like Buffett and Soros could have made so much money, in any other way. But Buffett and Soros enjoyed the great advantages of freedom of action and independence from conventional thinking – both the conventional thinking of practical men, who share and reflect each other's current opinions, and that of academics, who treat models like SEU and EMH as if they were true.

The New Economy bubble was the product of the self-serving puffery of corrupt analysts. The credit bubble was a game of 'pass the parcel' whose participants vied to dump risks on players less well informed. Both bubbles were based on systematic misrepresentations no less venal because they contained an element of self-deception.

The academic cheerleaders were, in the main, innocent dupes. Not especially well paid, generally centre-left in political orientation, they provided philosophical justification for greed and for rightist ideology, through a Panglossian message of markets efficient in both a broad and a narrow sense. The most public involvement of distinguished economists in cutting-edge financial practice would end in the fiasco of Long-Term Capital Management. They believed their own models.

But financial economics offers illuminating insights rather than truth. A more nuanced view acknowledges the ways in which the financial services industry has failed its taxpayers and retail customers. It recognises the economic importance of the financial services industry but does not equate the interests of businesses within it, or their employees, with the public good. In the last decade we have seen the abuse of retail customers during the New Economy bubble, systematic overcharging for investment management services, followed by reliance on taxpayers for support when the credit bubble jeopardised the survival of financial institutions. These events should be more than sufficient to dispel any sense that there is a close, or any, relationship between the profits of financial services businesses, the earnings of their employees, and the value of services rendered to society at large.

Where there has been abuse, there will be regulation. The primary objective of the regulation of financial services looking forward is that the casino should never again jeopardise the utility. Many people seem to think that the best method of achieving this is close supervision of the casino. This notion is misconceived. The junior officials of a public agency do not have the capability, or the authority, to advise bankers paid multi-million pound salaries and bonuses against what, with the benefit of hindsight, appear to be strategic errors in the conduct of their business. It is not realistic to imagine that they could have such capability or authority – after all, the boards of these institutions did not. Nor is it realistic to suppose that, if they did have such capacity, they could exercise it in a world in which the financial services industry is the most powerful political lobby in the country and the threat of judicial review hangs over every regulatory action.

The practical result of such 'more effective' regulation – which is inevitable – will be more international meetings of regulators and an expansion of the staff of regulatory agencies and of the compliance departments of financial services businesses. The additional rules which will be introduced as a consequence will be irrelevant to the next bubble, just as the Basle I and II capital requirements imposed on banks – the subject of so much regulatory and academic debate over the last two decades – were irrelevant to the credit bubble.

The better response is to separate the utility from the casino. Financial conglomerates are, as Senators Glass and Steagall recognised, a bad idea. They are a bad idea for their shareholders, victims of recurrent tension between investment and retail bankers within the organisation; a bad idea for customers, because conglomerates are riddled with conflicts of interest; and a bad idea for taxpayers, who have to pick up the bills when incompetent traders have gambled retail customers' savings away. Yet the collapse of the credit bubble has actually strengthened the role of conglomerates, because only retail banks have resources large enough to meet the capital requirements of players in the casino.

A new Glass-Steagall Act will not work, as the old Glass-Steagall ultimately did not work. Although diversified financial conglomerates do not serve the interests of those who work for them, own their shares or use their services, they do serve the interests of the greedy and ambitious men who run them. In the real world of modern politics those aspirations will challenge and find ways round any restrictions. Instead, structural rules should firewall the utility from the casino, by giving absolute priority to retail depositors (or the institutions which protect retail depositors) in the event of the failure of a deposit-taking institution. The players at the casino can then make such rules to govern their own activities (or none) as they think appropriate. There is a fundamental public interest in keeping crooks out of wholesale financial markets, but that is as far as public involvement need, or should, go. There is no obligation on regulators to provide liquidity for markets, especially when there is no evident public benefit from the market having come into existence in the first place.

The primary object of regulation should not be to ensure good practice in financial services businesses, but to protect retail customers. Its purpose should be consumer protection directed, not at removing information asymmetry, but to relieving its consequences. There is no escaping the stark contrast between the size and general profitability of the financial services industry and the poor service it delivers to its retail customers. The best advice that can be given on selecting products is, in most cases, to buy the cheapest and to do as much as possible yourself.

Neither regulation nor markets will ever ensure that ordinary retail investors receive good personalised financial advice. The economics of the business makes such provision impossible. We select clothes and food, furniture and cars, for ourselves from the shelf or the showroom floor because the services of skilled, knowledgeable, impartial intermediaries cost more than we are willing to pay. The cost of high-quality professional services is much greater. Bespoke legal advice is priced out of reach and medical advice accessible only because it is made free. The most that can be expected – and more than is available at the moment – is the confidence generated by a large supermarket, where you justifiably believe that the store's concern for its reputation means that the products you find will be fit for purpose and good value for money.

The metaphor of the casino invites both the citizen and the saver to treat financial services with less deference and respect. Bookmakers are prosperous, but most people regard them as slightly ridiculous. Their prosperity is the product of human frailty, deep cynicism indispensable to their success. Not many decades ago, stockbrokers, though drawn from a different stratum in the social hierarchy, were regarded in much the same way. This is probably how it should be.

If the City has changed, and public attitudes to it have also changed, it is partly because money has more and more become a determinant of status. The modern City is largely, though still not wholly, meritocratic. The cleverest people have intellectual capabilities that would win them success in many other walks of life. Yet the most successful people are, as always, distinguished by who they know rather than what they know. What they know is often not very much, and is largely the relaying of conventional opinions whose validity they have little opportunity, or inclination, to assess.

The major part of the work of the City is not very intellectually demanding (although, as we have seen, there are difficult concepts at the heart of its work and highly skilled professionals employed to apply these concepts). Many people in the City have genuine interest in ideas, and genuine concern for the public good, but these activities are, in the main, conducted outside formal business hours. There are also in the City some of the most selfish people outside prisons, who believe that no justification for their activities is required beyond the money they make from them.

The City of London is an important British export industry and deserves substantial credit for that. A process of change and reform will take the City less seriously than it takes itself, and less seriously than politicians have taken it. Neither the intelligent investor, nor the concerned citizen should be intimidated by the City, or unduly impressed by its increased but exaggerated expertise and professionalism. You are on your own. I hope this book can be your companion.

GLOSSARY

Absolute return The total return on a portfolio. Absolute return is measured without benchmarking or reference to market movements. 28

Acquisition The takeover of one company by another. 65

Acquisition accounting Accounting treatment designed to flatter the accounts of the acquiring company. 88

Active management (portfolio) Professional asset selection. Contrast with passive management, which simply follows an index. 46, 77

Agency costs Costs of intermediation which reduce the returns on financial investment relative to those of the underlying productive investment. 173

Allais paradox A problem in behavioural economics devised by the French economist Maurice Allais which demonstrates a 'Dutch book'. 24, 145

Alpha Outperformance of an investment or investment fund, relative to a benchmark, adjusted for risk (through *beta*). 121

Alternative investment Asset outside mainstream categories of shares, bonds and property. Traditionally alternative assets were mostly physical objects (such as paintings and commodities) but more recently the term is used to refer to private equity and hedge funds. 155

Alternative investment market (AIM) Market for shares in small companies which do not meet the standards for a London Stock Exchange listing. 161

American Depository Receipts (ADRs) New York traded versions of shares from countries other than the US. 29

Amortisation *see* Depreciation.

Anomalies Deviations from the efficient market hypothesis. 56, 65

Arbitrage A strategy to profit from divergences in the prices of similar or related securities. 36, 67

Arbitrageurs Traders using arbitrage strategies, especially those that trade between an acquirer's stock and that of the prospective acquisition. 46

Asset stripping Breaking up a company to realise the value of its
underlying assets. 95

Asset value The value of the assets underlying a security (which may
differ from the market price of the security). 45, 93

Asset-backed securities (ABS) An asset-backed security (ABS) can have
several tranches of security relating to the same asset pool: if the value
of the pool deteriorates, the senior tranches will be paid first. 162

Bagger (as in ten or twenty bagger) Speculative stock which increases
greatly in value. 24

Basis point Each percentage point of yield is 100 basis points.

Bayesian The view that degrees of belief can be expressed as probabilities
updated with new information. 112

Behavioural finance, behavioural economics Analysis based on
empirical or experimental studies of behaviour (especially
towards risk) rather than models of rational choice. 67, 124, 145

Benchmark The index specified to judge an investment manager's
performance. 77

Best execution The obligation to place a trade at the best price available
in the market. 7

Beta The predicted effect on the price of a security of a 1% movement in
the benchmark index. 121

Big Bang Deregulation of the City of London in 1986. 9

Black-Scholes model The most widely used model for pricing options. 152

Blue chips Shares in large companies. 97, 126

Bonds Securities with fixed interest rates and redemption dates. 34

BRIC Principal emerging markets – Brazil, Russia, India, China.

Buy side Investors and their advisers (contrast with sell side). 70

Call option The right to buy a security at a fixed price at a future date
(*see* Put option) 152

Capital asset pricing model (CAPM) A model that predicts that
expected rates of return will be determined by a combination of the
risk free rate and a risk premium determined by the asset category
and the asset *beta*. 122

Carry trade Arbitrage strategies which yield repeated small profits, usually
from interest rate differentials (*see* Taleb distributions). 157

Chartist (*see* **Technical analysis**) Someone who predicts security prices
by identifying trends from charts. 65

Chinese walls Measures (including rules and physical separation) to
prevent different divisions (principally buy side and sell side) of a
financial institution from exchanging information. 64

Closed end An investment fund whose shares can be acquired or
disposed of only by selling to another investor. Such a fund may

ISA (individual savings account) A scheme which allows share and
corporate bond holdings free of income or capital gains tax.   171

Junk bonds Bonds below investment grade.   38

Know your customer The regulatory obligation on a financial adviser
to base recommendations on specific knowledge of the investor's
circumstances.   12

Lemons Goods which the seller, but not buyer, knows to be of inferior
quality.   53

Leverage *See* Gearing.   41

Life insurance Insurance policy which pays on the death of the insured.
Most such insurance policies are packaged with savings products.   18

Likelihood The degree of belief in a narrative   130

Long Contrast with short: a positive position in a security.   149

Long end Bonds with long periods to run until redemption.   36

Long/short fund A fund which takes short positions as well as long
(a 130/30 fund will own shares worth 130% of its value and have short
positions equivalent to 30%).   156

Mark to market The practice of revaluing assets in line with current
market values.   48, 81

Market capitalisation The total value of the shares of a company.   31

Market risk The risk profile created by general market movements.   121

Mean reversion A tendency for variables to return to their long-term
average.   59

Mental accounting A tendency to treat different parts of an overall
portfolio as different portfolios.   147

Mergers The combination of two firms.

Momentum (*See* Serial correlation). Tendency for price movements to
continue in the same direction.   59

Monoliners Financial services firms that specialise in a single product or
product group.   16

Moral hazard The tendency for average product quality to deteriorate
when there is information asymmetry.   55

Mortgage backed security (MBS) An asset-backed security whose value
is based on a pool of mortgages.   162

New issues The sale of new shares for cash by a company (*see* IPO).   29, 69

Noise Short-term price movements without justification from changes
in fundamental value.   32

Noise traders Frequent traders who act on noise (*see* Day traders).   32

Nominal return The return on investments before taking account of
inflation.   24

Nominee account Holding securities in the name of a bank (necessary
to keep down dealing costs).   170

Non-recurring items Costs that a company does not want to charge against profits. 90

Normal distribution The most common – bell-shaped – statistical distribution. 108

Offset mortgage A mortgage product in which the balance in a savings account is used to offset the outstanding mortgage debt. 16

Open end fund investment company (OEIC) A fund which creates or redeems shares or units in line with investor demand. 44

Option The right to buy or sell securities at a price agreed in advance. 152

Over-rented A property on which the current rent exceeds the market rent. 44

Overweight No longer the result of long city lunches! Holding a larger proportion of one's portfolio in a particular security than the share of that security in the relevant index. 77

Passive fund, passive investment A fund or investment strategy which tracks an index. 46

Passive management (*See* Active management)

Payment in kind securities Bonds on which the interest rate increases as the creditworthiness of the borrower declines. 16

Payment protection insurance Retail product which meets loan repayments during sickness or unemployment. 19

PE ratio The ratio of the market price of the share of a company to its earnings per share. 31, 82

PEG ratio The ratio of the PE ratio and the growth rate of earnings. 83

Penny shares Shares whose value is only a few pence per share (even though there may be many millions of shares). Often issued to appeal to noise traders. 25

Personal pensions A scheme for long-term saving which allows tax relief on contributions and levies no income or capital gains tax on investment returns. 171

Personal probability, (subjective probability) Estimate of the probability of a particularly outcome of a single event. 112

Pound-cost averaging A scheme which reduces the average purchase cost of securities by regular investment. 194

Price-earnings ratio The ratio of the market price of a security to earnings per share after tax. 82

Principal The amount outstanding on a loan. 34

Private equity fund A fund which takes large stakes in unquoted companies. 60

Pro forma earnings The profits companies would like you to think they have earned. 89

Productive investment *See* Financial investment.

time periods. Short-term positive serial correlation is when price movements continue in the same direction (momentum). Long-term negative
serial correlation is the tendency for long-term movements to reverse.
(mean reversion).   59

Sharpe ratio The ratio of standard deviation (variability) to the return
from an asset.   111

Short end Bonds with early maturities.   36

Short-term positive serial correlation (*See* Momentum) The expectation
that short-term price movements will be followed by other moves in a
similar direction.   59

Short, short sellers A negative position established to benefit from the
fall in value of a share.   149

SIPP (self-invested personal pension) A tax advantaged scheme for
long-term investors.   171

Sophisticated or high net worth investor People who under FSA rules may
invest in a wider range of assets but lose certain regulatory protections. 11

Specific risks Risks which are specific to the investment concerned and
unrelated to movements in the general level of share prices.   120

Split level investment trusts Closed end funds with several different
types of share, e.g. some shareholders receive all income, others all
capital appreciation.   168

Spread betting (*See* Contract for difference) Betting on the rise and fall
of a security or index.   150

Statistical arbitrage Computerised trading systems for exploiting
short-term discrepancies between prices of similar securities.   67

Stock options The right (often given to senior executives) to buy the
company's shares at a future date at a favourable price.   78

Strike price The price at which an option is granted.   152

Strip A bond which has been divided into different components, e.g. one
group of holders receive the interest, another repayment of principal.   38

Structured product Security with complex relationship to the underlying
assets and liabilities. The result of financial engineering.   161

Subjective expected utility (SEU) A theory that individuals should or
do approach risk by maximising the expected value of payoffs using
subjective (personal) probabilities.   105

Sub-prime borrower, sub-prime mortgage Sub-prime borrowers have
poor credit ratings.   73

Survivor bias Misleading generalisation about performance based on
analysis of a population from which poor performers have been
removed.   135

Sustainable competitive advantage A competitive advantage which a
business can successfully maintain over time.   96

BOOKSHELVES AND BOOKMARKS

Do you want a small investment reference library? Both the *Financial Times* and *The Economist* offer guides that cover most investment topics – Glen Arnold's *Financial Times Guide to Investing* and Peter Stanyer's *Guide to Investment Strategy*. A book like Dominic Connolly's *UK Trader's Bible* has more extensive coverage of the mechanics of markets and trading. And there are several guides to the broader context of personal finance. See, for example, the *Which?* guides from the Consumers' Association, particularly those on *Be Your Own Financial Adviser* and on taxation. If you plan to buy individual stocks, you should have a book on how to read accounting statements, like Bob Parker's *Understanding Company Financial Statements*.

Do you want a book that contains the secrets of how to be rich? I hope not. But you might want advice from Soros and Buffett. The most relevant of George Soros's several books is *The Alchemy of Finance*, while Lawrence Cunningham offers an entertaining collection of extracts from the essays Buffett writes in his annual reports to Berkshire Hathaway shareholders (which are available on the company's website). Lowenstein's biography of Buffett (*Buffett: The Making of an American Capitalist*) is both entertaining and instructive (a new authorised biography by Alice Schroeder will shortly be published).

Lowenstein is one of the very few authors who write about finance and investment sufficiently well to make instruction pleasurable rather than painful (as in the history of LTCM, *When Genius Failed*). If you want a small shelf of books about the industry that are fun to read, you might consider Burrough and Helyar's *Barbarians at the Gate*, an account of the last days of RJR Nabisco; John Cassidy's *Dot.com* on the New Economy bubble (Rory Cellan-Jones describes the UK analogue in *Dot Bomb*); *Liar's Poker*, by Michael Lewis, is set in Salomon at its heyday. J K Galbraith's account of Wall Street in 1929, *The Great Crash*, is beautifully written and its lessons are all still relevant. A comparison of Tom Wolfe's *The Bonfire of the Vanities* and Anthony Trollope's *The Way We Live Now* reveals that while the actions and the instruments change, the fundamentals of financial follies do not.

Do you want another book like this one, which aims to provide practical advice with a rigorous intellectual basis? (I'm not sure whether I would like you to answer yes or no to that question.) The model that was in my mind from the beginning is Burton Malkiel's *A Random Walk Down Wall Street*, which has been for years what I recommended to the encouragingly numerous people who sought such a book. *Random Walk* has been through nine editions since it was first published in 1973, but its age shows, and the institutions and products it considers are American. So are the jokes, which are not to European taste. Still it remains a classic. The permanent classic is Benjamin Graham's *The Intelligent Investor*.

Other academics who have written popular books on investment are Jeremy Siegel, whose *Stocks for the Long Run* is an unashamed paean to the virtues of equity investment, and Robert Shiller, who had the good fortune to publish *Irrational Exuberance* just as the New Economy bubble was bursting. Similar books you might consider are William Bernstein's *Seven Pillars of Investing Wisdom* or either of David Swenson's volumes: *Pioneering Portfolio Management* and *Unconventional Success*. Swenson, Yale's much-feted investment manager, adopts a rather similar approach to that described here, but Swenson invests better than he writes.

The world of business and finance is notorious for writing that luxuriates in jargon and complexity. There are many books written on corporate strategy and for investment analysts, but not many target readers of this book would want to finish them. One of the few books that links corporate performance and investment is Jim Slater's *The Zulu Principle*, and I'm bound to recommend my own *The Hare and the Tortoise*, a distillation of *Foundations of Corporate Success*. Peter Bernstein's *Against the Gods*, on risk, is an exemplar of how to make complex concepts appear simple.

Do you want to pursue some of the more philosophical issues that have arisen in the course of this book? Quants and risk managers in the financial world make constant case of probabilities without much thought about what the numbers they readily deploy mean. Ian Hacking's *An Introduction to Probability and Inductive Logic* provides a good introduction to the underlying complexities. Questions about the nature of explanation – What does it mean to say a theory is illuminating but not true? – are at the heart of this book. People of a philosophical bent will appreciate the influence of Richard Rorty, whose related ideas are best set out in *Philosophy and the Mirror of Nature*. I found Wade Hands's *Reflections without Rules* an invaluable introduction to the central relevance of this sort of approach in modern economics.

Whatever books you put on your shelves, you will want to add some favourites to your computer. The internet gives you easy access both to products and information. But good websites cost money to build and maintain and, one way or another, he who pays the piper at least influences the tune. The fiercely independent Money Saving Expert has many useful financial tips, but unfortunately doesn't take you far into investment. You can access most financial services products through comparison sites such as Money Supermarket, though bear in mind that comparison sites are financed through commissions. All financial services organisations use websites to market and give access to their products, and competitive pressures ensure that most are easy to locate and use.

The internet also makes access to information much easier. Most companies have an investors relations section on their website, from which you can obtain annual reports and other financial information. Your stockbroker's site will probably have a research section that summarises this data and gives you other data about the company. The free elements of the *Financial Times* site give you similar access. Pricing and trading information is available on the London Stock Exchange's own website. This is one of several sources of regulatory news – companies are required to announce their results, large holdings and directors' dealings. Interactive Investor and ADVFN offer free access to information – and bulletin boards. While these are amusing, both the information and opinions should be treated with great caution.

Hemscott, the leading independent provider of company information, has recently merged with Morningstar, a leader in providing fund information, and the outcome may be premium services worth paying for. There are several sources of information on investment funds. Two sites, Cofunds and Funds Network, give access to funds at reduced charges. However, all these sites focus mainly on OEICS (unit trusts) which pay commission to intermediaries. Closed end funds are less well served – Trustnet is the main source for these. For exchange traded funds, you will have to go to the sites of the providers for information (Barclays iShares and Société Générale's Lyxor are the market leaders) and you will buy and sell them through your stockbroker's site. *Books mentioned above are listed in the Bibliography with ***

Bookmarks

ADVFN	**www.advfn.com**
Barclays iShares	**www.ishares.eu**
Cofunds	**www.cofunds.co.uk**
Financial Times	**www.ft.com**
Funds Network	**www.fundsnetwork.com**
Hemscott	**www.hemscott.com**
Interactive Investor	**www.iii.co.uk**
London Stock Exchange	**www.londonstockexchange.com**
Money Saving Expert	**www.moneysavingexpert.com**
Money Supermarket	**www.moneysupermarket.com**
Société Générale	**www.socgen.com**
Trustnet	**www.trustnet.com**

BIBLIOGRAPHY

Akerlof, G. (1970), 'The Market for Lemons: Quality, Uncertainty and the Market Mechanism', *Quarterly Journal of Economics*, Vol. 84, No. 3, Aug 1970 (pp. 488-500).

**Arnold, G. (2004), *Financial Times* Guide to Investing, *Financial Times/* Prentice Hall.

Samuelson, P.A. (1947), *Foundations of Economic Analysis*, Harvard University Press.

**Bernstein, P.L. (1996), *Against the Gods: The Remarkable Story of Risk,* John Wiley & Sons.

**Bernstein, W. (2002), *The Four Pillars of Investing*, McGraw-Hill.

**Buffett, W. (2002), *Essays of Warren Buffett: Lessons for Investors and Managers*, Wiley.

**Burrough, B. and J. Helyar, (2004, new ed), *Barbarians at the Gate*, Arrow Books

**Cassidy, J. (2002), *dot.con – The Greatest Story Ever Sold*, Allen Lane

**Cellan-Jones, R. (2001), *Dot Bomb: The Rise and Fall of dot.com Britain*, Aurum.

**Connolly, D. (2005), *The UK Trader's Bible: The Complete Guide to Trading the UK Stock Market*, Harriman House.

**Cunningham, L.A.(ed.), (2002), *The Essays of Warren Buffett*, Singapore, Wiley, (p.78).

Dimson, E.P., P. Marsh and M. Staunton, (2002), *Triumph of the Optimists: 101 Years of Global Investment Returns*, Princeton University Press.

Fama, E. and K. French, (1992), 'The Cross-Section of Expected Stock Returns', *Journal of Finance*, Vol. XLVII, No.2, June 1992.

**Galbraith, J.K. (1997), *The Great Crash 1929*, Houghton Mifflin.

**Graham, B. (new ed. 1991), *The Intelligent Investor*, HarperCollins

**Hacking, I. (2001), *An Introduction to Probability and Inductive Logic*, Cambridge University Press.

**Hands, D.W. (2001), *Reflection without Rules*, Cambridge University Press.

Jensen, M. (1978), 'Some Anomalous Evidence Regarding Market Efficiency', *Journal of Financial Economics*, Vol. 6 (p. 95-101).

**Kay, J.A. (1993), *Foundations of Corporate Success*, Oxford University Press.

Kay, J.A. (2003), *The Truth about Markets*, Allen Lane.

**Kay, J.A. (2006), *The Hare & the Tortoise*, The Erasmus Press.

Keynes, J.M. (1921), *A Treatise on Probability*, Macmillan.

Keynes, J.M. (1936), *The General Theory of Employment, Interest and Money*, Macmillan.

Knight, F.H. (1921), *Risk, Uncertainty and Profit*, Houghton Mifflin.

**Lewis, M. (1989), *Liar's Poker: Two Cities, True Greed*, Hodder & Stoughton.

**Lowenstein, R. (1995), *Buffett: The Making of an American Capitalist*, Weidenfeld & Nicolson.

**Lowenstein, R. (2000), *When Genius Failed: The Rise and Fall of Long-Term Capital Management*, Fourth Estate.

Lo, A.W. and A.C. MacKinlay, (2002), *A Non-Random Walk Down Wall Street*, Princeton University Press.

**Malkiel, B. (1973, 9th edition 2007), *A Random Walk Down Wall Street: A Time-Tested Strategy for Successful Investing*, Norton.

**Parker, R.H. (1999, 5th ed.), *Understanding Company Financial Statements*, Penguin Books Ltd.

Ramsey, F.P. (1931), *The Foundations of Mathematics and Other Logical Essays*, Kegan Paul.

**Rorty, R. (1979), *Philosophy and the Mirror of Nature*, Princeton University Press.

Savage, J.L. (1954), *The Foundations of Statistics*, Chapman & Hall.

**Shiller, R.J. (2005), *Irrational Exuberance*, Princeton University Press.

**Siegel, J. (2008, 4th edn), *Stocks for the Long Run*, McGraw Hill Professional.

**Slater, J. (1997), *The Zulu Principle*, Orion.

Smith, T. (1992), *Accounting for Growth: Stripping the Camouflage from Company Accounts*, Century Business.

**Soros, G. (2003), *The Alchemy of Finance* (2nd ed.), John Wiley & Sons Ltd.

**Stanyer, P. (2006), *Guide to Investment Strategy*, Bloomsbury Press.

**Swensen, D. (2005), *Unconventional Success: A Fundamental Approach to Personal Investment*, Free Press.

**Swensen, D. (2000), *Pioneering Portfolio Management: An Unconventional Approach to Institutional Investment*, Free Press.

Taleb, N.N. (2001), *Fooled by Randomness: The Hidden Role of Chance in the Markets and in Life*, Texere.

**Trollope, A. (1875), *The Way We Live Now*, Penguin Classics.

**Wolfe, T. (1991), *The Bonfire of the Vanities*, Picador.

www.johnkay.com

This website is a comprehensive guide to John Kay's activities and writing. On it you can

- find supporting material for *The Long and the Short of It*
- find details of John Kay's other books (and buy them)
- read and download a wide range of John Kay's articles
- search for materials on selected subjects
- receive advance notice of new publications
- order existing publications
- learn about current and coming events involving the author
- discover what is currently on John Kay's bookshelves
- obtain biographical and career details